COME, FOLLOW ME
7
SECOND EDITION

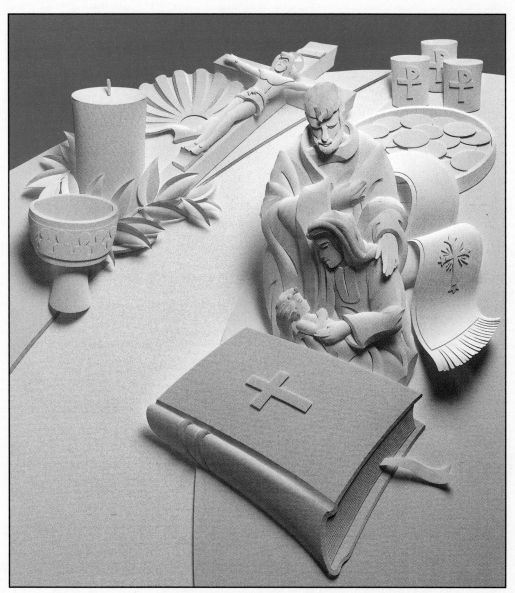

GENERAL EDITORS
Rev. Berard Marthaler, O.F.M. Conv.
Rev. Gerard P. Weber

CONSULTING EDITOR
Irene H. Murphy

BENZIGER
WOODLAND HILLS, CALIFORNIA

Writing Team Barbara Malone, Michael McKeefery, Sandra Sella Raas, Charles Savitskas, Margaret Savitskas, Helen Whitaker.

Design and Production Monotype Composition Company, Baltimore, Maryland

Cover Cover Design—Design Office, San Francisco, California; Paper Sculpture—Jeff Nishinaka

The Ad Hoc Committee to Oversee the Use of the Catechism, National Conference of Catholic Bishops, has found the doctrinal content of *Come, Follow Me, Second Edition,* to be in conformity with the Catechism of the Catholic Church.

Photographs Jagdish Agarwal/Unicorn Stock Photos: 174; Age Fotostock/FPG International: 113; Paul Almasy/Corbis: 146; James Amos/Corbis: 214; AP/Wide World Photos: 165; Bill Aron/PhotoEdit: 33; Tony Arruza/Corbis: 136; Billy E. Barnes/PhotoEdit: 193; Eric R. Berndt/Unicorn Stock Photos: 74; Robert Brenner/PhotoEdit: 10, 22, 113; Bill Conklin/PhotoEdit: 68; Corbis: 128, 145; Corbis/Bettmann: 169; The Crosiers/Catholic News Service: 127; Donna DeCesare/Impact Visuals: 209; Mary Kate Denny/PhotoEdit: 24, 39, 42, 62, 112, 179, 194; Hulton Deutsch Collection/Corbis: 169; Reinhard Eisele/Corbis: 121; Myrleen Ferguson/PhotoEdit: 5, 49, 87, 110, 112, 138, 158, 208, 228; Florent Flipper/Unicorn Stock Photos: 158; Wayne Floyd/Unicorn Stock Photo: 51, 187; Tony Freeman/PhotoEdit: 36, 105, 113, 117, 120, 152, 166, 210, 234; Philip Gould/Corbis: 38; The Granger Collection: 176; Jeff Greenberg/PhotoEdit: 106, 119; Jeff Greenberg/Unicorn Stock Photos: 19, 130; Peter Gridley/FPG International: 200; Chip Henderson/Tony Stone Images: 144; Martin R. Jones/Unicorn Stock Photos: 121; Jack Kurtz/Impact Visuals: 61, 93, 113; Robert Kusel/Tony Stone Images: 113; David Lees/Corbis: 154; Bill Losh/FPG International: 209; MacDonald Photography/Unicorn Stock Photos: 29, 137; Dennis MacDonald/PhotoEdit: 119, 140; Felicia Martinez/PhotoEdit: 192; Gunter Marx Photography/Corbis: 105; Lawrence Midgale/Tony Stone Images: 113; Karen Mullen/Unicorn Stock Photos: 148; Michael Newman/PhotoEdit: 17, 88, 108, 148, 149, 216, 221; Richard Nowitz/Corbis: 174; Alan Oddie/PhotoEdit: 113; Daniel J. Olson/Unicorn Stock Photos: 195; Vladimir Pcholkin/FPG International: 199; Jim Pickerell/Tony Stone Images: 63; Ed Pritchard/Tony Stone Images: 132; A. Ramey/PhotoEdit: 112, 208; Vittoriano Rastelli/Corbis: 158; A. Reininger/Unicorn Stock Photos: 185; Reuters/Corbis/Bettmann: 175; A. Rodham/Unicorn Stock Photos: 113; Jeffry Scott/Impact Visuals: 93, 172; Mark Scott/FPG International: 69; James Shaffer/PhotoEdit: 49; Nancy Sheehan/PhotoEdit: 122; Nancy Simmerman/Tony Stone Images: 127, 227; Steve Skjold/PhotoEdit: 217; Liba Taylor/Corbis: 184; Telegraph Colour Library/FPG International: 146; UPI/Corbis-Bettmann: 112, 170; Susan VanEtten/PhotoEdit: 121, 192; Greg Vaughn/Tony Stone Images: 105; Aneal Vohra/Unicorn Stock Photos: 40, 171; Tom Wagner/Odyssey/Chicago: 184; John Warden/Tony Stone Images: 104; Jim West/Impact Visuals: 92; Michael S. Yamashita/Corbis: 185; Dick Young/Unicorn Stock Photos: 123; David Young Wolff/PhotoEdit: 4, 19, 69, 129, 152, 218

Illustrations Kim Howard: 154; Susan Jaekel: 16, 24, 25, 26, 35, 38, 46, 52, 53, 58, 65, 66, 71, 72, 80, 86, 88, 91, 94, 102, 107, 216, 225; Jane McCreary: 22, 30, 32, 34, 37, 50, 54, 56, 60, 63, 101, 104; NJ Taylor: 20, 21, 28, 44, 45, 83, 95, 99, 205, 206; Stan Tusan: 189; Richard Wahl: 81, 173, 207; Jack White: 3, 9, 27, 55, 64, 70, 73, 84, 89, 125, 126, 133, 155, 161, 162, 164, 177, 178

Fine Art Alinari/Art Resource: 40, 56, 97, 196; Art Resource: 103; Arte Video Immagine Italia srl/Corbis: 41; Cameraphoto/Art Resource: 46; Corbis-Bettmann: 115; Girauden/Art Resource: 7; The Granger Collection: 47, 117, 141, 142, 185, 197, 201; Erich Lessing/Art Resource: 40, 100, 101, 153, 160, 163; Minneapolis Institute of Arts: 96; Nimatallah/Art Resource: 79; The Pierpont Morgan Library/Art Resource: 76, 190; Scala/Art Resource: 41, 43, 77, 98, 134, 156, 157, 184, 185; Tate Gallery/Art Resource: 151; Werner Forman Archive Museum Royal Afrique Centrale, Tervuren, Belgium/Art Resource: 157

Nihil Obstat Sister Karen Wilhelmy, C.S.J., Censor Deputatus

Imprimatur †Roger Cardinal Mahony, Archbishop of Los Angeles, March 4, 1997.

The nihil obstat and imprimatur are official declarations that the work contains nothing contrary to Faith and Morals. It is not implied thereby that those who have granted the nihil obstat and imprimatur agree with the contents, statements, or opinions expressed.

Send all inquiries to
Benziger Publishing Company
21600 Oxnard Street, Suite 500
Woodland Hills, California 91367

ISBN 0-02-655994-3
Printed in the United States of America.

6   079/043   03 02 01

This Year I Get To

- Discover more about Jesus, the Messiah.
- Act as a follower of Jesus.
- Celebrate Jesus' death and resurrection.
- Use the gifts of the Holy Spirit.
- Make Jesus present today through my actions and attitudes.

TABLE OF CONTENTS ....

4

5

COME, FOLLOW ME

de la Tour, *Saint Joseph the Carpenter.* 17th Century.

Jesus was truly human. He was born in the town of Bethlehem nearly two thousand years ago. He grew up in Nazareth. He was shaped by the influences of family, community, and faith. "Jesus advanced in wisdom and age and favor before God and man."   Luke 2:52

1 INTRODUCING JESUS

I am the way and the truth and the life.

JOHN 14:6

CONTENT KEYS

1. **Jesus helped many people.**
2. **Jesus' followers are called disciples.**
3. **Many people followed Jesus.**

I REMEMBER JESUS

Dear Friend,

My name is Mary. I come from the village of Magdala in Galilee. When I was a young woman, I made some choices that were harmful to me and to others.

Then I met Jesus. Jesus didn't seem to notice what was wrong with me. He noticed what was right with me. The first gift Jesus gave me was forgiveness. And the rest is history. I made up my mind to follow Jesus. I joined with the other women who followed him. I remember how completely crushed I was when Jesus was put to death. But do you know what? I was the very first one to see Jesus on Easter morning—the day he rose from the dead.

Even though Jesus returned to his Father, I know that he is still with us all. Knowing Jesus has made all the difference in my life. I am writing this letter that you may know Jesus better, may believe in him, and may follow him always.

Your friend,
Mary of Magdala

Dear Mary,

In the space, write a note to Mary. In the note, ask her two or three questions you have about Jesus. Share your questions with the rest of the class.

CONTACT WITH JESUS

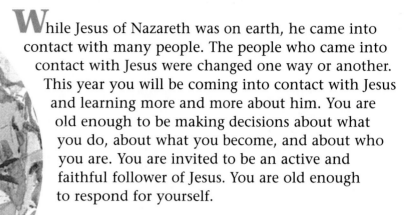

While Jesus of Nazareth was on earth, he came into contact with many people. The people who came into contact with Jesus were changed one way or another. This year you will be coming into contact with Jesus and learning more and more about him. You are old enough to be making decisions about what you do, about what you become, and about who you are. You are invited to be an active and faithful follower of Jesus. You are old enough to respond for yourself.

Imagine for a moment that many of the people who were eyewitnesses of the life and works of Jesus were all gathered in one place. Think about everything they would have to talk about.

EYEWITNESS NEWS

Miriam: This is Miriam, your Eye-on-Jerusalem reporter. With me today are several people who were eyewitnesses to Jesus of Nazareth, his life and his works. Let's hear what they have to say.

Mary: I was accused of adultery. I was supposed to be put to death. Jesus chased my executioners away. He told me to go and sin no more.

Zacchaeus: Jesus came to my house. I was so moved by his message and his kindness that I gave half of my possessions to the poor.

Nathan: I couldn't walk. Jesus told me to pick up the mat I was lying on and to walk. Would you believe it? I was cured.

Timaeus: I was totally blind. Jesus gave me my sight.

Ruben: I had the terrible disease of leprosy. No one would come near me. Jesus made me clean.

Jude: I was with Jesus in a boat. A storm came up, and we all thought we were goners. Jesus raised his hands and calmed the waters.

Abner: I saw Jesus feed thousands of people with a few loaves of bread and a couple of fish.

Rachel: I was on the hillside when Jesus taught about God's kingdom. I always want to be a part of that kingdom. He said that in that kingdom the poor are blessed.

John: I saw Jesus put to death on a cross.

James: I saw him alive after his death. I ate breakfast with him.

FIND JESUS

Choose three of the Gospel passages listed below. In the first column tell what happened. In the second column, tell in your own words what the passage tells you about Jesus.

1. Matthew 9:1–7
2. Luke 5:12–13
3. Luke 6:20–21
4. Luke 15:11–32
5. Luke 19:1–10
6. John 8:3–11

What Happened	In Your Own Words
1.	
2.	
3.	

COME, FOLLOW ME

When Jesus was on earth, he often gave a very simple invitation to those he met. "Come, follow me," he said. And often the strangest thing happened. People dropped everything and followed him. What an interesting reaction!

FOLLOWING Jesus

You already follow Jesus. You don't have any nets to drop or businesses to abandon. During the course of this year, you will be learning that following Jesus is something you do every day of your life. You learn how to do this from Sacred Scripture, from the teaching of the Church, and from the example of other followers of Jesus.

THE CAPERNAUM COURIER

Local Fishermen Abandon Business

Several residents of Capernaum witnessed a strange event yesterday. Simon bar Jonah, a longtime resident of this city, had been fishing all night—as usual. He had returned to shore and was cleaning his nets when a young traveling teacher—Jesus from Nazareth—spoke to him.

The teacher said, "Simon, put out into deep water and lower your nets for a catch."

Simon seemed annoyed at the suggestion and muttered to himself, "What does this fellow know about fishing?"

Simon answered, "We have worked all night and have caught nothing, but at your command, I will lower my nets."

Others on the scene were amazed at Simon's change of luck. He caught so many fish that he was almost dragged head first into the water. Simon needed help to pull in his nets.

When he returned to the shore, Simon ran and fell at the feet of the teacher. The teacher grabbed Simon by the elbow and helped him to stand. All the

teacher said to Simon was, "Come, follow me."

Here is the amazing part. Simon did just that. He left his boat, his nets, and the catch of fish, and he walked down the beach right after Jesus. And running along after the two of them went Simon's brother and business partner, Andrew.

Based on LUKE 5:1–12

Letters to the Editor

Write a letter to the editor. In the letter, give your reactions to what Simon and Andrew did.

LEARN ABOUT JESUS

When you get excited about something, you want to know more about it. If soccer excites you, you want to know how to play the game well. If you are into a computer game, you want to know all the tricks and traps. You talk with your friends about new techniques. If you have a favorite TV star, you are interested in what that star does—what he or she eats for dinner.

You are called to be one of Jesus' followers or **disciples.** You need to know all you can about Jesus and about what being a disciple means.

A PLACE TO START

Those who follow Jesus—the people of his time and the people today—all start with the belief that Jesus is the Son of God who came to announce God's reign of love. He saved all people from sin and from death. They believe that Jesus rose from the dead and returned to God the Father, and yet Jesus is alive and present in the world today. That is a good starting point for you, too.

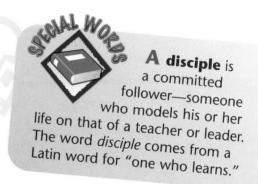

SPECIAL WORDS

A **disciple** is a committed follower—someone who models his or her life on that of a teacher or leader. The word *disciple* comes from a Latin word for "one who learns."

Jesus Makes a Difference

On the chart, there are three sayings of Jesus. Next to the saying is a real-life situation. In the space, write how learning about Jesus might make a difference to the people in each story.

Jesus Said	Real Life	The Difference
Blessed are they who mourn, for they will be comforted. MATTHEW 5:4	Lucy's best friend, Juanita, has moved away. Lucy is very lonely. She will never find another friend like Juanita.	
I am the resurrection and the life; whoever believes in me will live. JOHN 11:25	Donna just found out that her grandmother has cancer and has just a few months to live. Donna is scared and worried.	
Your sins are forgiven. LUKE 7:48	Mike is a seventh grader. He wanted to show off. He thought he would drive his mother's car around the block. He backed the car into a wall.	

JESUS CHANGES PEOPLE

Have you ever been changed by a new friend? Maybe your new friend liked to play table tennis, and so you learned to play the game, too. Maybe your friend read mysteries, and now you read mysteries, too.

Some friends of Jesus down through the ages have made some pretty big changes in their lives. Look at the grid below. It shows four friends of Jesus that the world knows as great saints. Read about their "before" and their "after." Then write how you have changed over the years that you have been a friend of Jesus.

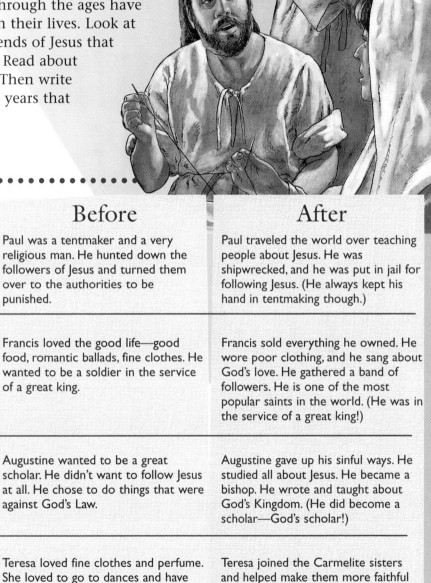

Friend of Jesus	Before	After
Saint Paul the Apostle	Paul was a tentmaker and a very religious man. He hunted down the followers of Jesus and turned them over to the authorities to be punished.	Paul traveled the world over teaching people about Jesus. He was shipwrecked, and he was put in jail for following Jesus. (He always kept his hand in tentmaking though.)
Saint Francis of Assisi	Francis loved the good life—good food, romantic ballads, fine clothes. He wanted to be a soldier in the service of a great king.	Francis sold everything he owned. He wore poor clothing, and he sang about God's love. He gathered a band of followers. He is one of the most popular saints in the world. (He was in the service of a great king!)
Saint Augustine	Augustine wanted to be a great scholar. He didn't want to follow Jesus at all. He chose to do things that were against God's Law.	Augustine gave up his sinful ways. He studied all about Jesus. He became a bishop. He wrote and taught about God's Kingdom. (He did become a scholar—God's scholar!)
Saint Teresa of Avila	Teresa loved fine clothes and perfume. She loved to go to dances and have fun with other young people.	Teresa joined the Carmelite sisters and helped make them more faithful followers of Jesus. She became a doctor of the Church. (Teresa still had some time for dancing with the sisters!)
You		

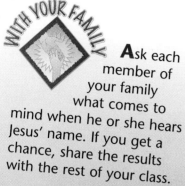
COVENANT

A covenant is a solemn agreement or promise. As you begin this year of meeting and learning about Jesus, it is a good idea to promise to do the very best job you can. Read and sign the Learning Covenant. On the covenant, write one way you can help the others in your class learn about Jesus.

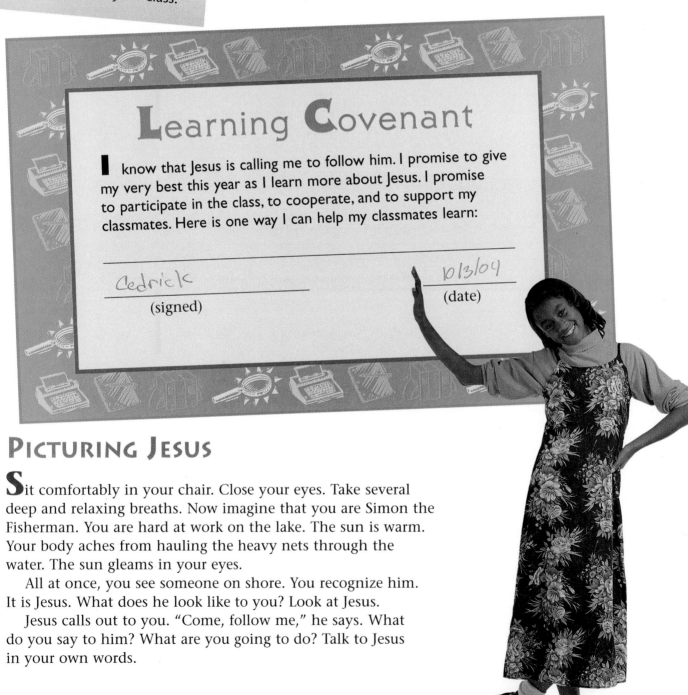

Learning Covenant

I know that Jesus is calling me to follow him. I promise to give my very best this year as I learn more about Jesus. I promise to participate in the class, to cooperate, and to support my classmates. Here is one way I can help my classmates learn:

Cedrick
(signed)

_10/3/04_
(date)

PICTURING JESUS

Sit comfortably in your chair. Close your eyes. Take several deep and relaxing breaths. Now imagine that you are Simon the Fisherman. You are hard at work on the lake. The sun is warm. Your body aches from hauling the heavy nets through the water. The sun gleams in your eyes.

All at once, you see someone on shore. You recognize him. It is Jesus. What does he look like to you? Look at Jesus.

Jesus calls out to you. "Come, follow me," he says. What do you say to him? What are you going to do? Talk to Jesus in your own words.

▼ REVIEW CHAPTER 1

CATHOLICS BELIEVE

1. Jesus is the Son of God, who came to announce God's reign of love.
2. Jesus died to save all people from sin and death.
3. Jesus rose from the dead and returned to his Father.
4. Jesus is present in the world today.

KNOW

Test what you already know about Jesus. In the spaces, write three things Jesus said and three things Jesus did. Try not to look back through the chapter to find the answers. See how much you can write from memory. Share what you have written.

What Jesus Said

1. Come follow me.

2. told peter to fish

3. blessed who they should be comforted.

What Jesus Did

1. rose from the dead

2. he caught many fish.

3. He healed people, Also provided heaven.

SUNDAY MASS

When you go to Sunday Mass, you will notice that many of the prayers at Mass end with the words, "Through Jesus Christ, your Son, our Lord." These words are used because community prayers are usually addressed *to* God the Father, *through* Jesus Christ. Next Sunday, pay very close attention. See just how many times the words "through Jesus Christ" are used at Mass.

2

CONTENT KEYS

1. **You learn from your family.**
2. **Jesus grew up in a Jewish family.**
3. **Jesus learned from his family.**

It's in the Mix

What goes into making you who you are? Use the following exercise to see how various people have influenced your life. Identify your physical characteristics, your personality traits, and your likes and dislikes. For each quality you identify, try to determine which parent or grandparent you most closely resemble. Write your answer in the appropriate vial. Traits that you can't trace back to a family member, place in the God-given vial. How are you influenced by your family?

And the Word became flesh and made his dwelling among us.

JOHN 1:14

ONE-OF-A-KIND

Sarah Louise is named for her two grandmothers. Everyone says that she looks just like her grandmother Louise, but acts just like her grandmother Sarah. Sarah Louise enjoys being compared to all of her grandparents. She knows that she owes them a real debt of thanks.

Like Sarah, you have received a great many traits and characteristics from your family. Is your hair red or black? Are you tall or short? Are you quiet and shy or loud and rambunctious? Whatever your looks or personality, you can thank your parents and grandparents. It is from them you inherited the genetic traits that make you who you are.

You have also been influenced by your family in other ways. Do you like sports or movies? Do you live in a small community or large city? Are you into gardening, auto repair, or helping others? Your family influences your choices by its attitudes, traditions, faith, and values.

(vials labeled: father, grandfather, grandmother, mother, grandfather, grandmother, God)

ALL IN THE FAMILY

Your study of Jesus begins with his life in a family. Jesus was a Jewish man. He had grandparents and great grandparents. He had a human mother and a human stepfather. Like you, Jesus was deeply affected by his family. Jesus was also shaped by the many stories of his Jewish ancestors.

How do families and the stories of their ancestors shape a person? Look at the lives of some seventh graders and see what you think.

What's in a Family?

1. Annie practically runs home every day after school. Her baby brother, Matt, is just learning to walk and talk. Annie never had any brothers or sisters before; now she thinks babies are the greatest people around. Annie's learning to take more responsibility around the house because of her new brother.

2. Annie's friend Rob has five brothers and sisters. He grew up babysitting and sharing a bedroom. Rob has learned that he is a role model for his younger brothers and sisters. Whatever Rob does, they try to do. Rob knows that if he acts out in anger, pretty soon everyone else in the house will be angry, too. Rob is learning to think before he acts.

3. Pete sits around after school and watches TV. His father and mother are divorced. His mother works the late shift, so she is not home when Pete comes home from school. Pete goes to bed before his mother gets home and leaves for school before his mother awakes. He feels very lonely and unloved. He wonders why he even bothers trying to learn, because no one seems to care.

4. Donna wants to be a sailor. Her Uncle Mark tells wonderful stories of all of the great sailors in their family's history. Donna spends every spare moment working on her small sailboat or trying to earn money to buy a bigger one. Her parents hope Donna receives a commission to the U.S. Naval Academy, another family tradition.

NOT EXACTLY AVERAGE

Four seventh graders, four families. Not exactly average—which family is?—but probably typical. You may know families like these. You may even be part of one. Whatever you do in life, you will always be influenced by your family.

Most people come to their faith in God through their families. Families and faith are interconnected, woven together like parts of a tapestry. Look at the language used to describe faith. God is called "Father." The family is called the "domestic church." You are a "child of God."

Although he was the Son of God, Jesus, too, grew up in a family. He experienced the ups and downs, joys and sorrows of family living, although the Gospel offers few stories about his early life. What he learned from his family and the stories of his ancestors definitely influenced his later ministry.

A MATTER OF INFLUENCE

Look again at the family lives of the four young people you've met in this chapter. How do each of their family situations offer opportunities for personal growth?

What could Annie learn from having a baby in the family?

_____

What can Rob gain from being a role model?

_____

How might Pete's sadness allow him to help other people?

_____

How has Donna's love for sailing been influenced by her family's naval tradition?

_____

Family Portrait

In the space provided, create a portrait of your family.

The Fourth Commandment asks you to honor your parents. When you honor people, you show them courtesy and respect. If you treat others with courtesy and respect, they will be more likely to treat you in the same way.

Roots and Wings

An old saying notes that the only two gifts parents can really give their children are roots and wings. Knowing your family history, what your family believes, and how your family acts can provide you with the roots of a stable foundation. It can help you feel attached to something important. Wings can provide you with the freedom to go out on your own, to try your own way, to make your own mark. Having roots can help you feel secure. Having wings can help you grow as a unique person.

Jesus' family provided him with deep roots. The attitudes and faith he learned from Mary and Joseph and his Jewish religious background are very important parts of his ministry. Both Matthew's and Luke's Gospels contain genealogies—family trees that trace Jesus' ancestry to David, the greatest king of Israel. Joseph, Mary's husband, was of the "house," or family, of David. It was this ancestry that brought the Holy Family to Bethlehem, the city of David, at the time of Jesus' birth (Luke 2:1–7).

Jesus' human family not only gave him roots, it also gave him wings. Jesus had the confidence and ability to do God's will, even at the cost of personal sacrifice. Jesus surely learned his great trust in God from the actions of Mary and Joseph, who showed total trust in God by their actions.

During his public ministry, Jesus relied heavily on his family roots. He knew Hebrew Scripture—including the Torah and the prophets—and taught from it. He followed the lead of his cousin John the Baptist and encouraged people to change their lives. His cousin James, who became the leader of the early Church in Jerusalem, was one of his earliest followers. His mother Mary is known as the first disciple.

Because of the great strength he gained from his family roots, Jesus was able to do great things. He was not afraid to challenge the rich and the powerful. He was not ashamed to be seen with the sick and the weak. He ate with sinners and tax collectors. He challenged the religious leaders of his time to go beyond fulfilling the letter of the law and show their love for God by loving their neighbor.

JESUS' FAMILY TREE

The Hebrew Scriptures contain the stories of Jesus' religious ancestors. Here is a quick sketch of some of the important people in Jesus' family tree.

God promised that Abraham would be the father of a great nation. Abraham believed God's promise and moved his family far from home to the land of Canaan. Abraham made a covenant with God. The descendants of Abraham and his wife Sarah would worship God alone, and God would make them the Chosen People. Abraham is remembered for his trust in God.

Ruth could have abandoned her Hebrew mother-in-law and stayed with her own people, the Moabites. But Ruth believed in the Hebrew God. Ruth's faithfulness is remembered in the book that bears her name because she was the great-grandmother of King David.

David united the twelve tribes of Israel into a strong nation. He was a military genius and an astute politician. David is also remembered for his great love for God. He was a musician who played and danced before the Ark of the Covenant. David is thought to have written some of the psalms.

GOD'S PEOPLE

Jesus had many other ancestors in faith. Read about one of the following and decide what Jesus would have learned from that person's story. Be prepared to share your findings with the class.

Sarah (Genesis 18:1–15)

Isaac and Rebekah (Genesis 24)

Leah and Rachel (Genesis 29:4–30:24)

Jacob (Genesis 32:23–33)

Deborah (Judges 4:1–5:31)

Solomon (1 Kings 3:1–28)

Elijah (1 Kings 18: 21–40)

Ezra (Nehemiah 8:1–6)

Esther (Esther 4–8:8)

Micah (Micah 4:1–5; 6:8)

THE HOLY FAMILY

Jesus would have been most influenced by his immediate family, Mary and Joseph. Mary was a young girl when God chose her to be the mother of Jesus. By agreeing to God's request, Mary allowed God's plan for salvation to be fulfilled. Her "yes" was a supreme act of trust in God.

Little is known about Joseph. Tradition teaches that Joseph was a craftsman in wood because Jesus was called the carpenter's son. What the Bible does say is that Joseph was brave and willing to follow God's will. He protected and provided for his family through very troubling times.

With their actions, Mary and Joseph taught Jesus to trust in the goodness of God, as they had. They taught Jesus the importance of being faithful through their love for each other and through living their Jewish faith. They were witnesses to the importance of accepting and living God's plan.

Mary and Joseph were also caring people. Mary rushed to the side of her aging cousin Elizabeth, who was pregnant *(Luke 1:39–56)*. Mary interceded on behalf of the newly married couple at Cana *(John 2:1–3)*. Joseph took a pregnant Mary into his home and cared for her son as his own. Although no details are supplied in Scripture, the care and compassion Jesus showed for the sick and the lonely, the sinner, and the social outcast proved that he came from a loving, caring family.

IN THE TEMPLE

When he was twelve, Jesus and his family went to Jerusalem to celebrate Passover. After Passover, Jesus' family started home, but Jesus was left behind. When they discovered Jesus missing, his parents—worried about his safety—hurried back to Jerusalem to search for him. They found Jesus in the Temple courtyard, calmly talking about the Law with the learned teachers. When asked what he was doing, Jesus said that he was doing his Father's work.

According to Luke 2:50, Mary and Joseph did not understand what Jesus said to them. Do parents ever understand their adolescent children? Luke adds, however, that Jesus returned to Nazareth with his parents and was obedient to them. "And Jesus advanced in wisdom and age and favor before God" *(Luke 2:52)*.

1. **Why are "roots" and "wings" important gifts for parents to give their children?**
2. **How was Jesus' mission shaped by his family?**

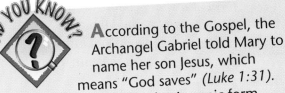

DID YOU KNOW?

According to the Gospel, the Archangel Gabriel told Mary to name her son Jesus, which means "God saves" *(Luke 1:31)*. His friends knew him by the Aramaic form, *Yeshua bar Yosef* ("Jesus, or Joshua, son of Joseph"). In Spanish, he is known as *Jesus* (Hay-SOOS); in Japanese, *Iesu* (Ee-ay-soo); in Vietnamese, *Jeisu* (ZAY-soo). What names for Jesus are common in your tradition?

TRUSTING GOD

Jesus would have learned from the stories of Abraham and King David that trusting God's will (or Divine Providence) takes a great deal of personal sacrifice. Most people find it difficult to give up what they want to do in order to follow God.

On the lines below, or in your journal, write about what you have learned from your family that will help you be a loving and caring person. Be sure to include your thoughts on the gifts and strengths God has given you, and some ways you can begin practicing trust in God right now.

_____

_____

_____

_____

_____

_____

_____

Look through family pictures with an adult family member who knows your family history. Talk about the important things that are part of your family heritage. Write a note of thanks to a living relative for what he or she has passed on to you.

A PRAYER OF BLESSING

Have among yourselves the same attitude that is also yours in Christ Jesus, who, though he was in the form of God, did not regard equality with God something to be grasped. Rather, he emptied himself, taking the form of a slave, coming in human likeness; and found human in appearance, he humbled himself, becoming obedient to death, even death on a cross.

PHILIPPIANS 2:5–8

▼ REVIEW CHAPTER 2 · · · · · · · · · · · · · · · · ·

CATHOLICS BELIEVE

1. Jesus grew in wisdom and knowledge.
2. Jesus received support for his divine mission from Mary, his mother, and Joseph, his stepfather.
3. Families are important in everyone's faith life.

KNOW

1. What are three ways that Jesus was influenced by his family?
2. What would Jesus have learned from the stories of these ancestors: Abraham, Ruth, David?
3. Why is it important to know about Jesus' immediate family and his Jewish ancestors?
4. Using the story of Jesus lost in the Temple, explain how Jesus was like any twelve-year-old child. How was he different?

SUNDAY MASS

After the Scripture readings at Mass, the entire congregation joins in saying the Prayer of the Faithful. These prayers include petitions for the entire world, the Universal Church, the local community, and parish needs. Join your prayers for your family to those of the whole Church family in the Prayer of the Faithful at Mass.

He shall be called a Nazorean.

MATTHEW 2:23

FAMILY CUSTOMS

Rosemary was excited. Her birthday was in two weeks and she was telling her friends about the great party she was going to have.

"My family always does the same thing to celebrate a birthday," Rosemary said. "My mother fixes our favorite dinner—I love pizza—and then we have an ice cream cake from Roberti's Bakery. Everyone sings Happy Birthday, and then we open presents. I hope I get a new CD this year."

Her friend Young-hee spoke up. "In my family, we honor the birthday person with a bowl of seaweed soup. That's how it's done in Korea."

"Seaweed soup!" Rosemary gasped.

"Oh, it may sound gross," Young-hee responded, "but it actually tastes delicious. You should try it sometime."

"No, thanks," Rosemary said.

"My family celebrates birthdays with a traditional Indian meal," Rekha chimed in. "My favorite is spinach cooked with rice, cooked pumpkin, and a homemade bread called *roti*."

"In Nicaragua we have cake and ice cream too, along with a piñata filled with candy," Alexis said. "But what I really like is the sweet homemade corn drink we call *chicha*. My father makes it especially for me."

"Wow," said Rosemary. "Families sure do celebrate birthdays in lots of different ways!"

we go to the Philippines for Christmas.

Our Way

How does your family celebrate birthdays, Christmas, and other special occasions? Choose one holiday and describe the way your family celebrates. Compare your findings with those of several classmates. How do your family's customs differ?

WHERE JESUS LIVED

People from different cultures have different ways of celebrating special occasions. Custom and culture affect how you celebrate special occasions. They influence who you are and how you think.

Jesus was influenced by the time and place where he lived, just like you are. To understand Jesus' message, you need to understand more about first century Palestine.

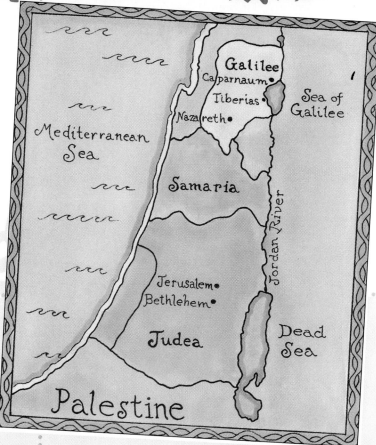

TIME-TRAVEL TOURS

Pilgrimage to the **Holy Land**
Overnight Stop: Jerusalem

Begin your pilgrimage in historic Jerusalem, capital of the southern province of Judea. King David made it the capital a thousand years ago. Visit the magnificent Temple, the center of the Jewish faith. Come and offer your sacrifice to God.

THE CITY OF DAVID

Only a few miles south of Jerusalem is the little town of Bethlehem, the city where David was born and anointed king. Did you know that Jesus the Nazorean was actually born in Bethlehem?

YOUR JOURNEY CONTINUES

Travel by caravan to the northern province of Galilee. Be prepared for an uncomfortable trip. The roads are hot and dusty. You will be walking unless you can afford to hire a donkey. Don't worry about the many violent bandits on the roads; you will be traveling with a large group.

Your journey will take you through the province of Samaria. Samaritans are disliked by Jews from Judea and Galilee because of the differences in their religious beliefs and practices.

The tour bypasses Tiberias, the capital of Galilee. Tiberias is shunned by the Jews as the seat of Roman rule and as an unclean city built on an ancient burial ground.

Choose between tending sheep with the local shepherds or picking grapes in an authentic vineyard.

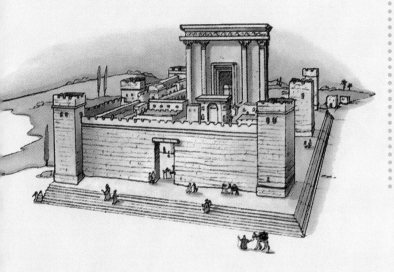

OVERNIGHT STOP: CAPERNAUM

Capernaum is a fishing town of about five thousand people situated on the Sea of Galilee, a freshwater lake. Jesus' disciples, Peter, James, Andrew, and Matthew, live in Capernaum. Jesus uses the town as a center for his teaching. You will have the opportunity to sail on the lake, but be warned that sudden dangerous storms are always a possibility.

Enjoy a journey of twenty-three miles through the fertile countryside of Galilee to the hillside village of Nazareth. Travel through fields of barley and wheat; vineyards; and groves of olive, almond, and date palm. Although Nazareth is home to only a few hundred people, its marketplace is a great spot to buy local produce and crafts, such as farm tools, woven baskets, and pottery. Often you can buy exotic foods and spices in the market, but be prepared to pay a higher price than you would in Jerusalem. This is Jesus' hometown, which is why he is called the Nazorean.

DELUXE ACCOMMODATIONS

You will spend each night of the trip with a local family (and their sheep, chickens, and goats) in a one- or two-room mud brick house. Dine on local foods, such as fruits (dates and melons), vegetables (beans and peas), bread, goat cheese, and olives.

Sleep on the floor inside the house or, if the weather is clear and warm, on the flat roof. Plan to sleep on a woven mat—the houses contain little or no furniture. Be sure to bring along a cloak to use as a covering, for the nights are very cool. Everyone in the family sleeps in the same area, so don't expect any privacy.

SPECIAL WORDS

The **Holy Land** is the land where Jesus lived. It is holy to three religions. Bethlehem, Nazareth, and Jerusalem are especially sacred to Christians. Jews believe this area is the Promised Land, given to them by God.

LIFE IN GALILEE

Jesus is called the Nazorean because he grew up in Nazareth two thousand years ago. There was no electricity, indoor plumbing, fast food, telephones, automobiles, or television then. People spent most of their time making a living. The work day ran from dawn to dark, and everyone in the family was expected to work. There was little time for leisure. Fathers taught their sons and mothers taught their daughters the skills they needed to survive.

The Roman province of Galilee was a crossroads for trade and culture. People from many races and nationalities lived there. (Jews referred to these people as Gentiles—non-Jews.) Caravans from all over the Roman Empire would pass through Galilee, bringing foreign treasures, languages, and beliefs into Jesus' community. Many people earned their living by trading with the caravans. Most people spoke Aramaic, but Latin, Hebrew, and Greek were also commonly used.

Although Galilee is very hilly and dry, most of the people there were farmers who raised wheat, barley, grapes, and olives. They also tended flocks of sheep and goats. Galilean farmers plowed with oxen and scattered seeds by hand. Most of the crops they raised went to feed their families. The farmers also used their produce for trade and to pay their taxes. Farmers depended on God's gift of weather for their very survival. Without the winter rains, their crops would fail. Some Galileans were also craftsmen, like Joseph, who was a carpenter. Jesus probably studied this trade as a boy.

Many Galileans also made their living from the freshwater Sea of Galilee. Jesus' first followers—James, John, Andrew, and Simon—all were fishermen. Rowing their boats out on the Sea of Galilee, the fishermen would toss their weighted nets toward a likely spot. When the net had sunk to the bottom, they would haul it into the boat. Then the fishermen would sort their catch. Even today, the most plentiful fish found in the Sea of Galilee are small, like sardines. Fishermen would work from very early morning (4 a.m.) to mid-afternoon to catch enough fish to eat and sell.

IN HIS OWN WORDS

Jesus proclaimed the Good News using stories based upon his life in Nazareth and Galilee. Look at these examples Jesus used to teach his followers. What was Jesus teaching in each story? Why would Jesus use these stories to make his point?

"If a man were to scatter seed on the land and would sleep and rise night and day, and the seed would sprout and grow, he knows not how" (*Mark 4:26–27*).

"The kingdom of God is like yeast that a woman took and mixed in with three measures of wheat flour until the whole batch of dough was leavened" (*Luke 13:21*).

"I am the good shepherd. A good shepherd lays down his life for his sheep" (*John 10:11*).

"I am the true vine, and my Father is the vine grower" (*John 15:1*).

"I am the bread of life; whoever comes to me will never hunger" (*John 6:35*).

"A city set on a mountain cannot be hidden. Nor do they light a lamp and then put it under a bushel basket; it is set on a lampstand, where it gives light to all in the house" (*Matthew 5:14–15*).

Following Jesus

You can follow Jesus by showing respect for the customs and traditions of others. Taste new foods. Don't make fun of the dress or customs of others. Try to learn as much as you can about customs that seem unusual to you. By showing respect in this way, you show that you care for other people.

Modern-Day Stories

Jesus used images from his time and place. What images would Jesus use to make his points today? Rewrite each of the above statements using modern images to make Jesus' meaning clear to adolescents today. Be prepared to read your statements aloud.

JESUS MADE CHOICES

Jesus was certainly shaped by his culture and his surroundings. The stories he told focused on a farmer sowing seeds, fishermen casting their nets, and a shepherd trying to do a good job. Jesus talked about God's presence in the everyday lives of the people he knew.

You may think that your life is very different from that of the young Jesus growing up in Nazareth two thousand years ago. After all, Nazareth was a tiny village, primitive by modern standards. You probably don't run across many flocks of sheep and goats on your way to school!

While the world has certainly changed since Jesus' time, many things remain the same. Families still struggle to make a living. People still complain about taxes and government. Crime is still a problem. And people are still pressured by friends or society to make decisions that are wrong and hurtful.

Jesus had to learn to make good choices, too, even though he was the Son of God. Luke 2:52 says that Jesus grew in wisdom, age, and favor. Jesus was not God acting as a human being, but was really human. He learned to make wise decisions through trial and error, just as you do. He had to choose which cultural influences he would follow and which he would ignore.

As Hebrews 4:15 says, Jesus is able to sympathize with your every problem because he "has been similarly tested in every way, yet without sin." Jesus was a person like you. He struggled with many of the same issues and problems that you face. In the face of these temptations, he chose to do God's will in all things. You are called in your own time and world to do the same.

1. **What evidence is there that Jesus' life in Nazareth influenced his teaching and ministry?**
2. **How does knowing something about Jesus' background help you understand him better?**
3. **What are some of the choices you have to make? What can you learn from Jesus to help you make better choices?**

INFLUENTIAL EFFECTS

Just as living in Nazareth shaped Jesus and his message, so your community shapes who you are and how you grow in faith. Take a moment to think of some of the values, events, and attitudes that influence you right now. In the space provided, write down as many influences as you can. Tell whether you think each influence is positive or negative. Describe how it affects your growth in faith.

Influence	Positive/Negative	How It Affects Me
_____	_____	_____
_____	_____	_____
_____	_____	_____

HALLOWING YOUR LIFE

Jesus, you taught us that God is our loving Father, who desires for us everything that is good. Therefore, we pray for God's blessing now on those we love, and on those who care for us. We pray for all those people who refresh us, inspire us, and shelter us. We ask you to be present in everything we do. Amen.

WITH YOUR FAMILY

Ask a parent, grandparent, or other adult family member to tell you a story about his or her childhood. Discuss how this person's community was the same as and different from your own. How does hearing this story give you more understanding of the person who lived it?

▼ REVIEW CHAPTER 3 ·····················

CATHOLICS BELIEVE

1. Jesus grew up in a particular time and place.
2. Jesus' environment influenced the images he used in teaching.
3. Jesus' life in Nazareth provides examples of how a person should live.

KNOW

Answer the following questions.

1. Where was Jesus born?
2. Why is Jesus called the Nazorean or the Galilean?
3. Who ruled Palestine during Jesus' life?
4. What are some of the chores Jesus might have done as a child?
5. What name is used for the part of the Middle East where Jesus lived?
6. What trade would Jesus have learned as a child? Why would he have learned this trade?
7. What are three examples of how Jesus was influenced by the time and community in which he lived?

SUNDAY MASS

You gather for Mass each Sunday with other members of your parish. This group of people has an influence on your life. At Mass this Sunday, identify the people in the parish that you know. Make sure to offer them the sign of peace.

4

CONTENT KEYS

1. **Jesus was Jewish.**
2. **The covenant is essential to Judaism.**
3. **Jesus fulfilled the covenant.**

You shall love the Lord, your God, with all your heart, and with all your soul, and with all your strength.

DEUTERONOMY 6:5

A PROMISE

Beth and Susan were good friends. Only two months ago, they made string bracelets together as a sign of their friendship. Blue was for Susan, green for Beth, and red for the bond between them. They swore always to be friends. They promised never to betray one another's trust. Susan thought of this as she fingered the friendship bracelet on her wrist, gently plucking the intertwined threads.

"Hey," said Rob. "You're not paying attention!"

"What?" Susan said.

"Does Beth like Jim or doesn't she?"

"I won't tell you."

"Ah, come on. Beth will never find out."

Susan plucked the bracelet again.

"Whether Beth finds out or not, I still won't tell. Beth asked me not to. I'd never betray Beth's trust."

Susan gave her bracelet a final tug. "You'll know soon enough, when Beth's ready to speak for herself."

A Strong Relationship

How do you and your friends show the strength of your relationship? Describe or draw a sign of friendship and explain what the sign means to you.

PEOPLE OF THE COVENANT

There are many signs that people use to show their relationship. Beth and Susan had a friendship bracelet. Married couples wear wedding rings to show their love and permanent commitment to each other. For the Jewish people, the **covenant** is the sign of their relationship with God.

Almost four thousand years ago, God formed a covenant with Abraham, the father of the Jewish people. God promised Abraham that if he were faithful to God, God would reward him and his descendants. Centuries later, God renewed this covenant through Moses.

Hebrew Scripture preserves the story of God's covenant with the Jewish people, especially in the first five books, known as the **Torah.** The Books of Leviticus and Deuteronomy in particular set out the laws Jews must keep if they are to remain faithful to the covenant. These laws are so central to Jewish faith that they have come to be known simply as "the Law," or "the Law of Moses."

Covenant between God and the Israelites

The Israelites will
Worship the one, true God
Obey the commandments
Keep the specific laws concerning worship, work, property, and family

God will
Make the Israelites God's Chosen People, dearer to God than all other people.

FULFILLING THE COVENANT

The covenant with God shapes every aspect of Jewish life. The covenant is fulfilled by living the Law. The Law spells out how Jews are to live, how family members are to behave toward one another, how business transactions are to be made, and how crimes are to be punished. As a sign of the covenant, Jewish males were circumcized.

Jews in Jesus' time would begin and end each day by following the teachings of the Law. In the morning, they would say a prayer of faith and thanks to God. They would also pray before washing, eating, and leaving or returning home. Specific laws were different for men and women, but each group was called to pray throughout the day.

In Jesus' time, Jews followed strict dietary laws. Certain animals—camels, hares, and pigs, for example—were considered unclean, and so were not eaten *(Leviticus 11)*. Creatures that lived in water, but that did not have scales and fins—lobsters, crabs, and shrimp for example—were also considered unclean. Even touching the dead flesh of one of these animals made a person unclean. An unclean person would have to be purified through an act of ritual sacrifice before he or she could again participate fully in the life of the Jewish community.

Jews in Jesus' time offered prayers and animal sacrifices to God in the Temple in Jerusalem, as required by the Law. When Jesus was presented in the Temple *(Luke 2:22–24)*, Mary and Joseph offered a sacrifice of two turtledoves or pigeons to fulfill the Law.

Jews gathered in the local synagogue three times on the Sabbath for prayer. The Sabbath was the day that God rested after creating the world *(Genesis 2:2)*. The Sabbath was kept from sundown on Friday until sundown on Saturday. On the Sabbath, most work was forbidden.

Jewish boys in Jesus' day attended school at the **synagogue** for at least eight years. The primary course of study was the Hebrew Scriptures, especially the Law of Moses, found in the Torah. Jewish boys would also study Jewish customs, traditions, history, and prayers. We know Jesus studied the prophetic books from Hebrew Scripture because he quoted them so frequently.

Many Jews—particularly Orthodox and Conservative Jews—continue to follow traditional Jewish customs and practices. Other Jewish groups follow a modern interpretation of Jewish law. All Jews continue to honor the covenant as a sign of their relationship with God.

> **SPECIAL WORDS**
>
> A **synagogue** is a place where Jews gather to pray, read, and study Scripture.

1. **How do Jews fulfill their covenant with God?**
2. **What are three examples of how keeping the Law shaped Jewish life?**

A Prophetic Tradition

Judaism has a long tradition of prophets. Prophets speak God's divinely inspired message, reminding people of how they should live. The prophets' task was never easy. They had the difficult task of calling the people of Israel back to faithfulness to the covenant. Prophets were abused, beaten, and generally mistreated because of their message. Jesus was a part of this prophetic tradition.

A Prophetic Voice

A scene at the Temple in Jerusalem.
Cast: The Prophet Micah, a judge, the crowd

Judge: We are here today to hear a complaint against the people of Israel. Who makes this complaint?

Micah: I do.

Judge: And who are you?

Micah: I am the prophet, Micah. God sent me to warn the people of Israel that they are not keeping the covenant.

Judge: What do you mean?

Micah: Look around you, Judge. People are angry and jealous with their neighbors. They lie, cheat, and steal. They forget to honor God, to follow the Torah, and to keep the Sabbath.

Crowd: Don't listen to him, Judge. What does he know? Who is he, anyway?

Micah: I told you. I am God's prophet. God called me and commanded me to speak. The words that come from my mouth are God's words. Repent! Change your ways, or God will punish you!

Crowd: Punish us? Not likely. It's you, prophet, who are in danger.

Micah: Do you threaten me?

Judge: I think the crowd only wants to remind you of what usually happens to prophets.

Micah: I know what happens to prophets. They are murdered because people cannot bear to hear the truth. They can kill me, too, but God will just send another prophet.

Crowd: Boo! Hiss! Get him out of here!

Micah: Repent! God is eager to forgive. Change your ways.

Crowd: We don't want to change! Stone him!

Judge: Wait! Too late. Another prophet is gone.

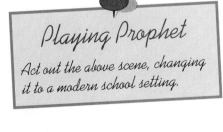

Playing Prophet

Act out the above scene, changing it to a modern school setting.

Jesus the Jew

Jesus was a Jew, brought up in the faith and traditions of Israel. He celebrated the Sabbath and the great feast of Passover, and he prayed in the Temple. Jesus was a student of the Law. During his public ministry, he was known as a rabbi, a master or teacher of the Law. Jesus followed a long line of Jewish storytellers and holy men. Jesus was also a prophet. He spoke God's word to the people.

When asked which was the greatest commandment (a question the Temple teachers argued constantly), Jesus answered with a statement about relationships.

> *You shall love the Lord, your God, with all your heart, with all your soul, and with all your mind. This is the greatest and first commandment. The second is like it: You shall love your neighbor as yourself. The whole Law and the prophets depend on these two commandments.*
>
> Matthew 22:37–40

Jesus simplified all 613 commandments in the Law of Moses into these two statements.

The things Jesus said about God's kingdom sounded new and strange to some people. His teachings made people feel uncomfortable at times because he challenged them to follow God more lovingly. Yet Jesus was careful to point out his faithfulness to the Law.

> *Do not think I have come to abolish the Law and the prophets. I have come not to abolish but to fulfill. Amen, I say to you whoever obeys and teaches these commandments will be called the greatest in the kingdom of heaven.*
>
> Matthew 5:17,19

Jesus asked people to look first at their relationship with God, and then determine how they would be faithful to the Law. He did not discard the Law of Moses; he asked people to live it more fully. He did not destroy Israel's covenant with God; he came to seal a new covenant in his own blood.

A New Covenant

Hundreds of years before the birth of Jesus, the prophet Jeremiah foretold the coming of a new covenant.

> *The days are coming, says the Lord, when I will make a new covenant with the house of Israel and the house of Judah. This is the covenant which I will make with the house of Israel after those days, says the Lord. I will place my law within them, and write it upon their hearts; I will be their God, and they shall be my people.*
>
> JEREMIAH 31:31,33

Jesus was to implement this new covenant through his words and actions.

On the night before he died, Jesus ate a Passover meal with his disciples. During this meal he introduced a new covenant. Lifting the cup of wine he said, "This cup is the new covenant in my blood; do this in remembrance of me" *(1 Corinthians 11:25)*.

1. Why would Jesus' teachings make some people uncomfortable or even angry?
2. Jesus said the greatest commandments were to love God and to love your neighbor. Explain how these two commandments sum up the entire Law of Moses.
3. What was the role of the prophets in Israel?

Covenant Words

These words describe people who follow God's covenant by loving God and their neighbor.

FAITHFUL
LOYAL
PATIENT
TRUSTING
OPEN

RESPECTFUL
GENEROUS
HOPEFUL
LOVING

You Are a Covenant Person

Read the following situations. Using the Covenant Words, describe a covenant person's response to each situation.

A man is standing on the side of the road with a sign that reads "Will Work for Food."

A neighbor has just returned from a week in the hospital.

Volunteers are needed to clean up abandoned lots and to paint over graffiti.

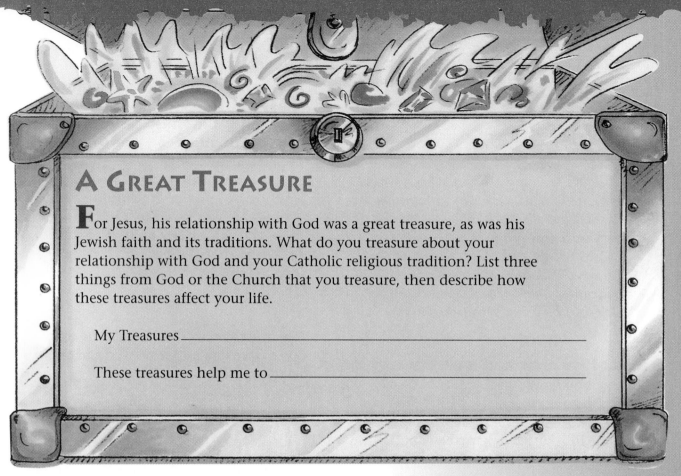

A GREAT TREASURE

For Jesus, his relationship with God was a great treasure, as was his Jewish faith and its traditions. What do you treasure about your relationship with God and your Catholic religious tradition? List three things from God or the Church that you treasure, then describe how these treasures affect your life.

My Treasures _____

These treasures help me to _____

GENERATION AFTER GENERATION

The psalms are a treasure for both Jews and Christians. As a class, pray these verses from PSALM 145. Your voices will be joining in a tradition that is three thousand years old.

Group 1: O God, I will bless your name forever and ever. Every day I will bless you.

Group 2: You are great Lord, and highly to be praised. Everyone praises your works and proclaims your might.

Group 1: The Lord is gracious and merciful, slow to anger, and of great kindness. The Lord is good to all, and compassionate.

Group 2: Let all your works give you thanks, O Lord, and let your faithful ones bless you.

All: The Lord is just in all things. The Lord hears our cries and saves us.

Adapted from PSALM 145:1–4—8–10, 13, 17, 19

WITH YOUR FAMILY

Pray a verse from PSALM 145 with your family as your prayer before meals this week. Be sure to pray for anyone who needs God's help.

▼REVIEW CHAPTER 4 ....

CATHOLICS BELIEVE

1. God formed a covenant with Abraham. Abraham and Sarah's descendants are the Chosen People.
2. The Hebrew Scriptures tell the story of God's covenant with the Chosen People.
3. Jesus was a Jewish rabbi and prophet.
4. Jesus formed a new covenant with his own blood.

KNOW

1. What was Jesus' faith tradition?
2. What was the task of the prophets? What often happened to prophets?
3. Explain the Jewish people's covenant relationship with God.
4. What is the Torah?
5. What is the new covenant?

SUNDAY MASS

At Mass, a psalm is usually sung or read in response to the first reading. At Mass this Sunday, consider how the psalm fits the first reading. Be prepared to discuss your findings in class.

MARY, MOTHER OF GOD

Mary is unique among all the women of the world. She was chosen to be the Mother of God. She alone was conceived without original sin. She is your most powerful intercessor, the one who prays for you before God. Mary is also the model for all Christian believers.

Fra Angelico, *Annunciation*. 15th century.

Mary is the model of faith. When the angel brought the news that she was to be the mother of the Messiah, she did not hesitate. She answered, "May it be done to me according to your word" *(Luke 1:38).*

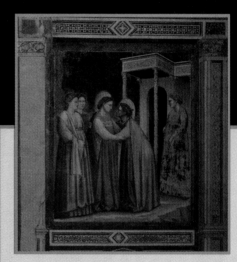

Giotto, *The Visitation*. 13th century.

Mary is a model of charity. She is the mother in faith of all people who follow Jesus. She is a witness to God's love. She offered great kindness to her pregnant cousin Elizabeth.

Zubaran, *The Young Virgin Praying*. 17th century.

Mary is the model of prayer. Her canticle, or song of praise, is one of the great prayers in Scripture. "My soul proclaims the greatness of the Lord; my spirit rejoices in God my savior" *(Luke 1:46–47).*

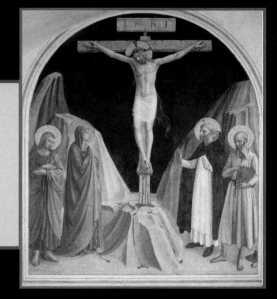

Fra Angelico, *Crucifixion*. 15th century.

Mary is a model of faithfulness. She stayed with Jesus throughout his entire ministry and beside him even as he died on the cross.

El Greco, *The Pentacost*. 16th century.

Mary is a model disciple. She followed Jesus, proclaimed his Good News, and lived as God commanded. She received the Holy Spirit at Pentecost.

Fra Angelico, *Coronation of the Virgin*. 15th century.

Through her Assumption into heaven, Mary shares in Jesus' resurrection. Mary's life in heaven looks forward to the resurrection of all Christians.

In Honor of Mary

Write a poem or make a drawing honoring Mary.

LEARNING

1. **Why do Christians follow Jesus?** Christians follow Jesus because he is the Son of God.
2. **Who is Jesus?** Jesus is truly God and truly man.
3. **Why is it important that Jesus grew up in a human community?** Because Jesus grew up in Nazareth, his life provides an example for all of his followers.
4. **Why is the Jewish religion significant to Christians?** Jesus was Jewish. He is the fulfillment of God's promises to Israel. Christian beliefs and practices grew out of the Jewish faith.

LIVING

You can call upon Jesus as a friend and companion any time you want. Memorize these short prayers and say them whenever you feel afraid, angry, or sad. These prayers will be like spare change in your pocket when you desperately need to make a phone call home.

> *"My Lord and my God."*
> *"O God, I trust in you."*
> *"Jesus, help me."*
> *"Come Holy Spirit."*
> *"Holy Mary, Mother of God, pray for us."*
> *"Lord, have mercy."*

ASKING

1. How is my life different because I am a disciple of Jesus?
2. What have I done recently to show that I am a disciple of Jesus?
3. What have I done recently to show my love for God and for my neighbor?

PRAYING

Group 1: Though he was in the form of God, he did not regard equality with God as something to be grasped.

All: Jesus Christ is Lord!

Group 2: Rather, he emptied himself, taking the form of a slave, coming in human likeness.

All: Jesus Christ is Lord!

Group 1: And found human in appearance, he humbled himself, becoming obedient to death, even death on a cross.

All: Jesus Christ is Lord!

Group 2: Because of this, God greatly exalted him, and bestowed on him the name that is above every name.

All: Jesus Christ is Lord!

Group 1: That at the name of Jesus, every knee should bend, of those in heaven and on earth and under the earth,

Group 2: and every tongue confess that Jesus Christ is Lord, to the glory of God the Father.

All: Jesus Christ is Lord!

PHILIPPIANS 2:6–11

Jesus the Messiah

Angelico, *Sermon on the Mount*. 15th century.

Jesus challenged his listener
To have absolute faith in God as a loving Father.
To place no limits on love.
To treat all people as neighbors.

GOD'S PROMISE FULFILLED

We have found the Messiah.

JOHN 1:41

CONTENT KEYS

1. **The Jewish people expect a Messiah.**
2. **Jesus begins his public ministry.**
3. **Jesus announces the reign of God.**

THE LONG WAIT

Simeon was tired and discouraged. His bones hurt, his eyes were failing, and he was ready to let go of life. Simeon lived for only one thing: to see God's promised Messiah. Each day Simeon went to the Temple and prayed that God's promise would be fulfilled.

How long, O Lord? Will you utterly forget me? How long will you hide your face from me? How long shall I harbor sorrow in my soul, grief in my heart, day after day? How long will my enemy triumph over me? Look, answer me, O Lord, my God!

PSALM 13:2–4

"The psalmist certainly had a way with words," Simeon thought. "I know that God's time is eternal, but mine isn't. How long, O Lord, must I wait?"

"Soon," God answered him. "Very soon. You will live to see the day. Watch and pray."

A couple entered the Temple to offer thanks to God for the birth of their son. "Could this child be the one?" Simeon wondered.

"Yes, as I have promised," God responded.

Simeon was overcome with joy. Taking the baby from the surprised parents, Simeon clutched him eagerly and gazed into his face. Unable to contain himself any longer, Simeon prayed.

Now, Master, you may let your servant go in peace, according to your word, for my eyes have seen your salvation, which you prepared in sight of all the peoples, a light for revelation to the Gentiles, and the glory of your people Israel.

Giving the boy back to his astonished parents, Simeon left the Temple singing God's praises. The long wait was over. God's promise had been fulfilled!

Based on LUKE 2:25–33

Keeping Watch

Tell a story about waiting for something that you really wanted. Describe what it's like to wait for something you want very badly. How did you feel when the wait was over?

A NATION WAITS

The nation of Israel was once an independent kingdom. Under the rule of the great kings David and Solomon, Israel experienced peace and prosperity. But by the time of Jesus, the Jewish people knew only oppression and foreign control. The nation had been split by civil war, defeated by the Assyrians, taken into captivity by the Babylonians, persecuted by the Persians, humiliated by the Greeks, and dominated by the Romans. After eighty years of Roman rule, many Jews anxiously awaited the birth of the Messiah foretold by the prophet Isaiah.

WHEN WILL THE MESSIAH COME?

Joshua and Zach had been on the road all day. The last thing they wanted was to be stopped and questioned by a Roman soldier. By the time the soldier let them go, Joshua kicked at the dirt in the road.

"It makes me angry," he snarled, "to have to answer to foreigners in my own country."

"The Romans think this is their country," Zach replied.

"Come on, Zach. God promised Abraham this land forever. One day, with God's help, it'll be ours again. A mighty warrior will appear in Jerusalem."

"You mean the Messiah?" Zach asked.

"Many people are expecting him," responded Joshua.

Zach shifted the load on his aching shoulders. "Some say he's here now," he said softly.

"Are you thinking of that prophet, John the Baptist? He's no Messiah. What a raggedy-looking fellow! I hear he dresses in camel hide and eats nothing but locusts and wild honey."

"He speaks with power," Zach said.

Joshua waved his arms in the air as if he were haranguing a crowd.

"I can just imagine," he said. "Repent! Change your ways! Prophets always sing the same song. I want to see the Romans overthrown, their palaces reduced to dust, and Israel restored to its former glory!"

SPECIAL WORDS

Messiah is the Hebrew word for "anointed one." The Messiah is the savior sent by God.

PREPARE THE WAY

John the Baptist attracted a great deal of attention in first-century Palestine. He dressed in rough robes of camel hide, and his hair and beard were long and shaggy. Although he lived in the desert, people from all over Judea came to see and hear him.

John didn't speak in synagogues. He stood knee-deep in the Jordan River, and preached a hard and challenging message of repentance to all who would listen.

"You brood of vipers," John told the crowd. "Who warned you to flee from the coming wrath? Even now the ax lies at the root of the trees. Therefore every tree that does not produce good fruit will be cut down and thrown into the fire."

"Repent, for the kingdom of heaven is at hand," John proclaimed. "Change your ways. Share your food with the hungry, your clothes with the naked. Take only what belongs to you. Treat people fairly. Be honest."

People heard John's message and were baptized by him in the Jordan River as a sign of their repentance.

Some people thought that John was the prophet Elijah or even the Messiah himself, but John denied being either.

> *I am baptizing you with water, but one mightier than I is coming. I am not worthy to loosen the thongs of his sandals. He will baptize you with the Holy Spirit and fire.*
>
> LUKE 3:16

John was a true prophet, pointing out sinfulness wherever he saw it. He chastised Herod, the governor of Galilee, for committing adultery. Herod promptly had John put in prison. (See *Matthew 3:1–12* and *Luke 3:1–20*.)

MESSIAH UPDATE

You are a reporter for the *Judean Times*. Using the information you have, write an article on John and the expected Messiah. What was the power of John's message?

John was more than a prophet—he prepared the Lord's way. He pointed out the sinfulness of the society in which he lived. Like earlier prophets, he was imprisoned and killed because his message threatened powerful people. According to the Gospel of Luke, John the Baptist was the child of Mary's cousin Elizabeth, and therefore Jesus' cousin. The Church celebrates the feast of Saint John the Baptist on June 24.

Vivarini, *Saint John the Baptist*. 17th century.

Jesus' Ministry Begins

Jesus was among the people baptized by John the Baptist in the Jordan River, although John was reluctant to baptize Jesus. John calls Jesus the "Lamb of God" (*John 1:29*). "I am not worthy to stoop and loosen the thongs of his sandals," John says (*Mark 1:7*).

The Gospel describes an amazing thing that happened at Jesus' baptism. As he came up out of the water,

> *the heavens were opened and he saw the Spirit of God descending like a dove and coming upon him. And a voice came from the heavens, saying, "This is my beloved Son."*

MATTHEW 3:16–17

Verrochio, da Vinci, *Baptism of Christ.* 15th century.

Jesus' baptism marks the beginning of his public ministry, a point made in each of the Gospel accounts.

Jesus did not begin to preach immediately after his baptism by John. First Jesus went into the desert to fast and pray for forty days. In the desert, he was tempted by the devil with offers of food, wealth, fame, and power (*Matthew 4:1–11*). Jesus overcame each of these temptations, completed his prayer, and returned to Galilee.

The Day of Power

The synagogue at Nazareth was filled. News of the new rabbi had quickly spread throughout Galilee, and people came from miles away to hear what he had to say.

Taking the scroll of the prophet Isaiah, Jesus found the passage where it was written:

> The Spirit of the Lord is upon me, because he has anointed me to bring glad tidings to the poor. He has sent me to proclaim liberty to captives and recovery of sight to the blind, to let the oppressed go free, and to proclaim a year acceptable to the Lord.

Then Jesus said to them, "Today this scripture passage is fulfilled in your hearing."

After going out of the synagogue, Jesus left Nazareth and moved on to Capernaum.

Based on LUKE 4:16–21

A Miraculous Cure

Scene: *Capernaum, early in Jesus' ministry*

Philip: I had heard about Jesus from my cousin Andrew. Was Jesus the one sent from God? Andrew thought so. I decided to find out for myself. That's why I went to the crowded synagogue in Capernaum.

Jesus: The kingdom of God is at hand! Turn away from everything that holds you back from God—greed, foolish pride, anger, and hatred. Unless you repent, you will not enter the kingdom.

Philip: I was amazed. I had never heard someone speak with such power. The room was unusually still. Then the silence was broken by a horrible shriek.

Daniel: *(screaming)* Go away. What have you to do with us, Jesus of Nazareth? Have you come to destroy us?

Philip: I recognized the man immediately as Daniel. Children made fun of Daniel because he mumbled to himself and shook his head constantly.

Daniel: *(hissing)* We know who you are, Jesus. You are the Holy One of God.

Philip: Jesus looked straight at Daniel, as if he could see through him. When he spoke, his words sounded like claps of thunder.

Jesus: Quiet! Come out of him!

Philip: Daniel sat down with a jolt and closed his eyes. When he opened his eyes a moment later, the evil spirit had left him. He was healed! What authority Jesus had! Even unclean spirits obeyed him. But that's not all. Later that day, I went with Jesus to Simon's house. The mother of Simon's wife was sick in bed.

Simon: Jesus, my wife's mother is ill. Can you help her?

Philip: Nodding his head, Jesus walked to the woman's room, took her hand, and ordered her to be well.

Jesus: Woman, be well.

Philip: The woman looked at Jesus, arose from her bed, and went to prepare dinner. You would never have known that she had been near death! Jesus worked many **miracles** that day. I believe that Andrew is right. Jesus is the Messiah.

Miracles are actions that are impossible for ordinary human beings to perform. They are dramatic signs of God's power and love at work in the world.

God's Chosen One

The Jewish people believed that God would send a Messiah to save them. There was much disagreement, however, about what the Messiah would save them from. Some people expected a military leader who would defeat the Romans. Others expected a politician who would create a great nation. Still others expected a spiritual leader. Few expected the Messiah to be like Jesus.

From prison John sent his followers to ask Jesus if he were the Messiah. Jesus responded:

Go and tell John what you hear and see: the blind regain their sight, the lame walk, lepers are cleansed, the deaf hear, the dead are raised, and the poor have good news preached to them.

MATTHEW 11:4–5

In everything he did and said, Jesus revealed that he was the Messiah. By his actions he showed that God's reign is present in the ordinary events of human life. He showed people that God was concerned with saving them from sin and death, not from the Romans. He showed that God's reign rules in people's hearts when they are open to God and act with love and kindness toward others.

Jesus spoke of God's kingdom as a place where the poor, the outcast, and the sorrowful are especially loved by God. Jesus also taught that people would be blessed if they were persecuted for following his teachings (*Luke 6:20–22*).

Jesus was truly the Messiah, the Savior promised to the Jewish people. The Son of God, he ushered in God's reign by freeing humankind from sin and death. He showed in his life and being that what God wants is for people to love God and each other.

1. **What did Jesus do to show that he was the Messiah?**
2. **How did Jesus' actions show that the reign of God was present?**

The Law of Love

Read Matthew 9:10–13 and 12:9–13. With these two passages as your source, describe the reign of God.

Following **Jesus**

Jesus healed people. That's one reason people believed he was the Messiah. You can be a sign of God's kingdom by working to heal others around you. Visit the sick and homebound. Perform small acts of kindness for people who are sad or tired. Your kind gestures will make someone else feel better.

CREATING THE KINGDOM

You have been asked by your pastor to suggest ways that your parish can be a sign of God's kingdom. Read the verses from the prophets. Describe how you can put the prophets words into practice.

EZEKIEL 37: 1-14

JEREMIAH 30: 12-22

ISAIAH 49: 8-20

MICAH 4:1-7

LOOKING FOR GOD

Gracious and holy Father, please give me the intellect to understand you, reason to discern you, diligence to seek you, wisdom to find you, a spirit to meditate on you, ears to hear you, eyes to see you, a tongue to proclaim you, a way of life pleasing to you, patience to wait for you, and perseverance to look for you.

Grant me your holy presence, a blessed resurrection, and life everlasting. Amen.

Prayer of Saint Benedict

WITH YOUR FAMILY

You don't need to be rewarded for every act of kindness you perform. Knowing that you've helped someone can be its own reward. Secretly help out at home by doing a chore or performing some other good deed for a member of your family. Watch your family try to figure out who is responsible for this act of kindness.

▼ REVIEW CHAPTER 5 · · · · · · · · · · ·

CATHOLICS BELIEVE

1. The Jewish people were expecting God to send the Messiah.
2. Jesus' public life began with his baptism by John in the Jordan River.
3. Jesus proclaimed the reign of God on earth.

KNOW

1. What is the meaning of the word messiah? _____
   _____

2. Who was John the Baptist? _____
   _____

3. What message did John the Baptist preach? _____
   _____

4. What did John the Baptist say about Jesus?
   _____

5. What were some of the expectations people had of the Messiah?
   _____

SUNDAY MASS

Jesus worked many signs to show that the reign of God was present in him. As you listen to the Gospel this Sunday, identify one thing that points to Jesus as the chosen one of God. Be prepared to share what you find with your classmates.

I have called you friends, because I have told you everything I have heard from my Father.

JOHN 15:15

CONTENT KEYS

1. Everybody needs friends.
2. Jesus' friends are called disciples.
3. The disciples spread Jesus' Good News.

THE IMPORTANCE OF FRIENDSHIP

Friendship is important to everyone. Read what these writers have to say about friendship.

No one can develop freely in this world and find a full life without feeling understood by at least one person.

Paul Tournier

God evidently does not intend us all to be rich or powerful or great, but God does intend us all to be friends.

Ralph Waldo Emerson

Two are better than one. If you fall, the other will be there to lift you up. Woe to you if you are alone. For if you should fall, no one will be there to help you stand.

Based on Ecclesiastes 4:9–10

Blessed are they who hunger for friends—for though they may not realize it, their souls are crying out for God.

Habib Sahabib

The impulse of love that leads us to the doorway of a friend is the voice of God within and we need not be afraid to follow it.

Agnes Sanford

Friendships begun in this world will be taken up again, never to be lost.

St. Francis de Sales

Here's What I Think

Express your thoughts on the importance of friendship.

You've Got a Friend

Mary Beth is writing a term paper on the value of friendship. As part of her research, she questioned some students in her class and recorded their answers. Here is a transcript of those tapes.

A Conversation with Bonnie

Mary Beth: I am speaking with Bonnie. Bonnie, do you think friends are important?

Bonnie: You know I do, Mary Beth. A year ago, when my parents divorced, I felt totally miserable. I couldn't do my homework. I went to class, but I didn't hear anything the teacher said.

I don't know what I would have done without my friends. They saw that I was unhappy and tried to cheer me up. I was too embarrassed to talk about my problem, but they helped me to do it. What a relief it was to know that I wasn't alone. They were real lifesavers.

Mary Beth: Thanks, Bonnie, that was great.

An Opinion from Ivan

Mary Beth: I am speaking with Ivan. Ivan, you're new in town. What can you say about the importance of friendship?

Ivan: Whoaa! I never appreciated my friends until I left them behind.

Mary Beth: What do you mean?

Ivan: Where I used to live I had lots of friends. Here I didn't know anyone. I spent the summer counting the cracks in my bedroom wall I was so lonely.

Mary Beth: How did you make new friends?

Ivan: The first day of school I was sitting alone on the playground rereading my favorite Star Trek book. Carlos saw what I was reading and joined me. Carlos is a major Trekkie! He knew more about the Enterprise than I did. That was the beginning of a great friendship. Through Carlos I've made a lot of other new friends.

Mary Beth: Would you say that friends are important?

Ivan: You know it.

My Friend

Help Mary Beth with her report. Write a story about best friends who support each other.

FOLLOW ME

You already know the story of how Peter and Andrew became Jesus' friends. The call of Matthew is no less dramatic.

Dear Diary,

I've just returned from the adventure of a lifetime. Two weeks ago, at dawn, I met Jesus and the other disciples outside the village as we'd planned. We came as Jesus asked—with only the clothes on our backs. We carried no walking sticks, no food, no sacks, and no money. We trusted that God would provide us with what we needed.

Jesus prayed with us before we left. He asked God to give us power to cast out demons and to cure diseases. Then Jesus sent us out in pairs to preach the Good News and to heal the sick.

Only one year ago, I collected taxes at the customs booth in Capernaum. I took money from my neighbors to give to the Roman oppressors (and, I must be honest, some extra for myself). I hated what I was doing, but I loved the money. I felt trapped. It was Jesus who finally freed me from my self-made prison.

I knew about Jesus and had heard him teach in the synagogue. My heart ached at his message of love and forgiveness. I longed to be forgiven. But how could God possibly love me after what I'd done?

Jesus changed all of that for me. He taught me that God's promise of forgiveness was true. He looked me in the eye and said, "Follow me." And I did. I accepted Jesus' friendship and God's forgiveness all at once.

Now it had come to this. Jesus was sending me on a mission. I was afraid that I would fail, that I would betray his trust in me. But I shouldn't have worried, Jesus gave me the power to succeed. I went out among the people. When I spoke of God's love and mercy, I saw the light of hope born in their eyes. I was never hungry, thirsty, or tired either, for God did provide.

I thank God for the day I said "yes" to Jesus' offer of friendship.

Based on MATTHEW 9:9 and MATTHEW 10:1–14

1. **What is the importance of friendship?**
2. **Read through Matthew's diary again. What did Jesus do to prepare Matthew for his ministry?**

Jesus' Friends

Jesus had many followers, or disciples. The Gospel of Luke mentions that the "Lord appointed seventy-two others whom he sent ahead of him in pairs to every town and place he intended to visit" (*Luke 10:1*). The disciples went all over Galilee teaching and healing in Jesus' name, with great success. When they returned they said, "Lord, even the demons are subject to us because of your name" (*Luke 10:17*).

Among his disciples, Jesus had many friends whom the Gospel mentions by name. You're familiar with the story of Mary of Magdala. Jesus was also a good friend of the family of Mary, Martha, and Lazarus. "Jesus loved Martha and her sister and Lazarus very much" (*John 11:5*). When Lazarus died, Jesus wept (*John 11:35*).

There was also a small group of disciples who became Jesus' closest followers. These friends learned from Jesus, and supported him in his work. This group is known as **the Twelve,** or the **Apostles.** The Gospel of Matthew names the Twelve as Simon (Peter), Andrew, James the Greater, John, Philip, Bartholomew, Thomas, Matthew, James the Lesser, Thaddeus, Simon the Cananean, and Judas Iscariot.

On the night before he died, Jesus told his friends what he expected of them.

This is my commandment: love one another as I love you. No one has greater love than this, to lay down one's life for one's friends. You are my friends if you do what I command you. It was not you who chose me, but I who chose you and appointed you to go and bear fruit that will remain, so that whatever you ask the Father in my name he may give you.

John 15:12–15,16

SPECIAL WORDS

The word **apostle** comes from the Greek for "one who is sent." In addition to the Twelve, Saint Paul is also called an apostle. The number **twelve** is very significant in Judaism. There were twelve tribes of Israel, descendants of Jacob's twelve sons. The number twelve suggests completion.

THE TRADITION OF THE APOSTLES

Jesus chose friends like Matthew and Peter to help him spread the Good News of the reign of God. Although they were simple people, not powerful leaders or learned scholars, the Twelve succeeded in their mission. They did their job so well that the Church is known as apostolic, meaning "in the tradition of the Apostles."

During his lifetime, Jesus sent the Twelve to preach and heal throughout Galilee. After Jesus' Ascension, the Twelve spread Jesus' Good News of salvation throughout the Roman Empire. James the Lesser led the Christian community in Jerusalem. Tradition has John preaching in the city of Ephesus, in modern day Turkey. Peter, the leader of the Twelve, led the Christian Community in Rome where he was martyred.

SPREAD OF CHRISTIANITY IN THE FIRST CENTURY A.D.

Although they spread the Gospel throughout the world, the Twelve did not leave any writings. The two Gospel accounts that bear the names of the Apostles John and Matthew were written by their followers based upon their teachings. The Good News of Jesus was not set down in written form until approximately A.D. 70.

The profession of faith known as the Apostles' Creed gets its name from the fact that it proclaims beliefs that are faithful to the teachings of the Apostles, not because it was written by the Apostles.

H. von Kulmbach, *Martyrdom of St. Peter.*

Loyalty is a virtue essential for friendship. Loyalty means that you can be counted on to keep your promises. It means that you can be trusted to be there for a friend when he or she needs your help. You grow in loyalty by keeping your word.

HOW THE GOOD NEWS GREW

Although the Gospels were not written by Jesus, they are based on historical fact. The Twelve learned directly from Jesus through his teaching and healing. They proclaimed the Good News to all who would listen. For years, these stories of Jesus were passed on through the **oral tradition** to new listeners. Eventually, authors familiar with the story wrote it in its present form.

The people who wrote the Gospels are called **Evangelists.** They were guided in their writing by the Holy Spirit. Like the authors of many biblical books, the names of the people who wrote the Gospels are unknown. Proclaiming God's Word was more important to the authors than receiving credit for their work.

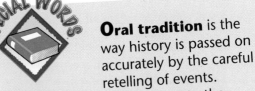

Oral tradition is the way history is passed on accurately by the careful retelling of events.

Evangelist is the title given to the author of a Gospel. The word *evangelist* comes from the Greek for "teller of good news."

ONE GOSPEL, FOUR ACCOUNTS

Each of the four accounts of the Gospel tells only part of the Gospel story. Three of the Gospel accounts—Matthew, Mark, and Luke—are very similar. These gospels are called *synoptic* (from the Greek word for seeing together) because they contain many of the same stories told in the same order. John's Gospel includes so many different stories about Jesus—and rearranges their order—that it is always considered separately from the other three gospels.

The Gospel authors used different types of writing to tell the Good News:

- Narratives and stories (*Luke 19:1–10, Mark 6:53–56*)
- Verses from the Hebrew Scriptures presented in a new context (*Luke 4:16–21*)
- Discourses, or long speeches, by Jesus (*JOHN 5:19–47*)
- Parables (*Matthew 13:1–9*) and proverb-like statements (*Luke 12:54–56*)

The Gospels are the heart of the Church because they are the main source of information about Jesus' life and teachings.

1. **Why is the Church considered apostolic?**
2. **Explain how the Gospels grew out of the teaching of Jesus.**
3. **What are some ways in which people today can be evangelists?**

You Are My Friends

Jesus calls you to be his friend and to proclaim the Good News. Read the following advertisement. Then write your own application, telling why you want to be a friend of Jesus. How are you qualified to spread the Good News?

Who is your best friend? What makes this person your friend? During this week, share information about your best friend with your family. Ask your family for suggestions on how you can be a better friend.

Teach Us to Pray

Jesus taught his friends to pray these words:
Father, hallowed be your name,
your kingdom come.
Give us each day our daily bread,
and forgive us our sins for we ourselves
forgive everyone in debt to us, and do not
subject us to the final test.

LUKE 11:2–4

Pray each line of this version of the Lord's Prayer slowly and thoughtfully. Pause after each phrase to think about what the words mean to you.

▼REVIEW CHAPTER 6

CATHOLICS BELIEVE

1. Friendship is important to all human beings.
2. From the beginning of his ministry, Jesus chose friends to share in his mission.
3. The Church is apostolic; it is founded on the faith that comes from the Apostles.

KNOW

1. People hated Matthew because he was a _____.
2. The word _____ means "one who is sent."
3. The Church is called "_____" because it is faithful to the _____ of the Apostles.
4. The writers of the Gospel are known as _____ because they bring _____ _____.
5. The Gospel accounts of Matthew, _____, and _____ are known as _____ because they are similar in content.
6. Jesus' closest disciples are known as the _____.
7. Jesus told the Apostles, "No one has greater _____ than this, to lay down one's _____ for one's _____."
8. Jesus sent his disciples to _____ the Good News and to _____ the sick.

SUNDAY MASS

The Gospel is proclaimed every Sunday at Mass. This Sunday, notice the special importance given to the Gospel reading. How is the Gospel set apart from the other readings? Who reads it? How is the congregation's response to the Gospel different from its response to the other readings?

7

EVERYONE IS WELCOME

This I command you: love one another.

JOHN 15:17

CONTENT KEYS

1. **Jesus offered God's love to all people.**
2. **Jesus taught Christians how to live.**
3. **When you care for a person in need, you care for Jesus.**

A WINTER NIGHT (A SCREENPLAY)

Act One

Fade in. Exterior. A City Street. Night.
A very cold night. Snow swirls along the pavement. The wind howls. There is not a soul in sight.

New Angle.
A solitary figure, bundled against the cold, appears at the end of the street. The figure struggles against the wind, head down, the very picture of misery and loneliness.

New Angle.
The camera draws back so that more of the street comes into view. The stranger is walking toward the only lighted window on the street.

Exterior. At the Window. Night.
The stranger stands outside the window looking in.

Interior. Dining Room. Night.
The stranger sees a group of people enjoying a Christmas feast. A fire burns in the fireplace. Lighted candles adorn the table. Lights from a Christmas tree cast a multicolored glow over the walls. The people talk and laugh. The table is laden with expensive food.

Exterior. Doorway. Night.
The stranger walks from the window to the door and knocks. His raps echo loudly through the night. Footsteps are heard. The stranger shrinks away from the doorway as if afraid. The door opens, shining light on the street.

Act Two

In the space provided, write an ending to this scene.

_____

_____

_____

_____

A Kingdom Banquet

In December 1972, the members of a Bible study group in El Paso, Texas, read these words of Jesus.

When you hold a lunch or a dinner, do not invite your friends or your brothers or your relatives or your wealthy neighbors, in case they may invite you back and you have repayment. Rather, when you hold a banquet, invite the poor, the crippled, the lame, the blind; blessed indeed will you be because of their inability to repay you. For you will be repaid at the resurrection of the righteous.

LUKE 14:12–14

After the reading, someone asked, "Has anyone here ever actually invited the poor to share a meal?" Everyone mumbled, "No." No one had even tried.

"THE POOREST PEOPLE I KNOW"

"But we could do it," one person said. "The poorest people I know live at the trash dump in Juarez, over the border in Mexico. Nobody cares about them. We could share our Christmas dinner with them."

The Bible study group gathered on Christmas morning, each person bringing food. After asking God to bless their work, the group set off for Juarez, carrying great quantities of delicious food—ham, burritos, traditional Christmas tamales, chocolate milk, and fruit.

Those members of the group who had never seen the trash dump were horrified at the sight. Whole families lived in shelters made of cardboard boxes covered with torn sheets of plastic. The homes were surrounded by garbage and filth. Nearly everyone was sick and the weather was freezing.

Not only did the people of the dump live in squalor, they were also divided into two groups that argued constantly. People from one side of the dump didn't get along with people from the other side, or set foot within their territory.

After talking to both sides, the Bible study group convinced the people of the dump to sit down to dinner together, even if they sat on opposite sides of a table set up in neutral territory. Only after everyone was seated did the visitors discover that 300 people had gathered, and they had food for only 120!

A CHRISTMAS MIRACLE

The decision was made to feed the children first, and to feed the adults with whatever was left over. After asking God's blessing, the visitors began serving the food. The hungry children ate and ate, and then stuffed their pockets, but the food did not run out.

Then the adults ate their fill. Plate after plate was emptied, and still there was food. "I couldn't understand it," said one of the visitors. "No one left the table hungry—and we had food left for a nearby orphanage!" Everyone was amazed.

A WONDERFUL SIGHT

There must have been something in the air that day. Not only were the people fed, but the feud that divided the dump was put aside in the festivities. As the visitors and the people from Juarez shared food, sang, and prayed, the feuding neighbors began to talk to one another.

The people from El Paso were also changed by the dinner. Although they had planned on serving only one meal, they now made a commitment to return each week to help the people of the trash dump improve their living conditions.

The people of El Paso kept their promise. Ten years later, the people of the trash dump had real houses, built with the visitors' help. They ran a cooperative salvage business that recycled materials from the dump. All the children were in school. And best of all, people in need were shown God's love by brothers and sisters who cared for them.

1. **What do you think made the biggest difference in the lives of the people of the trash dump?**
2. **Why is it important for people to know that someone cares about them?**

WELCOMING OTHERS

The people of the Juarez trash dump experienced poverty, dangerous living conditions, and illness and helplessness. But the worst evil they faced was exclusion from their society—being left out on the edges of life, forgotten and alone. The Christmas dinner changed all of that for the people of the dump.

Sharing a meal together is one of society's most powerful ways of showing that a person is part of a **community.** When you are invited to eat with someone, you feel accepted and welcomed. When you are excluded from a meal or a party, you feel unwanted and alone.

There is no better image of community and belonging than a banquet, a rich meal at which people share food and memories and love. This was Jesus' great image of God's kingdom—the banquet to which all people everywhere are invited.

SPECIAL WORDS

The word **community** literally means "those who live within the same walls." In the kingdom of God, the walls embrace all people.

BY HIS EXAMPLE

Exclusion is a sinful pattern in every human society. However, Jesus never accepted that pattern. Jesus proclaimed the saving love of God to all people. He announced the coming of a kingdom in which no one was an outcast, no one was left out, no one was alone.

At a time when women were often treated badly, Jesus welcomed women as his disciples. Mary Magdalene, Joanna, and Susanna traveled with him during his ministry (*Luke 8:2–3*). He encouraged his friend Mary of Bethany to sit at his feet and learn from him as a male student would learn from a rabbi (*Luke 10:38–42*).

Although the disciples thought children would bother Jesus, he welcomed them. (*Mark 10:13–15*).

Jesus also refused to discriminate against Samaritans, a group excluded from Jewish society for religious reasons. He preached the Good News to a Samaritan woman (*John 4:4–29*) and held up a Samaritan as an example of what it meant to be a neighbor (*Luke 10:29–37*).

In Jesus' world, people with certain diseases and disabilities were excluded from society. But Jesus reached out to lepers and the mentally ill, restoring them to health. Through his care for them, Jesus showed these people that they were loved by God. By healing them, he also integrated them into society (*Matthew 8:1–4; Luke 8:40–56; John 9*).

Who are the new people in your neighborhood? What can you do to make these people feel welcome?

WHEN I WAS HUNGRY

Through his actions, Jesus showed that everyone was welcome in God's kingdom. Jesus also gave clear instructions on how his followers were to treat others.

When you see someone who is hungry and feed him, thirsty and you give him drink, welcome a stranger, give clothing to someone who has none, comfort people who are ill, and care for people in prison, you care for me.

Based on MATTHEW 25:31–46

These acts of kindness described by Jesus are known as the Corporal Works of Mercy.

You may never see a leper, but you can care for others. Raise money to help the sick. Share your lunch with a friend. Read to a younger brother or sister. Give your parents a hug when they are sad. Above all, be aware of what other people are feeling and care for them.

FRANCIS AND THE LEPER

Francis of Assisi tried to follow Jesus completely. He had given up a military career to become a peacemaker. He cast aside his family's riches to become a poor friar. He seemed to exclude no one from his love. Francis even called God's lowliest creatures—rats, spiders, and fleas—"brother" and "sister"!

As caring as Francis was, however, he was not perfect. He was terrified of lepers! These disfigured people, whose contagious disease made them outcasts, frightened Francis more than war or rats. But if he was to follow Jesus completely, Francis had to overcome this fear.

One day, Francis came upon a leper begging at a crossroads. Francis tried to pass the leper quickly. After all, he had nothing to give—he was a beggar himself. And he certainly didn't want to look at the leper. But something forced Francis to look, and he was shocked by what he saw.

Instead of a hated monster, Francis saw a person, a brother in need. Francis was overcome with understanding: what he did for the beggar, he did for Jesus! Francis gave the man the only gift he had to give, his love. Francis hugged and kissed the man. Only then did he realize that following Jesus meant that he could exclude no one from his love.

BREAKING THE PATTERN

Sinful patterns of exclusion are present everywhere, even in your school and neighborhood. In the cases that follow, identify who is being excluded and tell how a follower of Jesus might solve the problem.

Janice and her close friends eat lunch together everyday. One day, they notice that Hillary is eating alone; she doesn't look very happy. If they invite her to join them, they won't be able to talk as freely as they'd like.

Everyone is talking about Dean's party on Saturday afternoon. You haven't gotten your invitation yet, but you're sure you will. Dean said everyone was invited except the class nerds.

A local restaurant recently posted the sign "We reserve the right to refuse service to anyone." Elizabeth has never seen anyone refused service, but when she suggests meeting her Hispanic friends there, they suggest somewhere else. Elizabeth wonders if the restaurant makes Hispanics feel unwelcome.

1. **What did Jesus do to make people feel welcome?**
2. **How is caring for people in need also caring for Jesus?**
3. **Explain in your own words the meaning of the story of Saint Francis and the leper.**

THE GIFTS YOU BRING

Jesus changed people's lives by showing them love and concern. Through his actions he showed that people are special and have valuable gifts to share.

Think about the gifts you have been given. Why does the kingdom of God need you? On the tags, describe the special gifts you bring to the Christian community.

Plan a special meal with your family. Decorate the table with flowers, a plant, or a centerpiece of your design. Make the table look special. Celebrate being part of a loving family.

A BOND OF LOVE

You can reach out to others as Jesus did by including them in your prayers. You don't need to know the names of the poor and forgotten ones of the world—God knows their names. You need only open your heart and ask God to help you care for them. Here is a prayer you can say for the whole human family.

Father, you have made us.

Red, yellow, brown, black, and white, tall and short, fat and thin, rich and poor, young and old—all are your children.

Teach us to cooperate rather than to compete, to respect rather than to revile, to forgive rather than to condemn.

Your son turned from no one.

May we learn, like him, to be open to the share of the divine that you have implanted in each of your sons and daughters.

Richard Armstrong

▼ REVIEW CHAPTER 7 . . . .

CATHOLICS BELIEVE

1. Jesus invited everyone to participate in the kingdom of God.
2. Jesus taught that when you care for a person in need you care for Jesus, too.
3. The Corporal Works of Mercy describe how Christians are to care for people in need.

KNOW

1. Who is invited to participate in God's kingdom? _____
2. Why is the image of a banquet appropriate for describing God's kingdom?_____
3. What inspired the Bible study group in El Paso to take a meal to the poor people in Mexico? _____
4. What did Saint Francis of Assisi learn from meeting the leper?
   _____
5. Why was it unusual for Jesus to allow Mary of Bethany to be his disciple?
   _____
6. Where in the Bible can you find Jesus' teaching of the Corporal Works of Mercy? _____

SUNDAY MASS

The Christian community is united around the altar through the Body and Blood of Christ. This Sunday, look for all of the other ways that people are brought together through the Eucharist. Be prepared to report on your findings.

8

THE AUTHORITY OF JESUS

> The crowds were astonished at his teaching, for he taught them as one having authority.
>
> MATTHEW 7:28–29

CONTENT KEYS

1. Jesus spoke with authority.
2. People use their conscience to make moral decisions.
3. Your conscience needs to be formed.

WHO'S IN CHARGE?

After school on Tuesday, Emma walked over to the gym to help with the school play. Mr. Scott had said they would begin work that day. Inside the gym, everyone was in a panic.

"Hey, Bart. Where's Mr. Scott?" Emma asked.

"He had to leave. Some kind of emergency. We're going ahead anyway. Are you here to help?"

"Sure," said Emma.

"Good," Bart said. "I want you to start painting the backdrop."

"She can't do that, Bart," said Jane. "We don't have the paint yet. You'd better go to the store, Emma, and buy the paint."

"Wait a minute," said Hank. "You can't buy the paint. We don't know what colors we need."

"I know, Emma," said Jerry. "Why don't you round up the cast and begin a read through?"

"Hold it, Jerry," said Amanda. "She can't do that. Mr. Scott hasn't assigned all the parts yet."

"I know what Emma can do," said Lester. "We have a scene where one of the actors has to fall off the balcony. Emma can jump off the second-story platform onto our mattress and see if there's enough cushion."

"Are you nuts?" asked Betsy. "She could get hurt. Hey, Emma. Where are you going?"

"I'll see you tomorrow," she said, "when Mr. Scott's back."

Taking Charge

What happens on projects when no one is in charge? Provide examples and demonstrate them for the class.

BY WHOSE AUTHORITY?

Emma walked away from the gym feeling very frustrated. What good was it to try to get any work done when there was no one to organize tasks or assign jobs? Without anyone in charge, it was even possible that someone could get hurt. Emma realized that the drama group needed someone with authority to make decisions.

The word *authority* comes from a Latin word that means "opinion," "decision," or "power." In English, the word *authority* also has several different meanings.

Look at the following meanings of the word *authority*. Provide an example for each meaning.

- Authority can mean "power over others." In this sense, parents, school principals, police officers, and other people in charge are the "authority figures" in your life.

- Authority can mean power that's shared. You can be authorized to do something by someone in authority.

- Authority can be connected to knowledge or experience. Someone who knows a lot about a particular subject is considered an authority.

- Authority can be based on knowledge of the truth. This is the ultimate, or final, authority. Truth can be counted on absolutely.

THE ONE WHO SENT ME

Jesus was a person of authority. According to the Gospel, crowds marveled at his words and actions. They saw power in him. They saw truth.

Jesus did not fit any of the usual patterns of authority, however. He was not wealthy. He did not have political power. He wasn't a Temple official. People wondered, therefore, about the source of his authority.

> *Is he not the carpenter's son?*
> (MATTHEW 13:55)
> *Where did this man get all this? What kind of wisdom has been given him?*
> (MARK 6:2)
> *By what authority are you doing these things? Or who gave you this authority to do them?* (MARK 11:28)

Jesus' answer to these questions was simple. His answer has been echoed ever since by Christians who choose to act for God's kingdom, even when acting for Jesus goes against the world's idea of what is right:

> *I cannot do anything on my own. I judge as I hear, and my judgment is just, because I do not seek my own will but the will of the one who sent me.*
>
> JOHN 5:30

Jesus could speak and act with such authority because he was the Son of God. Because his words and actions carried the power of truth, people looked at Jesus and saw God's love. Jesus the Messiah not only spoke God's word but is God's living Word. He is the fullness of **revelation.**

Jesus cried out and said, "Whoever believes in me believes not only in me but also in the one who sent me. I came into the world as light, so that everyone who believes in me might not remain in darkness."

Based on JOHN 12:44–46

1. **What does the word *authority* mean? Why do you consider someone an authority?**
2. **Where did Jesus claim his authority came from?**
3. **What does it mean to say that Jesus is the "fullness of revelation"?**

Revelation is the self-disclosure of God and the communication of divine truth.

MAKING MORAL JUDGMENTS

In Jesus' time, many people claimed to speak with authority as prophets who spoke for God. Jesus' friends asked him for help in sorting good advice from bad. Jesus gave them this answer:

> *Beware of false prophets, who come to you in sheep's clothing, but underneath are ravenous wolves. By their fruits you will know them. Do people pick grapes from thornbushes, or figs from thistles? Just so, every good tree bears good fruit, and a rotten tree bears bad fruit. A good tree cannot bear bad fruit, nor can a rotten tree bear good fruit. So by their fruits you will know them.*
>
> MATTHEW 7:15–18, 20

Growing in Christian **morality** means learning to avoid the wolves hidden in sheep's clothing. It means looking closely at the results—the fruit—of people's words and actions. It means making decisions based on real authority, not on whatever is the most popular, easiest, or exciting thing to do. It means, ultimately, that you conform your thoughts, words, and actions to those of Jesus.

GRAPES OR THORNS

You have a gift that helps you evaluate moral decisions: your **conscience.** Your conscience is a sign of God's presence within you. When your conscience is working properly, it helps you know what is right and what is wrong.

You were not born with a fully formed conscience. Your conscience has to grow and mature just as your body does. You need to learn to make wise decisions.

Look at the following cases. How does the person's age and maturity affect the choice made?

A toddler sees a shiny gold locket lying on a low table in someone's house. She picks up the locket and sticks it in her mouth. Is she stealing?

A thirteen-year-old sees a gold locket at a friend's house. Would it be stealing if she took it? What makes the difference in this situation?

A four-year-old hears a curse word and then repeats the word himself. Is the four year old cursing?

A thirteen-year-old gets angry and blurts out the same words. Is this person cursing?

Morality is the teaching that guides the choices you make. Christian morality calls people to make choices based on the teachings of Jesus.

Your **conscience** is a gift from God. It helps you recognize the difference between right and wrong.

SHAPING YOUR CONSCIENCE

Moral consciousness, or conscience, develops over time. The growth of moral consciousness doesn't happen automatically with your physical maturing, however. Outside influences affect how your conscience develops. Here are some of the things that can help you develop a healthy and mature conscience.

- *God's teachings,* especially the Ten Commandments and the teachings of Jesus recorded in the Gospel, such as the Beatitudes
- *Good examples* and advice from adults with well-formed consciences
- *Participation in the Sacraments,* especially the Eucharist and Reconciliation

Your conscience can also be affected by negative or harmful influences.

- *Peer Pressure.* Other people your age may act in ways that you know are wrong. Pressure to conform may lead you to follow their bad example.
- *Popular Culture.* The media places great value on wealth, pleasure, and power. You are encouraged to use harmful substances, such as cigarettes or alcohol, in order to belong.

You will make moral decisions throughout your life. Some of these decisions could change the course of your life. Think about these headlines. What different choices could these teens have made?

Thirteen-year-old Shoots Friend in Anger
Boy, 12, Arrested for Shoplifting
Teenage Girl Found Dead from Overdose

You can learn to make good moral decisions. Start by listening to the positive influences in your life and ignoring the negative ones. Think about the small decisions you make. How are they influenced by your faith in God? By learning to make small choices wisely, you will develop a mature conscience.

IDENTIFYING FALSE VALUES

What are some of the false values promoted by popular culture? What can you say or do to reject these false values?

A Life and Death Decision

Sir Thomas More had a wonderful life. He was Lord Chancellor of England and the most powerful man in the country after the king. He was a wealthy man with a wonderful wife and loving children. A scholar, Thomas had his own library, where he prayed, read, studied, and wrote.

In 1532, King Henry VIII asked the Church to annul his first marriage so that he could marry a younger woman. When the pope refused his request, Henry proclaimed himself the head of the English Church and granted himself a divorce! Concerned by the king's actions, Thomas quietly resigned as Lord Chancellor and retired to his home in the country.

King Henry was angered by Thomas's actions. He demanded that Thomas and his other subjects swear an oath proclaiming the king the rightful head of the Church in England. When Thomas refused to do so, he was arrested and sent to prison in the Tower of London.

Many people tried to talk Thomas into taking the oath, including members of his own family "What difference does it make if you tell a lie?" they pleaded. "It will get you out of prison!" His friends and family didn't understand Thomas at all. Telling the truth—and following what his conscience told him was the right thing to do—meant more to him than his own life. Because Thomas refused to take the oath, he was tried for treason and sentenced to death.

Sir Thomas More was blessed with wealth, power, and a loving family. He sacrificed everything rather than betray his conscience. His last words before he was beheaded were these: "I die the king's good servant, but I am God's servant first." Thomas was canonized as a saint in 1935.

1. **What is morality?**
2. **What is a conscience? How is your conscience formed?**
3. **What are some of the difficult decisions faced by young teens today? How can the teachings of Jesus help you make good decisions?**

Through the centuries many people have sacrificed their lives rather than recognize an authority greater than God's. These people are known as martyrs because they witnessed to Christ with their lives. You can be a witness to Christ by making your own good decisions and by setting a good example for others to follow.

GIVING WITNESS

As a follower of Jesus, you are called to give witness to Christ every day. One way to do this is to give good advice, or counsel, to others.

Think about the following situations. Based on the teachings of Jesus, what advice would you offer?

Dear Counsel,

My friends all want to see the new slasher film. I don't like blood and gore, but I don't want my friends to think I'm a wimp. Any suggestions?
Signed,
Pressured

Dear Pressured,

Dear Counsel,

My friend has a "D" average in math. He has asked me to help him cheat on a test "just this once." What should I do?
Signed,
Reluctant

Dear Reluctant,

WITH YOUR FAMILY

Discuss with a parent a situation that you find morally confusing. Ask a parent how he or she would handle the situation. Be prepared to discuss your parent's answer in class.

IMITATING CHRIST

When Jesus didn't know what to do, he prayed. In prayer, you can learn to recognize the truth. Use this prayer to help you recognize the truth.

Grant me, O Lord, the grace to know what I ought to know, to love what I ought to love, to praise what delights you most, to value what is precious in your sight, and to turn from what offends you.

Do not let me be content to judge according only to what I see, or to make decisions based only on what I hear from others.

Help me to discern with true judgment, to choose between what is momentary and what is lasting, and, above all, to seek always that which is pleasing to your will.

THE IMITATION OF CHRIST, Thomas à Kempis

CATHOLICS BELIEVE

1. People use their consciences to make moral decisions.
2. Jesus spoke with the authority that comes from God.
3. Jesus Christ is the full revelation of the Father.
4. To follow Jesus is to do God's will.

KNOW

1. What was unique about the way Jesus spoke with authority? Where did Jesus' authority come from?

2. Explain how Jesus Christ is the most complete revelation of God's saving love.

3. How does someone's age and maturity affect the morality of his or her actions?

4. Why do consciences need to be formed?

5. What are three things that help to shape a mature conscience?

6. Why was Sir Thomas More put to death? Why is More considered a martyr? What does the word *martyr* mean?

SUNDAY MASS

Except during Lent the Gloria is usually sung or recited at Sunday Mass. This ancient prayer is a doxology, or hymn of praise to God. It is the only hymn that is part of the official Order of the Mass. The Gloria celebrates the greatness of God. Sing along with the Gloria this Sunday, offering your own praise to God.

The Feast Days of the Apostles

The Church honors each of the Apostles with a special feast day. Based upon what you know about the Apostles, plan a celebration in their honor.

September 21
Feast of Saint Matthew

Matthew was also called Levi. Before becoming Jesus' disciple, Matthew was a publican—a collector of taxes—at Capernaum. One of the Gospels bears his name.

November 30
Feast of Saint Andrew

Andrew was Saint Peter's brother. Like Peter, he was a fisherman.

December 27
Feast of Saint John

John was the brother of the Apostle James and was part of Jesus' inner circle. He traveled to Asia Minor and led the Church at Ephesus, in modern-day Turkey. The Gospel of John was written by his followers.

October 28
Feast of Saints Simon and Jude

Simon the Zealot was from Cana, in Galilee. As a zealot, Simon wanted to overthrow the Roman rule of Palestine. Legend says that he was martyred.

Little is known about St. Jude. He is believed to have preached with Simon and to have been martyred there with him. St. Jude is the patron of lost causes.

Mazuronic, *Saint Simon*. 20th century.

El Greco, *Saint Jude Thaddeus*. 16th century.

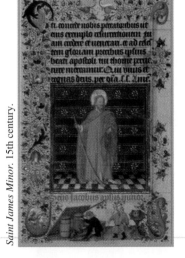

Saint James Minor. 15th century.

May 3
Feast of Saints Philip and James the Lesser

Philip came from Bethsaida, in Galilee. Before following Jesus, he was a disciple of John the Baptist. (See *John 1:43–48*.) The name Philip means "lover of horses."

James was a relative of Jesus. After Peter left for Rome, James became the head of the Christian community in Jerusalem. He was martyred in A.D. 62.

May 14
Feast of Saint Matthias

Matthias was selected an Apostle after Jesus' death to replace Judas Iscariot. (See *Acts 1:21–26*.)

de Conegliano, *Incredulity of Saint Thomas*

June 29
Feast of Saints Peter and Paul

Peter's name was Simon until Jesus called him Peter, from the greek word *petros*, meaning "rock." Peter was a fisherman from Capernaum and one of the first disciples called by Jesus. He was present at all the major events of Jesus' ministry. The Basilica of St. Peter's in Rome is built over his tomb. Saint Paul is the Apostle to the Gentiles. He is the only Apostle who did not know Jesus before the resurrection. Paul became the Church's greatest missionary, founding many Christian communities. Paul was martyred in Rome around A.D. 64.

July 3
Feast of Saint Thomas

Thomas is known as "doubting Thomas" because he refused to believe Jesus' resurrection until he had proof. Christians in India say that their country was evangelized by Thomas.

July 25
Feast of Saint James the Greater

James was a son of Zebedee and the older brother of the Apostle John. Like Peter, James was a resident of Capernaum and a fisherman on the Sea of Galilee. He was beheaded by Herod in Jerusalem around A.D. 44. He is the patron saint of Spain.

August 24
Feast of Saint Bartholomew

Little is known about Bartholomew, one of the Twelve.

LEARNING

1. What was the goal of Jesus' ministry?
The goal of Jesus' ministry was to proclaim the Good News of God's reign on earth.

2. What role did Jesus' friends play in his ministry?
Jesus had many friends and disciples who proclaimed the kingdom of God and healed in Jesus' name. After Jesus' death, the Twelve preached the Good News throughout much of the world.

3. What did Jesus command his followers to do for those in need?
Jesus told his followers to feed the hungry, give drink to the thirsty, clothe the naked, shelter the homeless, and visit the sick and imprisoned. These acts of kindness are called the Corporal Works of Mercy.

4. What is the basis of Jesus' authority?
Jesus' authority comes from God. God is revealed fully in Jesus Christ.

ASKING

1. How do I show that I love my neighbor?
2. On whose authority do I base my actions?
3. What do I do to make and keep friends?
4. What do I do to spread the message of Jesus?

LIVING

Write down one way you can develop each of the following qualities.

Quality	One Way I Can Develop It
Openness to people	_____
Faithfulness	_____
Commitment	_____
Right judgment	_____

PRAYING

All: God is love, and whoever remains in love remains in God.

Group 1: Beloved, let us love one another, because love is of God.

Group 2: Whoever is without love does not know God, for God is love.

All: God is love, and whoever remains in love remains in God.

Group 3: God sent Jesus so that we might have life through him.

Group 4: No one has ever seen God. Yet if we love one another, God remains in us.

All: God is love, and whoever remains in love remains in God.

Group 5: If we are to love God, whom we cannot see, we must love our neighbor, whom we can see.

Group 6: Jesus commanded us: love one another.

All: God is love, and whoever remains in love remains in God.

Based on 1 JOHN 4:7–21

Caravaggio, *Supper at Emmaus*, 16th century.

NO GREATER LOVE

CONTENT KEYS

1. **Jesus sacrificed himself for others.**
2. **Jesus freed you from sin and death.**
3. **You are called to sacrifice for others.**

He humbled himself, becoming obedient to death, even death on a cross.

PHILIPPIANS 2:8

HEROES IN THE NEWS

On almost any day of the week, you will find a story in the newspaper about people who risked their lives to help others. Here are two recent examples.

LOCAL HERO

ON THE BEACH

Fernandina Beach was very crowded. Lots of people were enjoying the Memorial Day sun. Lifeguard Chris French was tired after helping so many people all day. But when he saw people running toward the beach, Chris knew his day wasn't over. Seeing a swimmer having trouble out in the surf, Chris borrowed a surfboard and dove into the water. He reached for the man quickly and helped him to shore.

When he got to the beach, Chris was cheered by the crowd as a hero. Chris commented, "I only did what I was trained to do—save lives. What bothers me was that everyone else simply stood around watching. If I had been only a minute later the man would have drowned."

THE FLOOD

A severe thunderstorm dropped nine inches of rain on Eastern Texas, flooding roads and turning dry stream beds into raging rivers. When Allison Carver spun out on the wet road, she slid helplessly into a flooded ditch. Within seconds her car was filling with water.

Teenagers Louis Johnson and Eric Long saw the accident and jumped immediately into action. They reached the car in seconds, undid the seatbelt, and pulled Mrs. Carver to safety. If they had hesitated at all, Mrs. Carver would have drowned. When asked to explain why he had acted so bravely, Eric said, "I saw someone in trouble and I acted."

HEROIC ACTIONS

In the space provided, explain what it means to be a hero. Tell a story of someone risking his or her life to help others.

TO DIE IN HIS PLACE

The Poles called it Oswiecim, the Germans, Auschwitz. It was a place of death—a concentration camp where the Nazis imprisoned, tortured, and killed those they considered "undesirable." Many people found their ways onto this terrible list—resistance fighters, political protesters, priests, the disabled and mentally handicapped, Gypsies, and intellectuals. However, the majority of the prisoners were Jews, who were arrested because their very existence offended the Germans.

Over the gates to the camp was carved the ironic motto, "Work makes you free." Auschwitz was a work camp, part of a complex where millions of people were forced to do slave labor until they died of exhaustion, malnutrition, or torture. The dead were cremated or buried in mass graves. Those who survived the inhuman working conditions were often murdered outright.

Even in this terrible place, people managed to keep hope alive. Some even managed to escape. The price for those left behind, however, was death.

WHO ARE YOU?

Toward the end of July, 1941, a prisoner escaped from Cell Block 14. When he was not found after a few days, Commandant Fritsch, the officer in charge of the camp, called together all of the inmates of Cell Block 14.

"You know the rule," he shouted. "When one escapes, ten will die. Next time, it will be twenty."

The commandant walked up and down the rows of weak and terrified prisoners, stopping randomly to point out a man. When he had chosen ten, the commandant turned to order their execution. He was surprised to find his way blocked by Prisoner 16670.

"What do you want?" the commandant demanded.

"I wish to die in the place of one of these men," the prisoner replied.

"And just who are you?" snapped the commandant.

"I am a Catholic priest," the prisoner answered.

To the commandant, a Catholic priest was just another undesirable prisoner. It made no difference to him who died. "And whose place do you wish to take?" he grinned.

"That man," said the prisoner confidently, pointing at Prisoner 5659. "He has a wife and children. They need him."

"So be it," said the commandant. "You shall die in his place."

A Man for Others

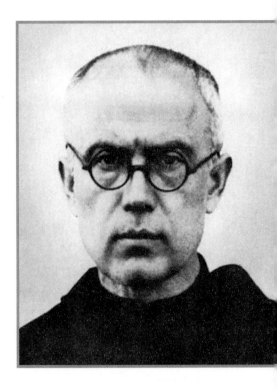

Prisoner 16670 was Father Maximilian Kolbe, a Polish Franciscan, well known throughout Europe for his writings and his devotion to Mary, the Mother of Jesus. The prisoner Father Kolbe replaced was a Polish soldier, Franciszek Gajowniczek.

Father Kolbe and the other nine prisoners were forced to suffer slow, painful deaths to discourage any other people who might think about escaping. They were locked away without food or water until death claimed them.

The ten prisoners faced their deaths bravely. Father Kolbe led them in prayers and hymns of praise until their mouths became too dry to speak. The songs they sang echoed through the surrounding barracks.

After two weeks, four of the prisoners—including Father Kolbe—were still alive. They were injected with poison by a camp doctor and died shortly thereafter. The last few, including Father Kolbe, died on the eve of the Feast of the Assumption of the Blessed Mother.

HE DIED FOR ME

The story of Father Kolbe's great sacrifice was remembered by those in the camp. It was retold to all who would listen. Father Kolbe was honored as a great hero and saint.

Before Father Kolbe was canonized by the Church, former prisoners of Auschwitz were interviewed about him. They talked about his kindness and generosity in the camp. They described how he shared his daily crust of bread with the hungry, and did the work of those too weak to stand. Father Kolbe also risked his life to lead prayers and hear people's confessions.

Franciszek Gajowniczek, whose place Father Kolbe had taken, offered his own thoughts about his rescuer. "His love for others was extraordinary," Gajowniczek said. "The most splendid confirmation of his heroic love came at the end, when he offered his life for none other than me."

Declared a saint in 1982 by Pope John Paul II, Saint Maximilian Kolbe left only one explanation for his actions. "Hatred is not creative," he told a fellow prisoner. "Our sorrow is necessary, that those who live after us may be happy."

1. **Why did Father Kolbe offer to take the place of another prisoner?**
2. **In what ways was Father Kolbe's sacrifice a sign of God's love?**

HE'S DEAD

Zachary was nearly exhausted by the time he reached home. He was surprised to see his friend Joshua there.

"He's dead, Zach. Jesus of Nazareth was crucified."

Zach gasped, "What happened?"

"Jesus entered Jerusalem several days ago, mobbed by the crowds. They threw their cloaks down in front of him, waved palm branches, and shouted, 'Hosanna to the Son of David!' Some called him king. I was excited, too. I felt certain Jesus was the Messiah."

Zach shook his head as if he doubted Joshua's story. "I can't believe this was the same man I heard in Galilee," he said. "What happened then?"

A VIOLENT END

Joshua continued, "Jesus' popularity frightened powerful people or something he said made them angry. I don't know. But in three days, the crowd went from calling him king to calling for his life.

"The Romans condemned Jesus to death. They whipped him severely, then mocked him by pressing a crown of thorns into his head. They made him drag his own cross to Golgatha, that horrible place. I watched the soldiers nail him to the cross."

"Did Jesus say anything?" Zach asked.

"He said, 'Father, forgive them.' I couldn't believe it. The man was in agony. People were torturing him. Yet he could forgive those who hurt him. I've never seen such faith."

Zach hung his head. "A sad ending," he said.

Joshua's voice grew louder. "You don't understand, Zach. It didn't feel like an ending. As I watched Jesus dying, I thought of something he had said earlier that week about dying for one's friends. I realized that's what Jesus was doing on the cross—dying for his friends.

"I knew I was looking at someone really holy, really God-like." Joshua ran his fingers through his hair in frustration. "I know that sounds crazy. He was dirty. He was bloody. He was helpless."

Zach rose and put his hand on his friend's arm. "I had hopes for Jesus, too," he said gently. "But we have to face facts. Our hopes are ended now. Just go on home, Joshua, and let me sleep. It's been a long day."

What Does It Mean?

Joshua and Zachary each are looking for meaning in Jesus' death. Explain in your own words what you think Jesus accomplished with his death.

THE SUFFERING SERVANT

The prophet Isaiah wrote of the one whom God would send to lead people to salvation.

He was spurned and avoided by all, a man of suffering, accustomed to infirmity. Yet it was our infirmities that he bore, our sufferings that he endured.
But he was pierced for our offenses, crushed for our sins, upon him was the chastisement that makes us whole, by his stripes we were healed.
The Lord laid upon him the guilt of us all.

ISAIAH 53:3–6

Jesus was this suffering servant promised by Isaiah. Jesus' violent death was not the result of chance, but was the fulfillment of God's divine plan to redeem all of humanity from the slavery of sin. As Saint Paul wrote, "Christ died for our sins in accordance with the Scriptures" (*1 Corinthians 15:3*). Indeed, Jesus said about himself, "Just so, the Son of Man did not come to be served but to serve and to give his life as a ransom for many" (*Matthew 20:28*).

Jesus died to reconcile all of the world to God's saving love. Although he did not sin, by becoming man, Jesus took responsibility for the sin of the world before God so that "we might become the righteousness of God" (*2 Corinthians 5:21*).

Through this act of redeeming love, Jesus overcame sin and death. Because of Jesus, people would no longer have to be slaves to sin or to fear death. Jesus' death and resurrection conquered sin and death for all time.

But now Christ has been raised from the dead, the firstfruits of those who have fallen asleep. For just as in Adam all die, so too, in Christ shall all be brought to life.

1 CORINTHIANS 15:20, 22

You can show your love for others by being aware of their needs and acting with the virtue of compassion. You show compassion when you try to understand what a person is feeling and try to help. Practice being a good listener. Be willing to go out of your way to help.

Jesus' death also showed God's love for creation.

God proves his love for us in that while we were still sinners Christ died for us. We also boast of God through our Lord Jesus Christ, through whom we have now received reconciliation.

ROMANS 5:8, 11

A **sacrifice** is something precious offered to God, or given up for the good of others. **Salvation**—the liberation from sin and death—is the result of Jesus' complete obedience to God's will.

THE GREATEST PUZZLE

When Franciszek Gajowniczek traded places with Father Maximilian Kolbe he experienced first hand what Jesus meant when he said, "No one has greater love than this, to lay down one's life for one's friends" (*John 15:13*). Gajowniczek was grateful for Father Kolbe's **sacrifice,** but he did not understand it.

Jesus' followers did not understand his death either. How could someone who was so popular, so important, willingly give up his life for others?

THE MYSTERY OF SALVATION

Jesus entered fully into human life. He did not sin, but by simply being human he took on the suffering, brokeness, and death that original sin brought into the world. And by doing so, Jesus showed that the way out of suffering and death lies in going *through* them. There are no shortcuts—no pills, no magic potions, no secret words—to life. What he did, in enduring suffering and death and rising triumphant to new life, offers the way of triumph for you.

But you cannot do it alone. The real mystery of **salvation**—to which Jesus' cross and empty tomb point—lies in sharing in Jesus' total obedience to God's will.

God the Father did not force Jesus to die, any more than God forces you to do anything. Jesus explained his devotion to the Father when he said,

This is why the Father loves me, because I lay down my life in order to take it up again. No one takes it from me, but I lay it down on my own. I have the power to pick it up again.

JOHN 10:17–18

Obedience that is forced is not obedience at all. Sacrifice offered grudgingly is not a gift. Jesus surrendered his life freely, trusting completely in God's love. In the same way, a mother will freely choose to go hungry so that her child may eat. Or you might risk your life to save a friend from crashing into a wall without a second's thought. Each time you make a sacrifice for the benefit of another, you follow Jesus' example.

1. **Why did Jesus suffer and die?**
2. **How do you share in the mystery of Jesus' suffering and death?**

MAKING SACRIFICES

As a follower of Jesus, you are asked to make sacrifices for the benefit of others. Every time you do something unselfish, every time you place someone else's wants and needs ahead of your own, you are following Jesus' example. The reward for your sacrifice (though you may not recognize it right away) is new life.

Use the chart below to list ways you sacrifice for others—and the reward of new life that each sacrifice brings.

Ways I Sacrifice for Others ~

Rewards ~

THE SIGN OF THE CROSS

For Christians, the sign of the cross is a sign of hope, of reconciliation, of redemption. Here is a prayer in honor of Jesus' loving sacrifice on the cross. Meditate on each line as you pray it.

By you, O Holy Cross, hell is ruined.
By you the world is renewed and made beautiful with truth.
By you sinful humanity is absolved, the condemned are saved, the slaves of sin are set free, the dead are raised to life.
By you, O Holy Cross.

Saint Anselm of Canterbury, 1033–1109

WITH YOUR FAMILY

Discuss with adult family members the important sacrifices they have made in their lives. How have they (and you) benefited from their sacrifices? Thank them for what they have done for you.

▼REVIEW CHAPTER 9

CATHOLICS BELIEVE

1. Jesus sacrificed his life for others.
2. Jesus' death saves people from sin and death.
3. Followers of Jesus are asked to make sacrifices for the benefit of others.

KNOW

1. Who was Saint Maximilian Kolbe? Why is he remembered?

   _____

2. Why did Jesus' followers have difficulty understanding the meaning of Jesus'

   death? _____

3. What was accomplished by Jesus' death and resurrection? _____

   _____

4. According to 1 Corinthians 15, how did Jesus' death overcome the sin of

   Adam? _____

5. How did the prophet Isaiah describe the suffering servant? How did Jesus

   fulfill that prophecy? _____

6. Define the words sacrifice and salvation. Use these words in a sentence in reference to Jesus.

   _____

   _____

SUNDAY MASS

Each week, people offer a sacrificial offering at Church. Through people's generosity, the Church is able to provide for the needs of the sick and the needy. Consider making a sacrificial offering in the collection this week with your own money.

10

CONTENT KEYS

1. **Jesus was raised from the dead.**
2. **Jesus appeared to the disciples.**
3. **Christians celebrate Jesus' resurrection.**

Why do you seek the living one among the dead? He is not here, but he has been raised.

Luke 24:5–6

LAID TO REST

"George, Mrs. Loria will be picking you up from school this afternoon. I've packed you an extra snack to eat after school."

"What's going on, Mom? Why can't I walk home like I do every day?"

"Aunt Mildred died during the night. Your father and I will be helping with the arrangements. On Thursday, you will miss school and go to the funeral with us," his mother explained.

"How'd she die?" asked George.

"Honey, Aunt Mildred was very old. Her heart finally failed her. She died peacefully and is now with God."

"Is there anything I can do to help?"

"I was hoping you'd ask, dear. Would you like to serve the funeral mass with your cousin Ruth Ann?"

"Sure. That would be neat."

Funerals are times of sadness because a person you love has died. You can no longer see or talk with the person. The spot the person filled in your life is suddenly empty. The funeral service provides people an opportunity to express their grief.

Funerals are also times of hope. Christians believe that when a faithful person dies, he or she goes home to God. While death is the end of life on earth, it is also the beginning of life with God in heaven.

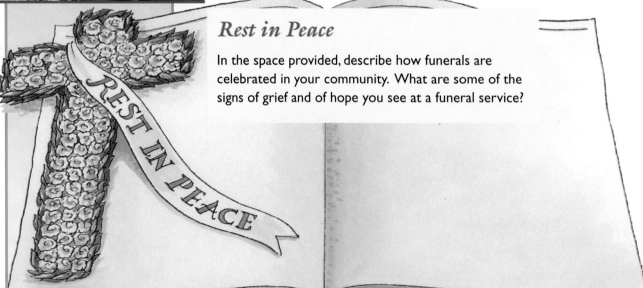

Rest in Peace

In the space provided, describe how funerals are celebrated in your community. What are some of the signs of grief and of hope you see at a funeral service?

I Have Seen the Lord

It was barely morning. There was no color at all in the garden, and the only sound came from the cooing doves, still invisible in their nests.

Mary of Magdala was up early. She hadn't slept much since Jesus' arrest. Mary thought she had finished crying, but here she was again, her face wet, her throat tight.

She'd rushed here hoping to fulfill the sacred ritual of anointing Jesus' body and wrapping it in clean burial linens. Because of the Sabbath, there hadn't been time on the day he died to prepare his body properly. "How silly of me," Mary thought. "How will I get past the guards or move the heavy stone?"

Approaching the tomb, Mary stopped in her tracks. The stone and the guards were gone! "They've moved his body," she thought. Frightened, she ran to tell the other disciples.

When Mary returned to the tomb, she was crying harder than before. Now Jesus was gone. She could not even give him the honor shown the dead. When the stranger spoke to her, Mary paid him little attention.

"Woman, why are you weeping?" the stranger asked. Thinking the stranger was the gardener, Mary begged "Please sir, if you carried him away, tell me where you laid him, and I will care for him."

The stranger said only one word in reply, "Mary."

Mary was overcome with joy. The stranger was Jesus, somehow no longer dead, but alive. "Rabbouni! (Teacher!)" she cried, rushing to hold him.

"Don't hold onto me, Mary. Go and tell the others that I am going to my Father," Jesus said to her.

As she ran to tell the others, Mary understood what Jesus had told them. Death was not the end, but the beginning.

Inspired by JOHN 20:1–18

FORSAKEN

When Jesus died, all of Peter's hopes were destroyed. His plans for a glorious reign of God here on earth had been crucified along with Jesus. He had given up everything to follow Jesus—his boat, his business, his reputation—only to see it all crumble like dust. Worst of all, the man he loved like a brother was no more.

Grief was not the only pain Peter was feeling. Peter was also ashamed. He'd promised to stand by Jesus through any danger. Yet when the soldiers arrested Jesus, Peter had fled in fear. Later, when asked if he were Jesus' disciple, Peter even denied knowing Jesus. Now all Peter could feel was loss, grief, and self-hatred.

Peter glanced around the room at the frightened group of disciples hiding behind a locked door. How much they had changed! A week ago, when the excited crowd cheered their entry into Jerusalem, they had felt like conquering heroes. Now they might as well be dead, walled up in this room as if buried in a tomb.

Peter laughed under his breath. Maybe they were more trapped than Jesus. Earlier in the day, Mary of Magdala had come to tell them that Jesus' tomb was empty. Peter and John had run to see for themselves. Truly, Jesus' body was gone. In death, Jesus had somehow managed to escape his tomb, while they were still trapped alive in theirs.

Peter wondered for a moment if he were losing his sanity. Certainly Mary of Magdala seemed to be losing hers. After they'd returned from Jesus' tomb, she'd come to tell the disciples that the Lord was alive. What craziness!

Suddenly, Peter heard a voice. It was a familiar voice—a beloved voice.

"Peace be with you," it said.

Peter's head flew up. Was he dreaming? There was Jesus, standing among them as large as life.

Every disciple in the room ran to the Lord. They couldn't believe their eyes. Jesus showed them his hands, pierced by the nails. It was true. He was real. Jesus was alive!

Jesus' words broke through Peter's hard shell of grief and disbelief. "Peace." Then Peter remembered what Jesus had told them weeks before: "The Son of Man must suffer greatly and be rejected and be killed and on the third day be raised" (*Luke 9:22*). Yes, that was it. Jesus had told them all along. He would die, but he would be raised. Why hadn't they understood?

Inspired by JOHN 20:19–23

He Is Risen!

What would you think and feel if someone you loved left your life, but then unexpectedly returned? Record your thoughts and feelings in this space.

HE IS TRANSFORMED

Bearing life and more fruitful than paradise, brighter than paradise, righter than any royal chamber, your tomb, O Christ, is the fountain of our resurrection.

ORTHODOX HYMN

When Peter and the other disciples first saw Jesus after the resurrection, some of them thought they were seeing a ghost. But Jesus was no ghost. He invited the disciples to touch him and to look at the marks of the nails on his hands and feet. He sat and ate with them. He explained the Scriptures to them. On at least one occasion, Jesus cooked breakfast for them. Jesus also told the disciples how to carry on the work of spreading the Good News.

However, Jesus' body was not the same as it had been before his death on the cross. The resurrected Jesus was transformed. He was no longer bound by limits of time or space. He appeared suddenly in a locked room and then, just as suddenly, disappeared. On the road to Emmaus, two of Jesus' disciples did not recognize him until Jesus revealed his identity.

Jesus was changed by the resurrection. His was not a dead body brought back to life, but a new one filled with the glory of eternal life. He was the Living Savior, the triumphant Son of God.

The resurrection is at the heart of the Good News. In a way, the Gospels begin with Easter, not Christmas. Every part of Jesus' life and mission takes on the light of that morning by the empty tomb.

Following Jesus

Because of the resurrection, Christian life is filled with hope. You can communicate to others your hope in the resurrection through your actions, words, or works. Your honest praise and support can give someone a feeling of new life.

A CHANGED PEOPLE

The people who encountered the resurrected Jesus were changed by that experience. Disciples who had been hiding in fear took to the streets to proclaim their faith in Jesus. Their personal witness to Jesus' resurrection has been passed down through an unbroken line of believers to this very day. Their witness is the foundation of the Christian faith.

The earliest Christian communities took their life from the message of the resurrection. In honor of the resurrection, Christians chose to worship and rest on Sunday, the Lord's Day. As Saint Justin Martyr wrote in the second century,

It is on Sunday that we assemble, because Sunday is the first day: the day on which God transformed darkness and matter and created the world, and the day on which Jesus Christ our Savior rose from the dead.

Every Sunday is a little Easter.

The first and greatest feast of the Church is Easter. At the Easter Vigil celebration, the new fire is blessed and the Paschal candle lighted in honor of "Christ, our light." The Scripture readings proclaim the triumph of God's love over sin and death.

At the Easter Vigil, the Church celebrates Jesus' death and resurrection by inviting people seeking to enter the Church (called the Elect) to die to sin and be reborn in Christ through the waters of Baptism.

The great acclamation of Easter is the Alleluia. The Hebrew word *alleluia* means "Praise the Lord!" Saint Augustine said, "The Christian should be a walking 'Alleluia.' We are Easter people, and 'Alleluia' is our song."

LIVING NEW LIFE

The signs and symbols of the Easter Vigil are part of your identity as a Catholic Christian. You are called to live Christ's resurrection every day. An anonymous second-century Christian recorded what this meant for the early Church.

There is something extraordinary about their lives. Condemned because they are not understood, they are put to death, but are raised to life again. They live in poverty, but enrich many. A blessing is their answer to abuse. For the good they do they receive punishment, but even then they rejoice, as though receiving the gift of life.

CHRISTIAN STARS

Where do you see signs of people living as "resurrection people" in your school or neighborhood? Tell stories of people reaching out to care for others, of people who share Jesus' love and joy by their attitudes and actions. Write their names in the space provided.

A Pilgrimage

Easter faith is alive today as the heirs of the Apostles continue to proclaim the resurrection. Every two years, young people from around the world gather at *World Youth Day* to celebrate the importance of Jesus in their lives. On August 15, 1989, 50,000 young people gathered at Santiago de Compostela, Spain, to hear the successor of Saint Peter, Pope John Paul II, preach a resurrection message.

The young people had traveled from all over the world—by plane, by boat, by train, by bus or car, on bicycles and in wheelchairs, some of them even on foot. They carried backpacks and sleeping bags, radios and tape players, and cameras and video recorders. They shared snacks and jokes and sang favorite songs.

Along with their radios, they carried rosaries. In their backpacks were Bibles. Along with the snacks and jokes, these young men and women shared the sacraments of Eucharist and Reconciliation. They were modern-day pilgrims.

WHAT DO YOU SEEK?

Pope John Paul II began by asking the young people the traditional question, "What do you seek, pilgrims?" Late in his talk, the pope prayed that the young people would find their answers in Christ.

Love is stronger than death. The cross and the resurrection together form the call to follow Christ. Our voices proclaim our faith and our hope. We want to kindle a fire of love and truth that will draw the whole world's attention to God's love.

1. In what ways was Jesus "changed" by the resurrection? How were his followers changed?
2. What is celebrated every Sunday? Why are these celebrations signs of hope?
3. How could belief in the power of the resurrection make a difference in your life?

DID YOU KNOW?

The Shrine of Santiago de Compostela has been a pilgrimage site since the seventh century. The shrine is dedicated to Saint James the Greater, who is said to be buried there. Pilgrims to the shrine brought back scallop shells from the Spanish beaches; these shells later became the universal symbol, or "badge," of pilgrims.

RESURRECTION PEOPLE

Christians are "resurrection people" because each day they show that Christ has risen by their beliefs, actions, attitudes, and behavior. What three things can you do this week to be a sign of Christ's resurrection? Write your plans below.

A RESURRECTION HYMN

All: Christ is risen from the dead, trampling down death by death, and upon those in the tombs bestowing new life.

Group 1: Where is your sting, O death? Where is your victory?

Group 2: Christ is risen, and death is overthrown.

Group 3: For Christ, having risen from the dead, became the firstfruits of those who slept in death.

Group 4: For by the cross, great joy is come into the world. Ever praising the Lord, let us sing his resurrection.

All: For he overthrew death by his death. To him be glory and majesty, now and forever, and unto ages of ages.

Based on the BYZANTINE LITURGY OF SAINT JOHN CHRYSOSTOM

WITH YOUR FAMILY

Make an "Alleluia" banner with your family. Decorate it with signs of Easter. Hang your banner where guests can see it.

▼ REVIEW CHAPTER 10

CATHOLICS BELIEVE

1. Jesus appeared to his disciples after the resurrection.
2. After the resurrection, Jesus' body was filled with the glory of God, and was capable of doing special things.
3. Easter is the most important Christian feast. Each Sunday is celebrated as a little Easter.

KNOW

1. Who were the first people to learn of Jesus' resurrection?

2. How did the disciples learn of Jesus' resurrection?

3. What is the message of the resurrection?

4. How did Saint Augustine describe Christians?

5. What Hebrew word is the song of Easter? What is the meaning of this word?

6. Why is the resurrection the most important Christian feast?

SUNDAY MASS

During the Eucharistic Prayer, at the Memorial Acclamation, the congregation expresses its faith in the resurrection. There are three acclamations that are commonly used to express this mystery of faith. This Sunday, listen to hear which of the acclamations is proclaimed. Report your findings to the class.

11

CONTENT KEYS

1. **Jesus is recognized as God's Son.**
2. **Jesus is true God and true man.**
3. **The Incarnation is a mystery of Faith.**

And the Word became flesh, and made his dwelling among us, and we saw his glory.

JOHN 1:14

WHAT DO YOU SEE?

There is a secret hidden in plain sight in this picture. Examine it carefully and describe what you see.

Things are not always as they appear at first glance. For centuries, people thought the sun revolved around the earth. They had all of the proof they needed: they saw it with their own eyes. Didn't the sun rise in the East and set in the West? It wasn't until Galileo perfected the telescope in 1609 that people learned that there was more to the world than what they could see with the unassisted eye. Galileo showed them that to see the heavens as they actually were, they would have to learn to see with new eyes.

Seeing with New Eyes

What are some examples of things that are different from what they seem? List your examples here.

Magritte, *Les Promenades d'Euclid.* 20th century.

MY CHOSEN SON

The sun had barely risen when Jesus called us aside to go up the mountain with him. Jesus liked to come to the mountains at times to get away from the crowds. Peter, my brother John, and I often shared such quiet times with Jesus.

When we arrived at the mountaintop, Jesus began to pray. The three of us prayed, too, each of us in our own way. As we prayed, we drifted off to sleep.

My brother John awoke first. He shook me. "James, look!" he whispered. His voice was filled with wonder. Peter stirred then, too.

Jesus was standing before us, but he was changed. His face was full of light— as though the light came from his face. His clothes were so white that it hurt our eyes to look at him. It was as though we were looking straight into the sun.

Two men stood with Jesus in the circle of light that radiated from him. I knew who the men were. I don't know how, but I knew.

One of them was Moses—the great liberator who had led God's People out of slavery in Egypt. It was Moses who had received the tablets of the Law from God on a mountaintop much like this one. The other man was the great prophet Elijah, who had raised the dead to life and been taken up to heaven in a chariot of fire.

As if in a dream, we heard their voices. They spoke of what Jesus would accomplish in Jerusalem. We stood in awe at what we saw and heard. We did not really understand what happened there, however, until after the resurrection.

Peter found his voice first. "Master," he stammered. "It is good that we are here. Let us build three tents—one for you, one for Moses, and one for Elijah."

Bellini, *The Transfiguration*. 15th century.

A Voice from the Cloud

John and I stared at Peter. What was he saying? I don't think he knew himself. But part of me understood. Yes, it would be good to capture this moment and make it permanent. It's what God's People have always done when God's presence broke into their lives. Even in the wilderness, the Israelites had stopped to make the beautiful Tent of Meeting as a shelter for the **Ark of the Covenant.**

As these thoughts raced through my mind, a great cloud came across the mountaintop, covering everything in a mist. When the cloud's shadow reached us, we were overcome with fear. I don't know about Peter and John, but I fell to the ground and hid my face. A soft yet powerful voice came from the cloud saying, "This is my chosen Son. Listen to him."

I knew in my heart that God had spoken.

When the cloud passed, and we dared to look again, Jesus was standing alone. He looked unchanged by the events, the same as he had always looked.

None of us spoke as we came down the mountain—for, eventually, we did go back down. In fact, Jesus asked us not to mention what happened to anyone else. But we knew in our heart who it was we followed, who we shared bread with, who we loved. In Jesus, God had come to live with us.

We had been with Jesus for so long, and yet never fully realized who he was. We had to learn a new way of seeing in order to recognize him as God's Son.

Adapted from Luke 9:28–36

Raphael, *The Transfiguration.* 16th century.

The **Ark of the Covenant** was the precious container in which the Israelites carried the tablets of the Law—the sign of God's covenant.

1. **What did it mean that Moses and Elijah were present on the mountaintop with the glorified Jesus?**
2. **Why do you think Peter wanted to build tents on the mountaintop? Why didn't he do it?**
3. **What helped the Apostles see Jesus more clearly?**

The Incarnate Word

The experience that Peter, James, and John shared on the mountaintop was an *epiphany,* from the Greek word for "showing forth." Jesus' transfiguration is an epiphany because through it, God was revealed.

There are other examples of epiphanies in the Gospel.

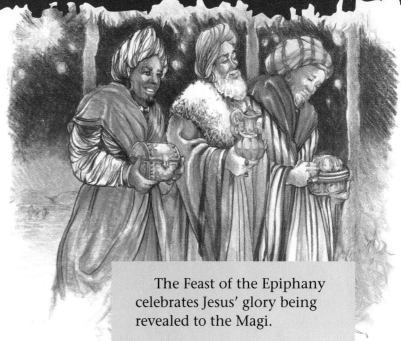

The Feast of the Epiphany celebrates Jesus' glory being revealed to the Magi.

At Jesus' baptism, the heavens opened and the Holy Spirit descended like a dove.

When Jesus appeared to the disciples after his resurrection, the experience was an epiphany.

All of these events point to the same truth: that Jesus is the Son of God, the eternal Word of God made flesh through the **Incarnation.**

SPECIAL WORDS

The mystery of the **incarnation** is the belief that God the Son was born the child of the Virgin Mary. The word **incarnate** means "in the flesh."

GOD, MAN, SPIRIT?

Understanding the true identity of Jesus was one of the most difficult challenges in Church history. The belief that Jesus is both God and man was a new idea. People could understand this truth with their hearts long before they could talk about it.

Over the years, there were many disagreements about who Jesus was. Some people believed that Jesus was nothing more than a very good person who showed other people the way to God. Others thought that Jesus was some kind of angelic spirit, neither God nor human. Still others thought that Jesus was God in disguise. They thought that God would never stoop so low as to actually become human.

The disagreements got ugly at times, with various groups excommunicating or imprisoning those who disagreed with them. It took four **ecumenical councils,** or worldwide gatherings of bishops, to determine the truths about the relationship between the Father, the Son, and the Holy Spirit. Pope Gregory the Great compared these councils to the four Gospels because they shed so much light on the person and mission of Jesus.

- The Council of Nicaea (A.D. 325) proclaimed that Jesus is truly God, equal and the same in every way to God the Father.
- The Council of Constantinople (A.D. 381) proclaimed that the Holy Spirit is God, equal to and the same as the Father and the Son.
- The Council of Ephesus (A.D. 431) taught that Mary, the Mother of Jesus, could be called the Mother of God because the child she carried was God.
- The Council of Chalcedon (A.D. 451) declared that divine and human natures are completely joined in the Person of Jesus, who is truly God and truly man.

These councils spelled out the mystery of

Bellini, *Madonna and Child.* 15th century.

the Incarnation that is celebrated in John's Gospel.

And the Word became flesh and made his dwelling among us, and we saw his glory, the glory as of the Father's only Son, full of grace and truth.

JOHN 1:14

During the Mass on Christmas Day, the Church recalls the Incarnation in these words:

In him we see our God made visible, and so are caught up in the love of the God we cannot see.

Ecumenical councils are gatherings of bishops from all over the world, meeting to discuss matters of faith and doctrine.

Madonna and Child (icon). 18th century.

GOD-BEARER

Alexandra peeked through the side door of Saints Cyril and Methodius Church. She was waiting for Aunt Katya to finish her prayers. Her eyes took in the beauty of the paintings that stood in front of the altar. "This Ukrainian Catholic church is very different from Saint John's," she thought.

The walls of the Ukrainian church were covered with icons. Their colors glowed softly in the reflected light of the hundreds of flickering candles. Aunt Katya knelt on the floor in front of the icon of the Blessed Virgin. The smell of incense filled the air.

Aunt Katya had just moved here from the Ukraine with her husband. She was eight months pregnant. Alexandria took her aunt's hand as they walked home.

"In Ukrainian, we call the Blessed Mother Bogoroditsa—the God-bearer," Aunt Katya said.

"Because she carried Jesus," Alexandra nodded. "Like you are carrying my new cousin."

"Not only for that reason," Aunt Katya said. "She is the God-bearer because she gave her Son to the world. You, Alexa, you are a God-bearer, too—and your mother, and your father, and Mr. Brooks, who gave Uncle Nicolai a job, and Peter."

Alexandra giggled. She couldn't help it—her brother, Pete, compared to the Blessed Mother? No way!

But Aunt Katya was serious. "Peter gave us his room," she explained. "That was a great sacrifice for him to make, but he did not complain. Your parents helped us come to this country, and the neighbors made us welcome. They gave us hope, and new life. That is what a God-bearer does—bring God's love to birth in the world."

Alexandra thought for a minute. "What about me?" she finally asked. "How am I a God-bearer?"

"You?" Aunt Katya smiled. "Who else could teach my baby how to laugh so well?"

1. What is the mystery of the Incarnation?
2. Why is "God-bearer" a good title for the Blessed Mother? Why is it a good title for Jesus' followers?
3. Tell one way that you are a God-bearer.

Following Jesus

You can be a God-bearer by sharing your joy with others. Smile often and help others to laugh. Be of good cheer—don't be a grouch. When things don't go as you'd like, don't whine and complain. People will see Christ in your actions.

READING THE SIGNS

The Incarnation is the major sign that God is present in the world. But you need only look with the eyes of faith to see God's glorious presence everywhere. Saints and mystics throughout the centuries have shown the way. Read some of their words below, and then write your own thoughts about finding God's glory.

One must see God in everyone.
Saint Catherine Laboure

The soul is in God and God is in the soul, just as the fish is in the sea and the sea is in the fish.
Saint Catherine of Siena

I knew my spirit was awake the day I first saw— and knew that I saw—all things in God and God in all things.
Mechtild of Magdeburg

The soul of one who loves God always swims in joy, always keeps a holiday, and is always in the mood for singing.
Saint John of the Cross

THE ANGELUS

The Angelus is prayed by Catholics throughout the world three times a day.

The angel spoke God's message to Mary, and she conceived of the Holy Spirit. (Hail Mary)
I am the lowly servant of the Lord: let it be done to me according to your word. (Hail Mary)
And the Word became flesh and lived among us. (Hail Mary)
Pray for us, holy Mother of God, that we may become worthy of the promises of Christ.
Let us pray. Lord, fill our hearts with your grace. Once, through the message of an angel, you revealed the incarnation of your Son. Now through his suffering and death, lead us to the glory of his resurrection. We ask this through Christ our Lord. Amen.

 **WITH YOUR FAMILY**

In your home, prepare a simple shrine to Mary. Place a statue, icon, or other representation of Mary in a special place. Decorate your shrine with flowers from your yard, with a candle, or with another special item. Use the shrine as a place of prayer.

CATHOLICS BELIEVE

1. Jesus' divine glory was revealed at the Transfiguration.
2. God becoming human is the mystery of the Incarnation.
3. Mary is truly the Mother of God.

KNOW

1. The revelation of Jesus' glory on the mountaintop is called the_____

    _____.

2. Jesus appeared in glory with _____and _____.

3. The phrase from John's Gospel "the Word became flesh" refers to the mystery of

    the_____.

4. The Council of Chalcedon proclaimed that Jesus was both _____

    and _____.

5. Mary received the title "God-bearer," or Mother of God, because Jesus was her

    _____.

SUNDAY MASS

The bishops at the Council of Nicaea taught that Jesus was truly God. This teaching is found in the Nicene Creed. This Sunday when you say the Nicene Creed, think about what it means to you that God became a man.

Christ Pantocrator (icon).

THE HOLY SPIRIT

Do you not know that the Spirit of God dwells in you?
1 CORINTHIANS 3:16

UNEXPLAINABLE FEELINGS

Tony looked forward to his family's camping trips. He enjoyed everything about them: hikes, hot chocolate, campfire sing-alongs—even sleeping on the ground. What he liked best, though, was staring into the campfire late in the evening. The deep red embers and shifting light made him feel safe and warm.

Erica had never been on a boat before, so she was nervous about going on her school's whale watching trip. Would she get seasick? What would happen if she fell overboard? As the boat moved quickly through the calm Pacific Ocean, she forgot all about her fear. As the fog lifted, Erica saw sea gulls hovering overhead. The wind and salt spray were exciting, not frightening. Erica was overwhelmed by the majesty and grace of the giant humpback and its baby as they surfaced nearby. She had never felt so alive!

Feeling Alive!

Use this space to describe or draw an experience that made you feel most alive. Include as many details as you can remember. Be prepared to share your experience with the class.

SIGNS OF THE SPIRIT

Certain natural elements have enormous power to affect human understanding. Who hasn't been enlivened by the wind, captivated by fire, or filled with joy by water? It is no wonder that, throughout the Bible, these elements have been associated with the Spirit of God, who gives life, hope, and grace to everyone.

The Holy Spirit is the very life and breath of God. (The word for spirit in Hebrew is *ruah,* which means both "wind" and "breath.") In the vision of the prophet Ezekiel, God's spirit came like a mighty wind to stir into life the dry bones of the house of Israel (*Ezekiel 37:1–14*). The presence of the Holy Spirit, the Advocate promised by Jesus, was signaled on Pentecost morning by "a noise like a strong driving wind" (*Acts 2:2*).

Water is a sign of God's life-giving Spirit, especially to people who live in desert climates, like the people of Israel. In the desert, even a little rain can turn a barren land into fertile ground. Water also has terrible power to destroy, ravage, and drown. That is why water is the sign for Baptism. You go down into the waters of death and are reborn into the new life of the Holy Spirit.

Fire, too, has the awesome power to destroy and kill. But it also provides warmth and light. People use fire to generate electricity, cook food, and forge metal. Fire is so important that Greek mythology explains how fire was stolen from the gods. In the Bible, fire from heaven is a sign of God's power (*1 Kings 18:36–39; 2 Kings 1:9–11*). At the coming of the Holy Spirit, "tongues of fire" came to rest on the Apostles (*Acts 2:3–4*).

THE SPIRIT OF GOD

*No one can say "Jesus is Lord"
except by the Holy Spirit.*

1 CORINTHIANS 12:3

*God has sent the Spirit of his Son
into our hearts, crying, "Abba!
Father!"*

GALATIANS 4:6

Jesus promised his disciples that he
would not leave them orphans. He
promised to send them an Advocate
(someone who will speak in their
behalf) to be with them until the end
of time. This Advocate is the Holy
Spirit.

Jesus described the Holy Spirit as a
Paraclete, or a "consoler." The Spirit
would be a teacher and a speaker of
truth.

*The Advocate, the Holy Spirit that
the Father will send in my name—
will teach you everything and
remind you of all that I told you.*

JOHN 14:26

Jesus kept his word. The Holy Spirit
came upon Jesus' followers on
Pentecost.

THE BLESSED TRINITY

The friends and followers of Jesus did
not put their experience of the Holy
Spirit in theological terms. But what
they had experienced was the three
persons in the one God, the mystery
of the **Blessed Trinity.**

- Through Jesus, they had come to
  know God as a Father who
  created the world and guided it
  with loving care.
- In Jesus, they recognized the Son
  of God, who revealed the Father
  and redeemed the world from sin
  and death.
- With the Holy Spirit, the disciples
  were set free from the fears that
  kept them hidden behind locked
  doors. The Spirit renewed their
  lives and filled their hearts with
  joy.

Just as it took the Church centuries
to develop doctrinal statements about
the identity of Jesus, so the Church's
understanding of the Blessed Trinity
unfolded over time.

1. **What images are used in
   Scripture to describe the Holy
   Spirit? Why are these images
   used?**
2. **Explain the mystery of the
   Blessed Trinity in your own
   words.**

The **Blessed Trinity**
describes the mystery of
the one God being Father,
Son, and Spirit.

Symbols of the Holy Spirit

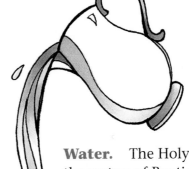

The Holy Spirit does not have a body. This is one reason why it is so difficult for people to imagine the Spirit. Yet the Spirit is very real and can be known through its results—just as the wind can be known only by its effects. These are some of the symbols that represent the action of the Spirit.

Water. The Holy Spirit empowers the waters of Baptism, giving birth to new life. Jesus said that the Spirit wells up in people like water to give them eternal life (*John 4:14*).

Anointing. Jesus was anointed by the Spirit. The title Christ means "anointed one." At Confirmation, Christians are anointed with the oil of the Spirit.

Fire. Fire symbolizes the transforming energy of the Holy Spirit. John the Baptist said that Christ would baptize with fire.

Dove. At Jesus' baptism, the Holy Spirit appeared in the form of a dove. In Christian art, the Spirit is often depicted as a dove.

Cloud and Light. In the Old Testament, God appears in the form of cloud and light. The Spirit of God overshadowed Mary at the Annunciation. The cloud appeared on the mountaintop at the time of the Transfiguration of Jesus. At the Ascension, Jesus was taken up into heaven in a cloud.

Spirit Signs

What image would you use to describe the Holy Spirit?

LIVING IN THE SPIRIT

As you might imagine from the language and symbols used to describe the Holy Spirit, being filled with the Spirit is not supposed to go unnoticed. Thunderous winds, tongues of flame, the ability to communicate with total strangers and be understood—all of these are signs of an experience that changes people's lives. The Apostles were so wild with joy on Pentecost morning that some bystanders accused them of being drunk on new wine! They were hardly being shy, or keeping the Good News to themselves!

What about you? You received the Holy Spirit when you were baptized. And if you have been confirmed, you were sealed in the Spirit then. When you receive the sacraments of Eucharist and Reconciliation, you share in the grace of the Holy Spirit. Why don't you hear whirlwinds or see flames? Did the working of the Spirit end with the Bible?

PEOPLE WILL NOTICE

The winds and flames described at Pentecost were external signs of the Spirit working within the disciples. There may not be loud noises and miraculous events when you act like a Spirit-filled person, but the Spirit will make a difference in you. People will notice who you are and what you do. They will know that you are following the Holy Spirit.

Saint Paul noticed how the Christians of Galatia (in Asia Minor) were behaving and wrote them a stern letter expressing his displeasure.

You seem to know very well how to do the things that don't show the Spirit. When you're fighting with one another, being selfish, chasing after false values, envying one another, getting drunk, and abusing God's gift of sexuality, you've turned your back on the Spirit.

Inspired by GALATIANS 5:19–21

Saint Paul did more than criticize the Christians of Galatia, however. He also explained to them the signs that would show that the Spirit was working in their lives.

In contrast, the fruit of the Spirit is love, joy, peace, patience, kindness, generosity, faithfulness, gentleness, self-control. If we live in the Spirit, let us also follow the Spirit.

GALATIANS 5:22–23,25

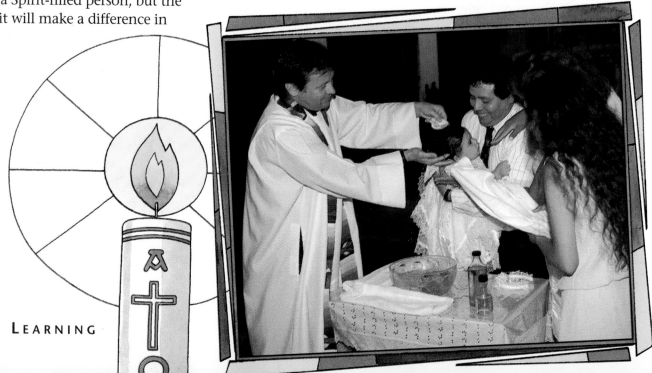

BEARING GOOD FRUIT

The qualities listed in the Letter to the Galatians don't seem, at first glance, to be spectacular—especially at a time when some people are famous for living the kind of life Saint Paul condemned! But what would the world be like without the fruit of the Spirit? As you read about each of the fruits of the Spirit, offer examples of how the Spirit makes a difference in your life.

1. **When did you receive the Holy Spirit?**
2. **Which fruit of the Spirit do you think is most needed in your life?**

Peace is the feeling of being tranquil and quiet, at one with the Lord. Peace is also the ability to resolve conflicts and bring different points of view into harmony.

Kindness means you help others because you care, not because you have to.

Faithfulness is the gift of being true to one's promises.

Self-control is the virtue of knowing when to act and when not to act.

Love is what binds you to your family and friends. Love heals and forgives. It makes you want to do good things for others.

Joy is a quality that's deeper than mere happiness. Joy lasts through tough times. Joyful people are energetic and spirited.

Patience is the quality of being able to wait and work for what is good. Patient people give others the time and room they need to succeed.

Generosity is the willingness to share what you have with others without needing to be repaid.

Gentleness means that you can make a difference without mistreating others.

With the Spirit's help you can have the courage to let others know how you feel about important issues. Write letters to your elected officials asking their help to end abortion, hunger, and homelessness.

LIVING THE GIFTS

The Spirit provides gifts to people to help them follow Jesus. The chart below lists the gifts of the Holy Spirit as they are outlined in the Rite of Confirmation. Tell what each gift means to you. Then tell one way you can use each gift in your life.

Gift	What It Means to Me	How It Helps Me
Wisdom		
Understanding		
Right judgment		
Courage		
Knowledge		
Reverence		
Wonder and awe		

COME, HOLY SPIRIT

Come, Holy Spirit, come! And from your celestial home shed a ray of light divine!
Come, the Father of the Poor! Come the source of all our store! Come, within our bosoms shine!
Bend the stubborn heart and will; melt the frozen, warm the chill; guide the steps that go astray.
Give them virtue's sure reward; give them your salvation, Lord; give them Joys that never end.
Amen. Alleluia!

From the VENI, SANCTE SPIRITUS

WITH YOUR FAMILY

Talk with family members about times when they've felt most alive. What makes family members feel hopeful, joyful, renewed, or refreshed? Do something refreshing together as a family.

▼REVIEW CHAPTER 12 . . . .

CATHOLICS BELIEVE

1. Jesus promised to send the Holy Spirit, the Advocate, to his disciples.
2. There is one God, revealed as the Blessed Trinity: The Father, The Son, and The Holy Spirit.
3. The Spirit gives people gifts with which to follow Jesus.
4. The fruit of the Spirit can be seen in the lives of people.

KNOW

1. Name three signs used for the Holy Spirit. Explain why each of these signs is appropriate._____

   _____

2. What is the Blessed Trinity?_____

3. In what sacraments is the Holy Spirit received?_____

   _____

4. What names did Jesus use for the Holy Spirit? What does each mean?

   _____

   _____

5. List the gifts of the Holy Spirit._____

   _____

6. Saint Paul told the Galatians that they could tell when the Spirit was working in their lives by the fruit they produced. Name these fruits._____

   _____

SUNDAY MASS

During the Liturgy of the Eucharist at Mass, the priest presider prays over the bread, "Lord, you are holy indeed, the fountain of all holiness. Let your Spirit come upon these gifts to make them holy, so that they may become for us the body and blood of our Lord, Jesus Christ." This is called the *epiclesis.* This Sunday at Mass, listen for other times the Holy Spirit is mentioned. Report your findings to the class.

THE WAY OF THE CROSS

For centuries, Christians have followed Jesus in his suffering and death by praying the Way of the Cross. The fourteen traditional stations of the cross help Catholics meditate on particular moments of Jesus' Passion. Jesus' suffering and death can also be experienced in the suffering of people today. As you pray these stations, think of the ways in which people still suffer. Under each picture, write a brief prayer.

1. Jesus Is Condemned to Death.

6. Veronica Wipes the Face of Jesus.

2. Jesus Takes Up His Cross.

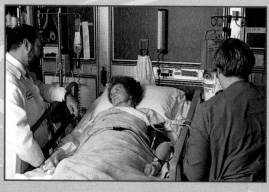

5. Simon of Cyrene Helps Jesus Carry the Cross.

3. Jesus Falls the First Time.

4. Jesus Meets His Sorrowful Mother.

7. **Jesus Falls a Second Time.**

8. **The Women of Jerusalem Weep for Jesus.**

9. **Jesus Falls the Third Time.**

10. **Jesus Is Stripped of His Garments.**

11. **Jesus Is Nailed to the Cross.**

12. **Jesus Dies on the Cross.**

13. **Jesus Is Laid in the Arms of His Mother.**

14. **Jesus Is Laid in the Tomb.**

15.

FIFTEENTH STATION

Draw a fifteenth station that celebrates Jesus' resurrection in people's ordinary lives.

LEARNING

1. **What is the significance of Jesus' resurrection from the dead?**
   The resurrection confirms Jesus' divinity, his works, and his teachings.
2. **What was accomplished by Jesus' death on the cross?**
   Jesus' death on the cross saves people from sin and restores them to communion with God.
3. **Who is Jesus?**
   Jesus is the second person of the Blessed Trinity, the only Son of God.
4. **Who is the Holy Spirit?**
   The Holy Spirit is the third person of the Blessed Trinity; the Holy Spirit dwells in people's hearts.

ASKING

1. When have I been aware of God's care for me?
2. What difference does God's care for me make in my life?

LIVING

The Holy Spirit is always involved in your life, whether you know it or not. In the space below, name at least one way in which the Spirit has been present to you in each of the following areas. Remember that the Spirit is experienced in moments of joy, love, kindness, and insight; you may not specifically be thinking of God.

In Nature _____

In a Person_____

In Music, Art, or Reading _____

In Church or Prayer _____

While Participating in a Sport or Hobby _____

PRAYING

All: Abba, Father!

Group 1: Those who are led by the Spirit are the children of God. For we did not receive a spirit of slavery and fear, but a spirit of adoption, through which we pray.

All: Abba, Father!

Group 2: We are heirs of God with Christ, if only we suffer with him so that we may also be glorified with him. What we suffer now is nothing compared to the glory that is to come, when, revealed as God's children, we will cry.

All: Abba, Father!

Group 3: We know that all creation is groaning in labor, waiting to give birth to the kingdom. We hope for our salvation. And the Spirit comes to our aid in our weakness, helping us cry, with Jesus.

All: Abba, Father!

Based on ROMANS 8:14–27

El Greco. *The Last Supper*. 16th century.

FOR I AM CONVINCED THAT NEITHER DEATH, NOR
LIFE, NOR ANY CREATURE WILL BE ABLE TO SEPARATE US
FROM THE LOVE OF GOD IN CHRIST JESUS OUR LORD.

BASED ON ROMANS 8:38–39

115

13

CONTENT KEYS

1. **Memories are important.**
2. **Signs and symbols help you remember.**
3. **Christians remember Jesus through the sacraments.**

For where two or three are gathered together in my name, there am I in the midst of them.

MATTHEW 18:20

WE REMEMBER

The Lancaster family celebrated Thanksgiving at the family homestead. After dinner, everyone gathered in the living room to honor a family tradition, the telling of the story of freedom.

"Francine," Grandmother said. "Now that you are a teenager, the time has come for you to tell the story for the family."

"I'm not sure I'll tell it right, Grandmother."

"Go on, child. You tell it, and I'll help if you need me."

Francine was nervous, but she didn't let it show. She began to speak in a clear, strong voice the words of the story she had heard so many times before.

"This is a story learned from my grandmother, and that she learned from her grandmother before her. This is the story of freedom.

"Our ancestors were a free people in Africa. They were farmers who tended the land, loved their families, and gave thanks to God for their happiness."

"You're doing fine, child," her grandmother whispered. "Tell it with pride."

"The slavers came and put our ancestors into chains. They whipped them, and starved them, and treated them worse than rats. Our ancestors suffered from exhaustion, from humiliation, from hate at the owners' hands. They suffered watching their own children being sold as slaves. They suffered because they were not free.

"After many terrible years, our freedom was won. So now we celebrate that great occasion with family because we remember when our families were torn apart. We are joyful because we remember the sufferings of slavery. And we make this promise, 'We will never be slaves again.' This we remember, this we celebrate, this we believe."

When Francine finished the story, she felt good about what she had done. She felt even better when her grandmother hugged her tightly and said, "You've learned well child. You've learned well."

Family Memories

Describe what your family does to remember special people, times, and events. What is accomplished by this act of remembering?

SIGNS OF REMEMBRANCE

For the Lancaster family, retelling the story of freedom was an honored custom and tradition. The story not only tells them about their past, it also tells them who they are in the present—a free, proud, and strong family. In retelling their story, they honor their ancestors for their courage and make a commitment to follow their example.

Besides remembering family stories, people use many other signs to help them remember important people and events. For example,

- In the United States, July 4 is celebrated with fireworks and festivities as a sign of the nation's independence.
- Most cities have statues erected in prominent places to honor and remember the men and women who were instrumental in helping the town to grow.
- Buildings, parks, and freeways are named after people who have made generous contributions to the life of the community.

THE IMPORTANCE OF SIGNS

When you want to communicate meaning and values, you have to use signs in order to be understood. Signs help you present ideas that cannot be seen physically. Think about the *idea* of friendship. You cannot see the idea, just as you cannot see your feelings of friendship, but that doesn't make your friendships unreal. You have friends, you know what it means to be a friend, and you use signs to show that you are a friend. What are some of the signs that you use to show friendship?

Signs allow people to communicate important ideas quickly. The Lincoln Memorial in Washington, D.C., effectively expresses the affection that Americans have for this great president. Francine's story of freedom recalls three hundred years of memories in a few brief sentences. When you make the sign of the cross, you are reminding yourself (and telling others who see you) that you are a Christian.

1. **What are some of the other ways that people are honored and remembered in your community?**
2. **How do signs help you remember important things?**

REMEMBERING JESUS

The disciples lived and learned from Jesus during his three years of public ministry. After Jesus' death, resurrection, and ascension into heaven, his disciples shared with others the Good News they learned from Jesus. They traveled throughout the Roman Empire, teaching what Jesus taught and doing what Jesus did.

As they proclaimed the Good News, the disciples remembered all that Jesus said and did. From these stories, they developed certain signs to remind them of Jesus. These signs flowed directly from Jesus' own actions.

Create signs to help you remember Jesus.

Gospel Signs

Look at the following examples of what Jesus taught and did during his public ministry.

1. Jesus fed the four thousand with only a few loaves and fishes. He gave thanks before breaking the bread and distributing the food *(Matthew 15:32–38).*

2. A crowd of people brought a woman accused of adultery to Jesus for him to judge. Jesus said to them, "Let the one among you who is without sin be the first to throw a stone at her." When no one condemned the woman, Jesus said to her, "Neither do I condemn you. Go, and from now on do not sin any more" *(John 8:2–11).*

3. Jesus was baptized in the Jordan River by John the Baptist. After Jesus came up from the water, the Spirit of God descended upon him *(Matthew 3:13–17).*

4. Jesus healed the centurion's servant with a word *(Luke 7:2–10).* He took Jairus' daughter's hand and said to her, "Arise" *(Mark 5:41–42).* Jesus laid hands on a woman who was crippled and she walked *(Luke 13:10–13).*

POWERFUL SIGNS

Although there are many different types of signs, some are more important than others. Think about the power of the American flag, the sign of the United States. During the Olympic Games, the American flag is raised each time an athlete representing the United States wins a medal. What do you feel when you see the flag raised and hear the national anthem played?

The sight of the flag has lead many people to act bravely. Soldiers in battle have died defending the flag. One of the most moving monuments of the Second World War is the Iwo Jima Memorial, which shows American soldiers raising the flag in the middle of a battle.

What is it about the flag that inspires such acts and feelings? There are many reasons why the flag is such a powerful sign. Among the most important reasons is that the flag stands for the hopes and dreams of America. It stands for the unity that joins 200 million Americans together as one. No other sign says "America" like the flag.

SIGNS OF CHRIST'S PRESENCE

As they preached the Good News of Jesus, the disciples used many signs to remember the Lord. They realized that some signs were more powerful than others as ways to remember the Lord. These signs were the things that Jesus himself did: forgive sins, honor marriage, celebrate the Lord's Supper, and make disciples. In these signs, the disciples realized that they weren't just remembering what Jesus did. Jesus was actually present with them as they prayed.

The disciples experienced Jesus' presence most clearly when they came together as a community to share the Good News, praise God, and celebrate the Lord's Supper. They also knew the Lord was present in particular acts of blessing and healing. The Lord was present when a married couple shared their love, when sins were forgiven, when a person accepted the Lord and was washed clean in water, and when people were healed.

The Church continues to celebrate using these signs instituted and given to it by Christ. In them, you can experience Jesus' presence directly today. Jesus is really present to you in the Scriptures, in the Eucharist, in the sacraments, and in the Church.

SIGNS OF THE LORD

Jesus is present to his followers in many ways, but he is especially present to them in the seven sacraments of the Church: Baptism, Confirmation, Eucharist, Penance, Anointing of the Sick, Marriage, and Holy Orders. The sacraments are signs of God's love and sources of God's grace. But the sacraments are more than just signs of what Jesus did. In the sacraments, Jesus continues to act through the Church.

The liturgical life of the Church revolves around the Mass and the sacraments. Jesus' presence gives the sacraments their power. When the Church celebrates the sacraments, Jesus is present and celebrating through the mission of the Holy Spirit. When one person baptizes another, Christ baptizes. When the priest, acting for the Church, forgives and heals the wounds of sin, Christ forgives and heals. When a man and a woman, in the name of Christ, commit themselves to each other in Marriage, it is Christ in whose life and love they are united.

Through the sacraments, Christians are united with God. By the signs of words and objects, your faith is nourished, strengthened, and expressed through the sacraments. In the sacraments you receive sacramental grace, the grace of the Holy Spirit.

IN THE SCRIPTURES

The Liturgy of the Word, which you celebrate each Sunday, comes from the first Christians. It reflects the Jewish Sabbath service of reading the Scripture, singing the psalms, and praying for God's blessings. The readings from the letters from missionaries like Paul and from the Gospel were added as these books were written. In sharing God's word, the community recognized that Jesus was present among them.

IN THE EUCHARIST

Jesus promised his friends, "Whenever two or three gather together in my name, there am I in the midst of them" *(Matthew 18:20).* The presence of Jesus is most clearly seen when people gather to celebrate the Eucharist, the Church's great prayer of thanksgiving.

Every Eucharist recalls Jesus' Last Supper with his friends. Jesus speaks in the Eucharistic Prayer, when the bread and wine are offered to God and become Jesus' Body and Blood.

The Mass and the sacraments are important sources of strength for Jesus' followers. Take advantage of the grace that God offers you by participating fully in the Mass and frequently celebrating the sacraments of Eucharist and Reconciliation.

CHURCH AS SACRAMENT

Although Jesus has returned to his Father, Christians know that Jesus continues to live and be present in the Church. The Church itself is a sacrament, a sign of Christ's presence because Jesus is present through the Church. And through the members of the Church, Jesus is present to the whole world.

Read the following examples and describe how Jesus is present in each incident.

A woman confesses her sins to a priest. The priest shares a Gospel reading with her, listens compassionately to her story, encourages her to change her life, and grants her forgiveness in the name of Jesus. She leaves the reconciliation room healed and ready to begin anew.

A man with no home, no money, no food, and no coat asks for help. Your parish Christian Service volunteers give him a coat, food, and a night's lodging. He is treated with respect and kindness.

Once a week, a small group of parishioners gather to study the Scriptures together. They share with each other their own life struggles and successes. They pray for each other and for their community.

1. **What are some of the signs that Jesus is present in the Church today?**
2. **What can you do to be a sign of Jesus' presence?**

YOUR PARISH

What signs do you see that Jesus is present in your parish community? Describe or draw two of these signs in this space.

Your Sign

As a part of the Church, the Body of Christ, you are a sign of Jesus still present in the world. In the spaces provided, describe how you are a sign of Christ's presence.

Offering forgiveness

Reaching out to heal

Being part of the community

Proclaiming the Good News

Being a peacemaker

A Hymn of Thanksgiving

Lord Jesus Christ, you gave us the Eucharist as the memorial of your suffering and death. May this sacrament of your Body and Blood help us to experience the salvation you won for us and the peace of the kingdom. Send me into the world in the power of your Spirit, to live and work for your praise and glory. Amen!

WITH YOUR FAMILY

Families hang a crucifix in their homes as reminders of what Jesus has done for them. Work with members of your family to hang a crucifix in your home in a place of honor. Use it as a sign to help you remember that you follow Jesus.

▼ REVIEW CHAPTER 13 . . . .

CATHOLICS BELIEVE

1. The Church remembers Jesus through signs and actions.
2. Jesus is present in the Scriptures, in the Church, in the Eucharist, and in the other sacraments.
3. Christians are called to be signs of Jesus' presence in the world.

KNOW

1. What are some of the special occasions that people remember? What signs do they use to help them remember?

   _____

   _____

2. What are some of the reasons why the flag of one's country is a powerful symbol? What are some of the feelings a flag inspires in people? _____

   _____

3. What are some of the signs the Church uses to remember Jesus? In which of these signs is Jesus present to the Church?

   _____

4. What are the sacraments? _____

   _____

5. What are some of the ways that Christians are called to be signs of Christ's presence in the world? _____

   _____

SUNDAY MASS

Jesus' voice is heard in the readings from the Gospel. You can prepare yourself to hear Jesus by reading next Sunday's Mass Scriptures in advance. Your teacher will help you find them. Discuss one of the readings with a friend. At Mass on Sunday, listen closely to the readings and the homily.

14

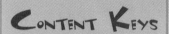

ONE IN CHRIST

CONTENT KEYS

1. **People are initiated into the Church.**
2. **The Church is the Body of Christ.**
3. **You are a member of Christ's body.**

> For in one Spirit we were all baptized into one body and we were all given to drink of one Spirit.
>
> 1 CORINTHIANS 12:13

INITIATION

My name is Martin and I am a Junior Lifeguard. I am proud to wear my lifeguard badge because it shows what I have accomplished. For two months I got up at six-thirty every morning to be at the pool by eight o'clock. There were warm-up drills and then hours of swimming. I was so tired when I got home each day that I usually skipped dinner and went straight to bed.

When we finished our training, we had a special awards ceremony at which we officially became Junior Lifeguards. I've never been prouder than when I walked forward to receive my certificate. I couldn't wait to put on my Junior Lifeguard pin, T-shirt, and swim trunks.

As soon as the ceremony was over, I raced to the changing rooms with the other new Junior Lifeguards. I felt important wearing my new uniform. But I was totally surprised by what happened next. As we came out of the changing rooms, Coach Hayes and all of the other lifeguards doused us with buckets of water. I was soaked and very annoyed. But I couldn't stay angry for long. Not when everyone started laughing and shaking our hands.

"Congratulations, Martin," Coach Hayes said. "You have now passed your final test. You are a fully initiated Junior Lifeguard."

Join the Club

Many clubs and organizations have special uniforms, badges, and initiation ceremonies. In the chart below, describe some of the ways groups initiate new members.

NAME OF GROUP	SYMBOL OF MEMBERSHIP	INITIATION

124

In the Holy City

"My dear sisters," Egeria began, after dipping her quill in ink. "The light of the oil lamp is flickering on the walls of this tiny room in the pilgrims' hostel. What a joy it is for me to be here in Jerusalem. I give thanks to God that I was born into a family that believed in educating daughters. Thanks to my parents and tutors, I can share with you what I am experiencing on this pilgrimage. I will be your eyes and ears through this journal.

"What wonders I have to share with you. I will describe for you in great detail the sea voyage from Spain to Constantinople and the long and painful donkey ride over the mountains. But nothing compares with what I have seen and done in Jerusalem—the Holy City itself.

"I have been in Jerusalem for most of Lent. I walked the Way of the Cross with the other pilgrims on Good Friday. How wonderful it was to walk in the Lord's footsteps! But tonight's celebration of the Lord's resurrection at the Easter Vigil was the most thrilling moment of all.

"My dear sisters, you can't imagine how it felt to stand there in that cave, in the church built right over the Lord's tomb, holding candles and welcoming the Light of Christ!

"The joy and wonder I felt was reflected in the eyes of the newly baptized, who came to us robed in white, straight from the saving waters. The bishop anointed them with chrism, and they ate at the Table of the Lord, receiving his Body and Blood.

"On this night, sisters, they do everything here just as we do at home. The elect, those catechumens who were received into the Church, have been preparing through prayer and study all during Lent. The bishop explained the Creed to them, and one by one they recited it back to him. They prayed the Lord's Prayer from memory. They chose new names and promised to turn their backs on their old lives. I was moved to tears by what I saw."

LEARNING THE MYSTERIES

"The night is far advanced and I am very tired, but I want to share with you all I saw this night," Egeria wrote. Her mind and heart were full of the events she had witnessed.

"You know, of course, that the elect are never told about the ceremonies of initiation ahead of time. The symbols of water and oil and bread and wine, the beautiful words of blessings—how could they understand these things before they experience them?

"So now begins their time of **mystagogia** (mys-ta-go-gi-a), when they come to know and believe that they are joined to the Body of Christ. For the next eight days, they will go every morning with the bishop to the mountain where Jesus himself taught his disciples. They will eat breakfast with the bishop, and he will teach them the meaning of the mysteries they experienced.

"How I envy them! Imagine coming to know the Lord and his Church in this Holy City, in the very place where our faith began. Truly, their baptism is the beginning of a new life.

"Now dawn is breaking over the city of Jerusalem. I leave you with the Easter anthem, The Lord is risen, Alleluia."

WORDS FROM THE PAST

In 1884, a musty, damaged volume was discovered in a monastery in Arezzo, Italy. It was an eleventh-century copy of the journals kept by a fifth-century traveler named Egeria. She was probably a nun from Spain or Gaul. Her writing shows that she was well-educated for a woman of that time. She also had the wealth to make a very long and difficult pilgrimage through Turkey, Egypt, and the Holy Land. This suggests that she was from a wealthy and noble family.

Egeria's journals have been a great legacy for the Church. They provide a detailed account of how the Catholics in fifth-century Jerusalem celebrated the sacraments—especially the sacraments of initiation. Egeria's record influenced the renewal of the sacraments that resulted from the Second Vatican Council (1962–1965).

1. **According to Egeria's journal, how was the Easter Vigil celebrated in Jerusalem?**
2. **What is the mystagogia? Why do you think the candidates had to wait until after they were initiated to have the ceremonies explained to them?**

SPECIAL WORDS

The Greek word **mystagogia** means "teaching of the mysteries." Mystagogia is a time of study and reflection on the Scriptures and the sacraments.

THE TRADITION CONTINUES

Today, as in Egeria's time, new Christians receive the sacraments of initiation—Baptism, Confirmation, and Eucharist—at the Easter Vigil. This tradition—and receiving the sacraments in this order—dates back to the earliest years of the Church.

Adults and children old enough to participate in catechesis prepare for these sacraments through study and prayer. During Lent, special ceremonies are conducted to help them prepare to fully enter the Church. The whole parish community supports the candidates with prayers and fasting during this time of preparation.

New Christians receive the sacraments of initiation at the Easter Vigil because it is the most important feast day of the year for Christians. The Easter Vigil is the celebration of Jesus' saving sacrifice and resurrection. Those who receive the sacraments give witness to the whole Church of the need for conversion and rebirth in Christ.

Whether you receive the sacraments of initiation all at once at the Easter Vigil or over several years (as people usually do who are baptized as infants), these three signs and sources of God's grace all do the same thing: they join you to the Body of Christ and the **Communion of Saints.** Initiated into the Body of Christ you can truly say with Saint Paul, "I have been crucified with Christ; yet I live, no longer I, but Christ lives in me" *(Galatians 2:19–20).*

SPECIAL WORDS

The phrase **Communion of Saints** refers to the unity that exists within the Church of all followers of Jesus, whether they are living or dead, who share in the Body and Blood of Christ.

CHRISTIAN INITIATION

Adults and older children join the Church through the Rite of Christian Initiation of Adults (RCIA). This ancient process is accomplished by a journey of several stages. Each person covers the journey at his or her own pace. Certain steps are always part of the process: the candidates for baptism hear God's word, accept the Gospel and seek conversion, profess the faith, are baptized, receive the Holy Spirit, and are admitted to the Eucharistic communion.

There are several stages to the RCIA, which is also known as the catechumenate.

- *Pre-catechumenate.* In this stage, a person inquires about the faith and hears the Gospel. There is no formal commitment to the Church.

- *Catechumenate.* A person is enrolled in the order of the catechumenate when he or she has made an initial decision to follow Jesus. This is a time of study and prayer.

- *Election.* When people are ready to commit their lives to Jesus, they enter the order of the Elect—they become part of God's Chosen People. During Lent, they fast and pray in preparation for Baptism.

- *Mystagogia.* For fifty days after their initiation, the newly baptized learn about the mystery of faith.

SACRAMENTS OF INITIATION

The initiation process prepares the catechumen for baptism, confirmation, and eucharist. Through these sacraments, people are made part of the Body of Christ, receive the Holy Spirit, and share in the Lord's Supper.

In Baptism, you take on Christ's suffering and death, die to sin, and are reborn in Christ through the waters of new life. Baptism is like a cleansing bath, but it is more; it is the sign of the covenant—the special commitment—that binds you to Jesus and the Church.

The anointing of Confirmation seals you with the Holy Spirit, just as Christ ("the Anointed One") was sealed. Through Confirmation, you accept Jesus' mission to bring the Good News to the world. Now you have been marked by the seal of the Holy Spirit, and you can never be separated from Jesus. In Confirmation, you receive the strength you need to be Jesus' disciple.

In the Eucharist, you are joined to Jesus in the closest possible way. When you eat his Body and drink his Blood, Jesus lives within you. It is through the Eucharist that all Christians are joined together into the Body of Christ.

1. **Describe how the sacraments of Baptism, Confirmation, and Eucharist initiate new members into the Church.**
2. **What does it mean to say that you belong to the Communion of Saints? What is the importance of belonging to this communion?**

THE BODY OF CHRIST

When you became a Christian through Baptism, you became part of the Body of Christ (the Church) and a member of the Communion of Saints. Through God's grace, you became an adopted child of God and a member of God's family. In you flows the life of God. When you say yes to God, all of the members of the Church become your brothers and sisters. That's part of the deal.

When you recognize that you are part of one body in Christ, you agree to accept other people as part of your family. That means everybody—no exceptions! You cannot choose some and discriminate against others because they are the wrong sex, color, or class.

Responsibility (the ability to respond to another person's needs) and respect (the virtue of seeing and treating all people as children of God) are two important skills for living as members of the Body of Christ. When you take responsibility for your actions and treat others with respect, you are putting the Gospel into action.

For all of you who were baptized into Christ Jesus have clothed yourselves with Christ. There is neither Jew nor Greek, there is neither slave nor free person, there is not male and female; for you are all one in Christ Jesus.

GALATIANS 3:27–28

If you saw your brother or sister without food to eat, a place to sleep, or warm clothes to wear, what would you do? The answer is obvious. You would help them immediately, even if it meant making a personal sacrifice. As a member of the Body of Christ, you are called to act the same way toward all the members of Christ's Body.

If a brother or sister has nothing to wear and has no food for the day, and one of you says to them, "Go in peace, keep warm, and eat well," but you do not give them the necessities of the body, what good is it?

JAMES 2:15–16

The First Letter of John precisely states how Christians are to act.

The way we came to know love was that God's Son laid down his life for us; so we ought to lay down our lives for our brothers and sisters. If you see a person in need and refuse compassion, how can the love of God remain in you? Children, let us love in deed and truth.

Adapted from 1 JOHN 3:16–18

Signs of Belonging

People who are initiated into the Church are called to conversion, to change the way they live and act as followers of Christ. Conversion is a lifetime process; you will need to examine your actions your entire life.

Look at the following situations. How can each be an invitation for conversion?

Situations	My Thoughts
1. On your way to school each day, Mr. Cirelli smiles and waves to you. One day it occurs to you that Mr. Cirelli might be lonely.	
2. You have a short temper and get angry at the slightest offense. Last night you screamed at your little sister for tearing your favorite book. Now she runs away from you.	
3. You have competed against Andy in school for five years. Every chance he gets, Andy puts you down. You manage to get back at him every time. Lately you've tired of the competition.	

A Cloud of Witnesses

Belonging to the Communion of Saints means that you are never alone on your journey of faith. You are surrounded by the saints of heaven who pray for you and Christians on earth who pray with you. Join your prayer with them through this litany. After each name respond "Pray for us."

Holy Mary, Mother of God, Saint Michael and the holy angels, Saint John the Baptist, Saint Joseph, Saint Peter and Saint Paul, Saint Andrew and Saint John, Saint Mary Magdalene, Saint Stephen, Saint Ignatius and Saint Lawrence, Saint Perpetua and Saint Felicitas, Saint Agnes, Saint Basil and Saint Gregory, Saint Augustine, Saint Martin and Saint Benedict, Saint Francis and Saint Dominic, Saint John Neumann, Saint Elizabeth Seton, Saint Frances Cabrini, All holy men and women.

WITH YOUR FAMILY

You can participate in your parish's initiation process by adopting a catechumen. Find out the name of a person seeking to join the Church. As a family, pray for this person by name. Write a letter to tell this person you are praying for him or her.

▼REVIEW CHAPTER 14 . . . .

CATHOLICS BELIEVE

1. Baptism, Confirmation, and Eucharist are the three sacraments of initiation.
2. The Church is the Body of Christ.
3. Christians are called to care for all people as their brothers and sisters.

KNOW

1. What is the purpose of the Christian initiation process?

   _____

   _____

2. When does the Church initiate new members? Why is initiation most appropriate on that day? _____

   _____

3. What are the stages of the Rite of Christian Initiation of Adults?

   _____

   _____

4. What are the sacraments of initiation?

   _____

5. What does it mean to say that all people are called to change their lives and follow Jesus? _____

   _____

SUNDAY MASS

In many parishes, catechumens leave the Mass after the homily. They are going with their catechists to study and pray about the Scripture readings and to learn more about the Church.

15

THE HEALING PRESENCE

Your faith has saved you. Go in peace.

LUKE 7:50

CONTENT KEYS

1. **Everyone needs forgiveness and healing.**
2. **Jesus healed people and forgave them their sins.**
3. **You are healed and forgiven by the sacraments.**

A STUPID MISTAKE

Hank sat dejected in the hospital emergency room. A few doors away, his friend Rick was being examined by a doctor.

"Please, God, let Rick be okay," Hank whispered.

Hank hadn't meant to hurt Rick, just frighten him. It was supposed to be a joke. When Rick was high up on the ladder, Hank gave it a little shake. But Rick lost his balance and fell a long way, hitting his head on the pavement. Rick was still unconscious when the ambulance arrived.

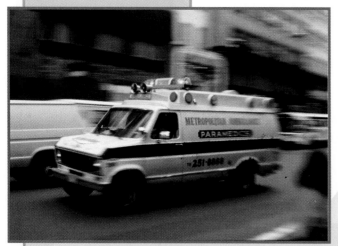

When Rick's dad came into the emergency room, Hank burst into tears. "I'm sorry, Mr. Fisher," he sobbed. "Rick is my best friend. You know I'd never do anything to hurt him."

Mr. Fisher gave Hank a hug, "Everything's all right, Hank. Rick has a concussion, but he's going to be fine."

"Can you ever forgive me?" Hank asked.

"I forgive you, Hank. And so does Rick. You can go in to see him now if you want."

"You bet I do. I owe him a big apology," Hank said, starting to smile.

Seeking Forgiveness

Describe a time when you did something you knew was wrong and had to seek forgiveness. What does it take to admit that you've done wrong? How does it feel to be forgiven?

YOUR SINS ARE FORGIVEN

I don't know which hurt me more: the fact that I couldn't walk or the anger I felt at those who could. All my life I've borne the pain of seeing other people do what I could not.

Recently my cousin Aaron came to my home with three of his friends. "There's a holy man here in Capernaum!" he said. "A healer. Jesus of Nazareth. We've come to take you to him." They quickly grabbed my mat and carried me out the door.

A very large crowd had gathered to see the holy man. We could not even get close to the house, much less through the door.

"Forget it, Aaron," I said. "Thank you for trying, but there's no way we can get in."

Aaron never gives up, no matter how difficult the challenge. He looked at me, grinned, and then said to his friends, "If we can't go through the door, we'll use the roof." In a flash, we were at the top of the outside stairs.

They wasted no time removing the tiles. Soon they had an opening big enough to lower me through. I landed right in front of Jesus. He stopped his preaching, smiled at me, and said, "Your sins are forgiven."

At first I didn't know what he meant. Couldn't he see that I needed healing? Why was he offering me forgiveness? But then I realized that my bitterness was more of a burden than my paralyzed legs. By forgiving my sins, Jesus had freed me from my anger.

Some of the people in the room were upset with Jesus. "Who does he think he is offering forgiveness from sins? Only God can forgive sins," they said. Jesus looked the people in the eye and said, "Which is easier, to say 'Your sins are forgiven,' or to say, 'Rise, pick up your mat, and walk?' He looked at me again and said, "I say rise, pick up your mat, and go home."

And that's what I did.

Inspired by MARK 2:1–12

1. **What are some of the ways that a person can be crippled by sin?**
2. **How can being forgiven of your sins help you to get well?**

A Lost Lamb

I've been an outcast for so long I can't remember ever being anything else. I was twelve when my parents died, and there was no one to take me in. I lived on the street, begging for food and sleeping in hidden corners of the village. One day a man offered me money for sex. I took it, and I never went hungry after that.

Still, it was a lonely life. Men shunned me. Women turned their faces when they saw me coming. I told myself that even this was better than starving. But what kind of a life was it? I was trapped like a caged animal in my sinful life and I could see no way out.

My life changed when the rabbi Jesus of Nazareth came to my village. Jesus spoke about how much God loved everyone, even sinners like me. He compared God to a shepherd who leaves his flock of ninety-nine sheep to find one lost lamb. I knew I was that lost lamb. According to Jesus, all I had to do was seek forgiveness and change my life.

All day, I followed Jesus through the streets. At one point, I bought a small alabaster jar of costly oil from a street vendor. I guess I had some vague idea of offering it as a gift to Jesus. But even with my gift in hand, I couldn't gather enough courage to go up to him. What if he turned away from me in disgust?

That evening, I followed Jesus to the house of Simon the Pharisee. I waited until the servant had left the door, and then slipped inside the house. The men were reclining around the table, eating.

Gathering all my courage, I ran across the dining room and went straight to where Jesus was reclining. I was too ashamed to look him in the face, so I dropped to my knees and began to kiss his feet. I washed his feet with my tears and dried them with my hair. Then I poured the oil from the alabaster jar over his feet.

The men at the table wondered how Jesus could let me touch him, what with me being a sinner and all. In response to their dirty looks, Jesus asked the men a simple question, "Which person will be most grateful, the one who is forgiven a little debt or the one who is forgiven a large debt?" The men all answered, "The person forgiven the large debt, of course."

Then Jesus answered them, "This woman has much to be grateful for, for her many sins have been forgiven. That is why she shows such great love."

Jesus turned and spoke to me in a gentle voice, "Your sins are forgiven. Your faith has saved you. Go in peace."

Inspired by LUKE 7:36–50

Your Faith Has Saved You

Read the story of the woman with the alabaster jar in *Luke 7:36–50*. Write a modern story of great forgiveness.

Jesus as the Good Shepherd (icon).

PENANCE AND RECONCILIATION

The Gospel is filled with stories about Jesus healing people of their infirmities and forgiving them from their sins. Jesus made it clear in John 9:2–3 that illness is not a punishment for sin. But Jesus also knew that sin and illness can trap people and keep them from responding fully to the offer of God's love.

You may never be crippled by anger or cause a friend to fall off of a ladder, but you do sin. Maybe you feel guilty for something you've done or said. Perhaps you regret not being as kind as you wanted to be. No matter what you've done, sin affects your life. But you do not have to be trapped by it forever. Jesus continues to offer you healing and forgiveness through the Church.

> *Those who approach the sacrament of Penance obtain pardon from God's mercy for the offense committed and are, at the same time, reconciled with the Church which they have wounded by their sins.*
>
> VATICAN II, CONSTITUTION ON THE CHURCH 11.2

The sacrament of Reconciliation celebrates God's healing love. Jesus forgave sins and shared this ministry and power with his Church. The word *reconciliation* means "coming back together again." The sacrament celebrates the return of the sinner to God and to the community. In the sacrament, people return to the Lord, recognize their sinfulness, confess their sins, are forgiven by God through the priest's sacramental absolution, and are reconciled to God and the Church.

Absolution ("to loosen, to set free") is the forgiveness of sin offered in the sacrament. To receive absolution you must confess your sins, express sorrow for having done wrong, express a willingness to do penance, and promise to do better with God's help.

Only God forgives sins, but Jesus gave this power to the Church to be exercised in his name. The Church is the sign and instrument of his forgiveness and reconciliation.

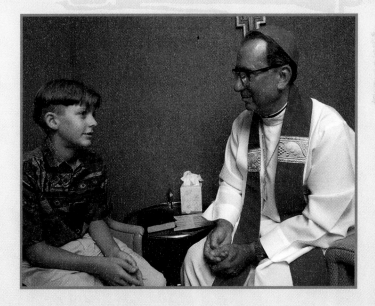

Confession to a priest is an essential part of the sacrament. By virtue of the sacrament of Holy Orders and the authority of the bishop, priests are empowered to forgive sins in the name of the Church. When he celebrates the sacrament, the priest is the sign and the instrument of God's merciful love.

FREEDOM AND PEACE

The seventh-graders of Saint Camillus parish had gathered to celebrate the sacrament of Reconciliation. Before beginning the service, Father Conseco asked if anyone had any questions. Quite a few hands went up.

"Father," Jonathan asked, "Why do I need to go to confession? Couldn't I simply ask God to forgive me?"

"Of course you can ask God to forgive you," the priest replied. "God's forgiveness is not limited to the Church. But there is something very freeing about admitting your faults to another person. It helps you to be honest and take responsibility for your own actions. Besides, in the sacrament, Jesus absolves you from your sins and fully reunites you with the Church."

"Father Conseco," Liz said. "Do I have to go to confession if I haven't committed a mortal sin?"

Father Conseco looked at Liz. "That's a good question. Let me try to answer it briefly.

"You're right. The sacrament of Reconciliation is required only for the forgiveness of mortal sin. That means that you freely and intentionally reject the love of God. You can't commit mortal sin unknowingly or by accident. But there are many reasons why you should receive the sacrament often, even if you only have committed venial sin."

IN TRAINING

"How many of you play a sport or a musical instrument?" Many of the youths raised their hands. Pointing to Kevin he asked, "How many hours a day do you practice?" Kevin answered him, "I practice on my flute at least 45 minutes a day." Cathy answered him next, "If I don't practice dribbling the ball for an hour each day, I lose my touch."

Father Conseco continued, "That's right. In order to do anything well, you've got to practice and train. Celebrating the sacrament of Reconciliation is like being in training for the Christian life. Celebrating the sacrament frequently helps you to work on your bad habits and overcome venial sins. You'll feel better about yourself, be better able to overcome temptations, and draw closer to God all at the same time."

Father Conseco smiled. "It seems you would want your soul to be in shape and healthy, just like your body. What do you say? Shall we celebrate God's love for us?"

1. **Why is it important to celebrate the sacrament of Reconciliation frequently?**
2. **How does the sacrament of Reconciliation help you to train for the Christian life?**

When you celebrate the sacrament of Reconciliation, you need to be truthful with yourself and with God about your faults and weaknesses. By admitting your sinfulness in the sacrament, you recognize what you have to do to improve your life.

IN BODY AND SPIRIT

Jesus often combined forgiveness of sins with physical healing. In carrying on Jesus' healing work, the Church ministers to the ill, the aged, and the dying through the sacrament of the Anointing of the Sick. With the anointing, the Church asks the Lord Jesus to heal those who are suffering.

Jesus did not heal all of the sick in Israel. He healed people as a sign of the coming of God's kingdom. These healings announced that, in Jesus, sin and death were conquered. Through his death, Jesus gave new meaning to suffering: by suffering, you are united with the Lord's redemptive passion.

In the same way, the Anointing of the Sick does not promise physical cures. What people receive in the sacrament is Jesus' healing presence and the spiritual and mental well-being and strength this creates. They are united with Christ, who bears their burden and shares their pain. This grace is a gift of the Holy Spirit.

The Church has cared for the sick from apostolic times.

Is anyone among you sick? He should summon the presbyters of the Church, and they should pray over him, and anoint him with oil in the name of the Lord, and the prayer of faith will save the sick person, and the Lord will raise him up. If he has committed sins, he will be forgiven.

JAMES 5:14–15

The sacrament may be celebrated with anyone who is seriously ill; you have to suffer from more than the flu or a toothache to receive the sacrament. You may receive the sacrament many times, for example, if your illness gets worse, you need an operation, or if you are elderly.

Anointing of the Sick is a liturgical and communal celebration. The sacrament begins with readings from Scripture and a statement of repentance. The priest then lays hands on the sick and prays that they may be healed. Finally, the sick are anointed with blessed oil. The sick often receive the Eucharist after being anointed.

DID YOU KNOW?

In 1858, a young peasant girl named Bernadette Soubirous saw a vision of a beautiful lady who called herself "the Immaculate Conception." The lady told Bernadette to dig in the mud, from which a spring of fresh water bubbled up. Over the years, many people have come to this place, called Lourdes and have been healed in these miraculous waters. It is a place that celebrates the healing power of Jesus.

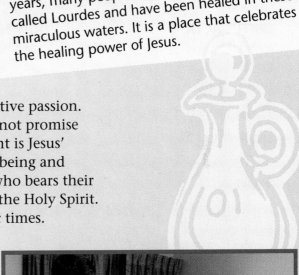

1. **What sickness have you or members of your family gone through? What is it like to be ill?**
2. **Have you ever received or witnessed the Anointing of the Sick? Talk about the experience.**

A CHECK-UP

In order to receive the sacrament of Reconciliation, you must first examine your conscience to see how well you have followed Jesus. Using the list below, tell how each sinful action hurts the sinner and his or her relationship with God and others. Then privately examine your own conscience. How do these sinful actions hurt you?

SINFUL ACTION	HOW IT DAMAGES A RELATIONSHIP WITH		
	SELF	GOD	OTHERS
Hurtful Words			
Lying			
Stealing			
Using Drugs			
Fighting			
Selfishness			

THE POWER OF PRAYER

Because Christians are members of one body, all are hurt by what physically or spiritually hurts one. Here are a two short prayers you can pray for the sick members of the Body of Christ.

Lord, touch the hearts of those who have abandoned you through sin. Call them back to you, and keep them faithful in your love.

From RITE OF RECONCILIATION

Lord, heal their sickness and forgive their sins; expel all afflictions of mind and body; mercifully restore them to full health, and enable them to work for your kingdom, for you are Lord forever and ever. Amen!

From RITE OF ANOINTING OF THE SICK

Make a list of family members and friends who need your prayers. At mealtime or during family prayer, say a family litany and remember each person by name. Pray that they might be healed of their illness and brought to spiritual health.

▼ REVIEW CHAPTER 15 . . . .

CATHOLICS BELIEVE

1. The Church celebrates Jesus' healing power in the sacraments of Reconciliation (Penance) and the Anointing of the Sick.
2. The sacrament of Reconciliation offers forgiveness for sins and reconciles Christians with the Church.
3. The Anointing of the Sick offers strength and healing to those who are ill or nearing death.

KNOW

1. What does the sacrament of Reconciliation celebrate?
   _____

2. What takes place in the sacrament of Reconciliation?
   _____

3. What must you do to receive sacramental absolution?
   _____

4. Who forgives sins in the sacrament of Reconciliation?
   _____

5. How is God's presence seen in the sacrament of Reconciliation?
   _____

6. Why should you receive the sacrament of Reconciliation frequently?_____

7. Who may receive the Anointing of the Sick? How often may the sacrament be received? _____

8. What takes place in the Anointing of the Sick? _____

SUNDAY MASS

The sacrament of Anointing is often celebrated as part of the Sunday Mass. These services dramatize the communion of saints: the well-being and health of every individual member of the Church is important to the entire Body of Christ. If you can, participate in a healing service. Your prayers are needed by the sick.

16

THE CALL TO LOVE AND SERVICE

As the Father has sent me, so I send you.

JOHN 20:21

CONTENT KEYS

1. Jesus taught his followers to serve others.
2. In Baptism, Christians receive the vocation to serve others.
3. Marriage and Holy Orders are sacraments of service.

ASPIRATIONS

Ed was in the hospital room when his grandmother Anna died. Ed was really impressed with the kindness and thoughtfulness of the priest who prayed with Grandma Anna at her death and then consoled the family. Ed began to wonder if God was calling him to be a priest.

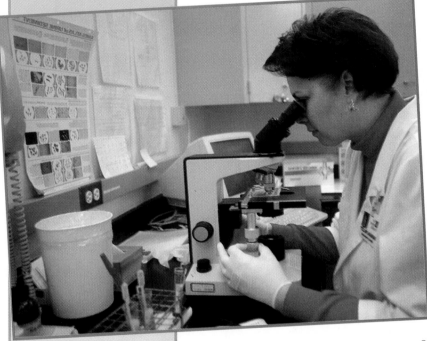

Sister Helen is a microbiologist. She is working to develop chemical-free ways of removing pollutants from drinking water. Sister Helen says that, "When I was a child, my family camped often. I loved the woods and lakes of Minnesota. I came to my love for God through that grandeur of nature. I've dedicated my life to serving God and all of God's creation."

For a school project, Lisa wrote about her parents and how much she admired them. One of the things she liked most about her parents was the way they showed affection. They always seemed to have a hug and a kiss for each other and for their three children. They were also very generous with their time. Lisa was proud of the way her family worked at the parish food bank once a month.

The Person I Admire

Write a brief essay about a person you admire because of the good they do for others. Be sure to mention specific examples that show why you admire this person.

TRUE TO THE CALL

Jesus' call from God—his **vocation**—was to serve others, and lead them to the Father along the road of loving service. Jesus remained faithful to this call throughout his life.

The Gospel mentions that Jesus was tempted to abandon his call. After his baptism, Jesus spent forty days in the wilderness praying and fasting. While there, Satan tempted Jesus to give up his mission and instead choose wealth, fame, and power. Jesus overcame these temptations in the wilderness, but he was to be tempted by them throughout his public ministry.

When Jesus fed five thousand people near the Sea of Galilee, the crowd wanted to make him a king *(John 6:14)*. They saw Jesus as a new Moses who fed people with manna from heaven. The crowd believed that if Jesus were king, they would never again have to work for or worry about their next meal.

Satan had offered Jesus the same easy way to be a hero, urging the hungry Jesus to turn the desert stones into magical bread. Jesus answered Satan, "One does not live by bread alone, but by every word that comes forth from the mouth of God" *(Matthew 4:4)*.

Botticelli, *Temptation of Christ (detail).* 15th century.

Even the people closest to him sometimes misunderstood Jesus' calling. Members of his own family begged Jesus to go to Jerusalem to celebrate an important religious feast and to work miracles there to impress the visitors to the city. "No one works in secret if he wants to be known publicly," these relatives pointed out *(John 7:4)*.

Satan, too, had tempted Jesus to gain fame with cheap tricks. In a vision, Jesus found himself on the topmost part of the Temple wall, hundreds of feet above the city. "Throw yourself down," Satan dared Jesus. "If you are truly the Son of God, God will send angels to catch you. That will get people's attention" (based on *Matthew 4:5–6*).

NOT FAME OR FORTUNE

Jesus did not give in to Satan's temptations or those offered by his friends. Jesus was sure of his vocation. His mission in life was to call people to repentance and to proclaim the Good News of the reign of God. He did not need to work magic tricks to get people's attention. God's message was powerful enough on its own.

Although Jesus was clear about his mission, his disciples did not always understand what he was about. Sometimes they got caught up in the gossip, joining the crowds in wanting to name Jesus king. "Let us sit at your right hand and your left hand," James and John pleaded. "Give us the highest places in your kingdom" (based on *Mark 10:37*).

Giotto, *Scene from Life of Christ.* 14th century.

Satan offered Jesus the same temptation in the wilderness. Taking Jesus to a tall mountain, Satan showed Jesus the whole world. "This can be yours if you only bow down and worship me." Jesus' answer to this offer was, "Get away from me, Satan. God alone is to be worshiped" (based on *Matthew 4:8–11*).

Jesus did not give in to the offers of wealth, power, or fame he received. These trappings of society meant nothing to Jesus. Jesus knew what was really important. As he told his disciples,

Whoever wishes to be great among you will be your servant; whoever wishes to be first among you will be the slave of all. For the Son of Man did not come to be served, but to serve, and to give his life as a ransom for many.

Based on MATTHEW 20:26–28

1. **What are some of the temptations seventh-graders experience today? What are some things that you can do to overcome these temptations?**
2. **What's the first image that comes to your mind when you hear the word *vocation*? What do you think about that image?**

Following Jesus

The washing of the feet at the Holy Thursday Mass is a celebration of what it means to follow Jesus. In performing this humble action for his friends *(John 13:1–6)*, Jesus made it clear that his followers were to serve others.

MINISTRY OF LOVE AND SERVICE

Jesus asked all his followers to love God and serve others. The vocation to service that all Catholics receive in Baptism can be lived out in many different ways: as a married or single lay person, as a religious sister or brother, or as a deacon or priest. The service vocations of Marriage and Holy Orders are sacramental signs of Jesus' presence in the Church.

ANOINTED FOR SERVICE

The seventh graders were stumped. It was the youth group's turn to nominate people for the "Christian of the Week" Award for the parish bulletin, and they didn't know where to begin.

Ted, the youth group advisor, looked around at the puzzled faces of the young people. "Maybe we need to start out by thinking about what it means to be a Christian," he suggested.

"Christians are followers of Jesus," Ray said.

"Right," answered Ted. "But there's something even more basic. You know that the title **Christ** means anointed one. So Christians are literally anointed like Jesus. Why was Jesus anointed, or sent?"

"I know," Rebecca replied. "He was sent to serve God's people."

Ted nodded. "Good. So that means?"

"That Christians are people who serve other people, the way Jesus did," Laura continued.

"And we're anointed, too," Judy added. "In Baptism and Confirmation, right?"

"Right," Ted said. "Now, do you know someone who fits that description?"

NOMINATE
Make your own nomination for "Christian of the Week." Tell how the person serves others.

LIVES OF SERVICE

The seventh graders came up with three nominations.

Sister Mary Steinberger. Nurse at Mercy Hospital. Seventh-grader Laura Dillon reports, "When I had my appendix removed, Sister Mary sat with me when my mom couldn't be there. She's great!"

Ted Cruz. Youth group advisor. The seventh-graders say, "Ted really expects a lot from us. He shows us how to live our faith, not just talk about it. He's always ready to talk or to listen to us."

Bernadine Johnson. School crossing guard. Seventh-grader Judy Wilson says, "We've all grown up with Mrs. Johnson waiting at the corner! But most people don't know she helps to raise three grandchildren and volunteers in the anti-drug program."

CHRISTIAN OF THE WEEK — Bernadine Johnson. School crossing guard. Seventh grader Judy Wilson says, "We've all grown up with Mrs. Johnson waiting at the corner! But most people don't know she works another job on weekends to help raise three grandchildren. And she's a volunteer in the anti-drug program." Mother of Renee, grandmother of Ricky, Don, and Frannie.

THE SACRAMENT OF MARRIAGE

Carl Meyers and Gloria Budanski had come to the rectory to make the final plans for their wedding.

"I love weddings!" Father Gorski said. "I think Jesus must have loved them, too. He often described God's kingdom as a wedding feast. You're getting married at Mass, right?"

Carl and Gloria nodded.

"Good!" Father Gorski answered. "The Eucharist is the best way to celebrate your love for each other."

"It won't be a big wedding," Gloria explained. "Just our family and friends, the people closest to us."

Carl laughed. "Still, that's a lot of people. The Meyerses and Budanskis are big families."

Father Gorski smiled. "No matter how many people are present, however, you will still be making your wedding **vows** to the whole community."

"What do you mean? Gloria asked.

"You're going to promise to love and be faithful to each other throughout your lives," Father Gorski explained. "You're going to commit yourselves to accepting and loving children as gifts from God. That's pretty powerful stuff—and it affects the whole Body of Christ."

"I think I see," Carl said thoughtfully. "Because we are part of Jesus' body, the love we share and the sacrifices we make affect the whole community."

"The way Jesus showed love," Gloria added.

"Exactly!" Father Gorski beamed. "Marriage takes everyday, ordinary people and gives them the grace to follow Jesus every day of their lives."

I DO

The Church recognizes the vocation of marriage as a gift from God. God witnessed the love of a man and a woman at creation and declared it good. God blessed the human union and said to them, "Be fruitful and multiply" *(Genesis 1:27–28)*. The health of the Church and Christian society is closely tied to healthy married life.

At a Catholic wedding, the spouses, as ministers of Christ's grace, mutually give the sacrament to each other by expressing their consent before the Church. This consent must be freely given. You can't cross your fingers or plan to quit if you don't like it. A couple's promise to love and be faithful to each other is a lifetime commitment. The wedding rings a couple exchanges are a sign of that unending promise.

A vow is a sacred promise made in the presence of God and the Christian community.

THE SACRAMENT OF ORDERS

Holy Orders is the sacrament through which the mission of Christ, entrusted to his Apostles, continues in the Church. It is the sacrament of apostolic ministry. There are three levels to this sacrament: *episcopate* (bishop), *presbyterate* (priest), and *diaconate* (deacon).

The essential rite of the sacrament of Holy Orders consists of the bishop laying hands upon the head of the man to be ordained, along with the prayer of consecration, and asking God to send the Holy Spirit upon this person.

No one has a right to this sacrament. People who celebrate Holy Orders must be called by God and the Church. Candidates to the Roman Catholic priesthood are men who are **celibate** for the "sake of the kingdom" *(Matthew 19:12)*.

DEACONS

Deacons are ordained into the ministry of service. Deacons assist the bishop and priest in preaching the Gospel, celebrating some of the sacraments, and serving the needs of the people. Unlike priests and bishops, deacons may be married.

PRIESTS

Priests are co-workers with the bishop in serving God's people by celebrating the sacraments, preaching the Word, and leading the community in prayer. A baptized man becomes a priest when a bishop lays hands upon him and prays that the Spirit will consecrate the man. The priest receives special sacramental powers that continue the presence and work of Jesus in the Church. The priest becomes an "other Christ." Through Holy Orders, priests are consecrated to preach the Gospel, lead the community, and celebrate the Eucharist. It is in the celebration of the Eucharist with the community of faith that the sacred office of the priesthood is exercised most completely.

Priests can exercise their ministry only with the approval of their bishop. At **ordination,** priests make a promise of obedience to the bishop. In communion with the bishop, priests serve the People of God and proclaim the Gospel to the world.

BISHOPS

Bishops, as the successors of the Apostles, receive the fullness of Holy Orders. By virtue of the Holy Spirit, bishops take the place of Christ himself as teachers, shepherds, and priests, and act as his representative. They are the true and authentic teachers of the faith. With the pope, bishops lead and teach the universal Church by virtue of their episcopal office.

Bishops are entrusted with the pastoral care of a local church (called a diocese). At the same time, bishops are responsible for the apostolic mission of the Church.

1. **What signs do you see in marriage that show the presence of Christ?**
2. **Describe the ministry of bishops, priests, and deacons. How is each a sign of Christ to the world?**

SPECIAL WORDS

The word **celibate** means "single, one who is not married." **Ordination** is the reception of the sacrament of Holy Orders. To ordain means to "set aside for a special purpose."

HEARING THE CALL

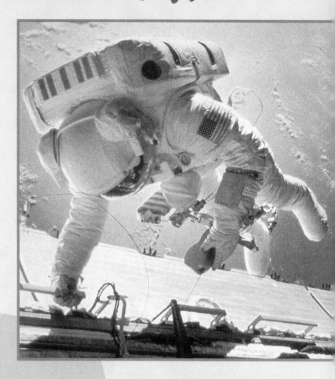

God is calling you to a special vocation, although you may not yet be aware of what it is. Your ideas about a vocation may change repeatedly over the next few years. But you can listen for God's call and prepare for your future vocation right now. One way to do this is to learn about fields that interest you.

On the lines below, list one area of life that really interests you. What can you do to learn more about this area? How can your interest in this area help you to serve God's people better?

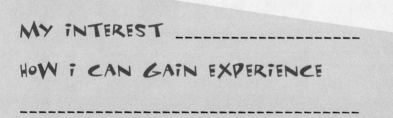

MY INTEREST _____

HOW i CAN GAIN EXPERIENCE

HOW i CAN SERVE GOD'S PEOPLE

_____

INIGO'S PRAYER

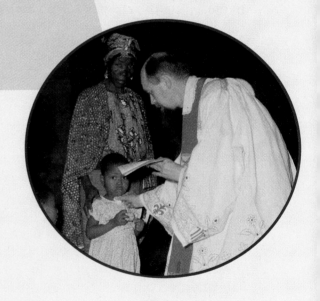

Saint Ignatius Loyola composed his prayer of surrender to God's will when he was still uncertain about his life's direction. This is a good prayer for all Christians. You can pray these words as you seek your vocation—your call to make your life a great adventure in the service of God's people.

Lord Jesus Christ, take all my freedom, my memory, my understanding, and my will.
All that I have and cherish, You have given me. I surrender it all to be guided by your will.
Your grace and your love are wealth enough for me. Give me these, Lord Jesus, and I ask for nothing more.

WITH YOUR FAMILY

As a family, identify people in your parish whom you admire because of the way they follow Jesus. Write letters to these people and thank them for being such good examples of Jesus' love.

▼ REVIEW CHAPTER 16 ....

CATHOLICS BELIEVE

1. Jesus taught his followers to serve others.
2. In Baptism, Christians receive the vocation to serve others.
3. Marriage and Holy Orders are sacraments of service.

KNOW

1. What does it mean to have a vocation? What vocation does every Christian receive at Baptism?_____
   _____

2. How did Satan tempt Jesus to abandon his vocation? How did Jesus respond to Satan? _____
   _____

3. What did Jesus tell his disciples was a sign of greatness? How did Jesus demonstrate this sign to his disciples? _____
   _____

4. What are some of the ways that people can live out their vocation? Which of these ways are recognized as signs of Christ's presence? _____
   _____

5. What vows does a couple make at the sacrament of Marriage? Why are these vows important to the faith community? _____
   _____

6. What are the three levels of the sacrament of Holy Orders? Describe how each is a sign of Christ's presence. _____
   _____

SUNDAY MASS

During the Eucharistic prayer, the community asks God to care for and guide the pope, the local bishop, and all those who serve the Church in every vocation. Remember to join your prayers to those of the community, asking that the Church be served with skill and charity.

THE PARTS OF THE MASS

The Mass is like a great musical symphony in four movements. The rhythm of the Mass moves through each movement, carrying the worshiper through the celebration.

The First Movement
INTRODUCTORY RITES

The First Movement sounds all the themes for the Mass, including the human need for mercy and God's greatness and glory.

The Entrance Hymn symbolically unites the people in one body.

The priest enters, reverences the altar, and greets the congregation.

The people begin their worship by asking forgiveness of sins and giving glory to God.

The Second Movement
THE LITURGY OF THE WORD

In the Second Movement, God speaks through Scripture and the people respond with faith and prayer.

The congregation listens to readings from the Hebrew Scriptures, the Epistles, and the Gospel.

The congregation responds to these readings with the Responsorial Song.

The Homily by the priest relates the readings to contemporary life.

The people profess their faith and exercise their common priesthood in the Prayer of the Faithful.

The Fourth Movement
CONCLUSION

The Mass ends with the Fourth Movement as the celebrant sends people out to love and serve the Lord.

The Mass continues in people's lives long after they leave the Church.

The Third Movement
THE CELEBRATION OF THE EUCHARIST

In the Third Movement, the people commune with God, who humbly comes to them under the appearance of bread and wine. Through their common sharing in the Eucharist, the people are joined to God and to each other.

The bread and wine become the Body and Blood of Christ.

People pray the Lord's Prayer and share a sign of Christ's peace.

The community shares in Christ's sacrificial meal.

LEARNING

1. **What are the seven sacraments?**
   The seven sacraments are Baptism, Confirmation, Eucharist, Penance, Anointing of the Sick, Holy Orders, and Marriage. These are special signs that Jesus is still present in the Church.

2. **Which three sacraments join people to the Church?**
   People are joined to the Church through the sacraments of Christian initiation: Baptism, Confirmation, and Eucharist.

3. **Which two sacraments are considered sacraments of healing?**
   There are two sacraments of healing: Penance and the Anointing of the Sick. The sacrament of Penance offers forgiveness for sins; Anointing of the Sick offers strength and healing from physical, mental, and emotional illness.

4. **What are the two sacraments of service?**
   Marriage and Holy Orders are the sacraments of service. All Christians are called by God to lives of service.

LIVING

Symbols are important for keeping and sharing the faith. Through symbols, invisible realities are made visible. Describe or draw your own symbol for each of the following.

Love   **Faith**   **Hope**

Friendship   **Joy**   **Church**

PRAYING

All: Lord, help us serve your people in love.

Group 1: I remind you to stir into flame the gift of God that you have through the imposition of my hands. For God did not give us a spirit of cowardice, but rather of power and love and self-control.

All: Lord, help us serve your people in love.

Group 2: He saved us and called us to a holy life, not according to our works but according to his own design, and the grace bestowed on us in Christ Jesus before time began.

All: Lord, help us serve your people in love.

Group 3: Take as a model of sound teaching the words you have from me, in the faith and love that are in Christ Jesus. Guard this rich trust with the help of the Holy Spirit that dwells within us.

All: Lord, help us serve your people in love.

Based on 2 TIMOTHY 1:6–14

ASKING

1. When have I recently gone out of my way to help others?

2. In what ways am I willing to be of service to others?

Jesus, the Truth

Brown, *Jesus Washing Peter's Feet.* 19th century.

AS I HAVE LOVED YOU, SO YOU ALSO SHOULD LOVE ONE ANOTHER.

JOHN 13:35–36

THE FACES OF CHRIST

He is the image of the invisible God.

COLOSSIANS 1:15

CONTENT KEYS

1. **Images of the divine can help you grow closer to God.**
2. **Christian art teaches about Jesus.**
3. **People express their love of Jesus through art.**

WORTH A THOUSAND WORDS

There is an old saying that goes, "A picture is worth a thousand words." Look at the pictures on this page and explain the significance of each.

Why do people keep photographs of one another? What photographs do you carry with you?

FILL IN THE FRAME

Draw a picture of the person who is most important in your life. Explain why this person is so important.

Give Me That Water

Although she was only eight, Teresa loved to look at the painting of Jesus speaking with the Samaritan woman. It reminded her of just how kind and loving Jesus was.

Jesus had walked many miles that morning and was hot and dusty. When he saw the well, he stopped to rest. That's when he met the woman. She came in the middle of the day rather than in the morning with the other village women because they treated her badly and called her names.

Jesus said to the woman, "I'm thirsty. Please give me a drink."

The woman was amazed by Jesus' request. By his accent, she could tell that he was from Galilee, not Samaria. Surely this man knew that Jews and Samaritans avoided each other as if the other had leprosy. How bold of him to ask her for a drink.

"Sir," she replied. "How can you, a Jew, ask me, a Samaritan woman, for a drink?"

"Woman, I am thirsty," Jesus replied. "But if you ask, I will give you living water."

"Sir, you do not even have a bucket and the cistern is deep. Where can you get this living water?" the woman asked.

Jesus said to her, "Everyone who drinks this water will be thirsty again; but whoever drinks the water I shall give will never thirst; the water I shall give will become a spring of water welling up to eternal life."

The woman answered, "Sir, give me this water so that I may not be thirsty."

Based on JOHN 4:13–15

de Flandes, *Christ and the Samaritan Woman at the Well.*

As an adult, Saint Teresa of Avila wrote this:

Oh, how often do I remember the living water of that Gospel. I have loved it ever since I was quite a child and I used often to beseech the Lord to give me that water. The picture of the Lord at the well hung where I could always see it. It bore the inscription: "Lord, give me that water."

This picture inspired Teresa to do great things. Her life, her work, her writings, and her spiritual experiences have inspired others to a deeper faith for over four hundred years.

THE POWER TO INSPIRE

People have been inspired by sacred art and images for thousands of years. Sacred art includes statues, paintings, wood carvings, mosaics, and stained glass windows. There are many stories of people being moved to acts of greatness by these images. Here are two of those stories.

GO HENCE, FRANCIS

The youthful Saint Francis of Assisi often prayed at the deserted and half-ruined chapel dedicated to San Damiano, a fifteen-minute walk from the town of Assisi. Francis was drawn there by the Byzantine crucifix that hung on the wall. For some reason, the crucifix helped him to pray.

One day while he was deep in prayer, Francis heard a voice coming from the crucifix. "Now, go hence, Francis," the voice said, "and build up my house, for it is nearly falling down!"

Francis recognized that it was Jesus who was speaking to him, but he did not at first understand the command. He started immediately repairing San Damiano chapel. Only later did Francis understand that Jesus meant for him to repair the whole Church.

BE MY HANDS

An American soldier on a European battlefield during World War II came upon a bombed out church. As he knelt to pray at the ruined altar, the soldier noticed a statue of Jesus. Although knicked and cracked from the force of the bomb that destroyed the church, the statue was all in one piece except for one thing: Jesus had no hands.

Staring at this battered statue, the battle-hardened soldier was moved to tears. As he was crying he heard the words, "You must be my hands." The soldier had no idea who spoke the words he heard, or if he had only imagined them. But where they came from didn't matter. He knew the truth when he heard it. From that moment on, the soldier worked to rebuild a world destroyed by war.

1. **Why was the picture of Jesus important to Saint Teresa of Avila?**
2. **Tell a story of a time when you were inspired by a work of art.**

THE POWER OF IMAGES

The first commandment prohibits worshiping false gods or graven images. To fulfill this commandment, Judaism and Islam do not allow any images at all. Christianity, does not have such a prohibition. Christians are encouraged to use pictures and statues to help them worship God.

There was a time in the Church's history when the use of sacred images was forbidden. During the fourth century, laws forbade people to make or worship before icons (or images) of Jesus and the saints. This movement was called *iconoclasm,* which means "image breaking."

Emperor Leo III and Patriarch Anastasius destroyed any sacred image they found. But people loved their icons and refused to give them up. They hid the icons away where they could not be found. Saint John of Damascus is remembered for his efforts at preventing the iconoclasts from destroying these popular signs of faith.

During the Reformation, many Christians who separated from the Catholic Church also believed that praying before images was idolatry. A few of these groups smashed stained glass windows and destroyed religious statues and paintings. A few Christian groups even today do not allow the use of sacred art.

NO GRAVEN IMAGES

Deuteronomy 4:15–16 prohibits the making of images of God because no image can ever hope to capture the wonder and grandeur of the Creator. But even with this prohibition, the Hebrews made sacred images at God's command; the bronze serpent (*Numbers 21:4–9*) and the cherubim in the Temple (*1 Kings 6:23–28*) are two examples.

The Christian veneration of images is not idol worship. In the year 787, the second Council of Nicaea approved the veneration of icons—not only of Christ, but also of Mary the mother of God, the angels, and the saints. As Saint John of Damascene wrote, "Whoever venerates an image venerates the person portrayed in it." So when you pray before a statue of Jesus, or remember a saint, you are not worshiping an idol. You are simply using these images to help lead you to God.

1. **How does looking at an image of Jesus help you to pray?**
2. **Why is honoring an image of Jesus not idol worship?**

Images of Jesus

No one knows what Jesus looked like. No one painted a portrait of him while he walked the earth. Over the ages, Christians have pictured Jesus in many different ways. How artists represented the Lord was affected by the culture in which they lived.

The earliest paintings of Jesus are found in Christian burial places. Jesus appears as a young beardless man, carrying a sheep on his back. Jesus described himself as the Good Shepherd who lays down his life for his sheep *(John 10:14–15)*. During these times of persecution, Jesus' followers needed to be reminded of Jesus' loving care for them.

Christ as the Good Shepherd.

In the later years of the Roman Empire, Jesus was often depicted as a ruler. Especially in large churches, Jesus could be seen as the Pantocrator, or "all-powerful ruler." The Pantocrator is many times larger than life and often dominates the arch or dome over the altar.

Christ, the Pantocrator.

Reni, *Jesus is Scourged.* 17th century.

Of course, Jesus identified himself with the poor and lowly rather than with earthly rulers. The image of Jesus suffered with the poor and lowly during the long centuries when the people of Europe suffered through wars and plagues and poverty. The Man of Sorrows—whipped, crowned with thorns, dying on the cross—appears in the art of suffering, oppressed people everywhere. It is a way of saying, "Jesus is one of us. He shares our pain."

Through the centuries, many artists have painted Jesus in the arms of his mother. This image makes a powerful statement about the Incarnation. The Son of God, Jesus, was born an infant.

Raphael, *The Madonna and Child Jesus.* 15th century.

As Christianity spread around the world, the artistic traditions of Asia and Africa have been adapted to Christian subjects.

FOLLOWING Jesus

You may not always know what to say or do when you find yourself in a new or difficult situation. At these times, a conversation with Jesus can help you make the proper decision. Many people find it easier to pray when they focus on an image of Jesus in their minds. The next time you pray, try to imagine Jesus sitting and having a conversation with you.

SEEING THE LORD

Even if the iconoclasts had succeeded in destroying all the painted and carved images of Jesus ever created, people would still be able to look at one another and see the face of the Lord. Every human face is an icon, a living image of Jesus.

Look at these pictures. Write a brief sentence describing how Jesus is present in each one.

Look around your home for images of Jesus, Mary, or the saints. Ask a parent why these images were chosen for your home. As a family, use the image as a source of inspiration and prayer.

THE HOLY NAME

There are many titles for Jesus, just as there are many images. As you pray each of these names slowly to yourself, form an image to go with it.

Jesus, Son of the living God. Jesus, Splendor of the Father. Jesus, the Everlasting Light. Jesus, King of Glory. Jesus, Dawn of Justice. Jesus, Prince of Peace. Jesus, Gentle and Humble of Heart. Jesus, Our Refuge and Strength. Jesus, Servant of the Poor. Jesus, the Way, the Truth, and the Life.

▼REVIEW CHAPTER 17 . . . .

CATHOLICS BELIEVE

1. Christian art expresses the Gospel message through visual images.
2. Visual images help people express their devotion to Jesus and feel close to him.
3. Honoring an image or picture of Jesus is actually a way of honoring Jesus.

KNOW

1. Saint John of Damascus is remembered for _____

_____

2. The word *iconoclasm* means _____

_____

3. Some of the first images of Jesus show him as _____

_____

4. Three other images of Jesus include _____

_____

5. People's images of Jesus are affected by _____

_____

6. Three of the titles given to Jesus are _____

_____

7. Images of Jesus as a baby in Mary's arms remind people that

_____

8. Paintings of Jesus as the Man of Sorrows tells people that

_____

SUNDAY MASS

Examine your parish church closely at Mass this Sunday, looking for images of Jesus. Look for statues, stained glass windows, and paintings that show Jesus, God, or the saints. How are these images included during the Mass? How do people use these images for personal prayer and devotion? Prepare a report on your findings.

FAITHFUL WITNESS

CONTENT KEYS

1. Jesus' followers are called to be witnesses to him.
2. Some of Jesus' followers died for their faith.
3. You can be a witness to Jesus today.

Whoever loses his life for my sake and that of the Gospel will save it.

MARK 8:35

BISHOP IGNATIUS

All of us in Antioch who followed Jesus knew Bishop Ignatius. He had preached to us the Good News about Jesus and baptized us as Christians. Bishop Ignatius preached to us the importance of belonging to the Church, a church that was open to anyone who believed in Jesus. He was our leader, our teacher, and our friend. What a shock it was to see him bound in chains and led away by the Roman soldiers. As long as I draw breath, I'll never forget that sight.

As he was being led away, Bishop Ignatius told us not to worry over him. He was honored to be persecuted for worshiping Jesus. What he asked us to do was pray that he might have the strength to die as a faithful witness to Jesus.

Bishop Ignatius thought of us often on his long journey to Rome. Like the great apostle Paul, Ignatius sent us letters encouraging us to live as Jesus asked. I don't know where he found the strength to write letters so full of warmth, humor, and practical advice. Obviously his faith in God was very strong.

In one of his last letters, Bishop Ignatius wrote to us:
Pray for me, that God will give me the grace not just to be called a Christian, but to be one. I am God's grain, and I go to be ground by the teeth of wild beasts into the bread of Christ. Do not try to stop me; believe me, I know what is right for me. Only now am I beginning to be a true disciple.

When my time to be persecuted comes, I pray that I can have the faith and courage to be such a wonderful witness for Christ.

1. **How was Bishop Ignatius a witness for Jesus?**
2. **What did Bishop Ignatius mean when he said he wished to be ground into bread by the teeth of lions?**

Stephen's Witness

Stephen was an early follower of Jesus. He loved the Lord completely and dedicated his life to following him. The Apostles chose Stephen as one of the first deacons to care for the sick, widows, and orphans in the Christian community. Now Stephen stood before the Sanhedrin accused of blasphemy because he preached about Jesus.

Finally given a chance to address his accusers, Stephen spoke of his love for God, the covenant, and the Temple. But he didn't stop there. He went on to remind the Jews of how they had rejected every prophet God had ever sent them. And now they were doing it again, only this time they were rejecting God's son.

"If you ask me what I believe," Stephen concluded, "it is this: Jesus, who lives, has the power of God within him. Even now I see him standing at the right hand of the Father."

The angry crowd did not like Stephen's comments. They grabbed him and dragged him outside the city gates. There they prepared to punish him in the traditional way—death by stoning.

Even as the rain of sharp stones came at him, Stephen continued to testify to the wonder and greatness of the Lord Jesus. He did not try to dodge the stones or use his arms to block them. Instead, he stood still and accepted each blow, just as Jesus accepted death on the cross.

Finally Stephen could take no more punishment. Lying on the ground, bloodied and battered, Stephen looked up to heaven and said, "Lord Jesus, receive my spirit." Then in his final breath, Stephen forgave those who murdered him. "Lord," he prayed, "do not hold this sin against them."

Stephen is honored as the first Christian martyr, the *protomartyr* ("first witness" in Greek). He was the first person, after Jesus, to give his life for the Gospel. The Church celebrates the martyrdom of Stephen on December 26 to show his closeness to the Lord.

A Brother's Testament

My sister Perpetua and I grew up in a wealthy household in Carthage, an African province of the Roman Empire. Although still a girl, Perpetua was married and had a baby son. After we heard a disciple speak about Jesus, she and I decided to become Christians.

In the year 202, while Perpetua and I were still catechumens, Emperor Septimus Severus issued an edict requiring every citizen to offer sacrifice to the pagan gods. Many Christians, including Perpetua and four other catechumens, were arrested when they refused to offer the sacrifice.

While imprisoned, Perpetua and these other catechumens were secretly baptized. Their religious instructor, a holy man named Saturus, turned himself over to the authorities so that he could share the martyrdom of his brothers and sisters in Christ.

My father tried to convince Perpetua to make a sacrificial offering to the pagan gods. It was such a small thing to do, he said, in order to save her life.

Perpetua pointed to her clay water jug and asked, "Is that water jug a tree or a bird?"

"No," my father answered, puzzled.

Perpetua spoke softly. "Nor can I say that I am not a Christian."

When Perpetua was led to trial, my father was among the crowd in the street as they passed. "Think of your mother," he called to her. "Think of your aunt and your baby." But Perpetua did not yield, not even when she was condemned to death.

Perpetua and her companions were led to the amphitheater on March 7, in the year 203. They were the entertainment offered in honor of the Emperor's birthday. I was present with a group of Christians who had come to witness the martyrdom of our friends and to pray for them.

The men offered no resistance and were killed quickly by a bear. Perpetua and the other women were kicked and gored by a mad bull, but it did not kill them. Seeing us in the crowd, Perpetua encouraged us to remain true to the faith and to love one another. I could barely see her through my tears.

After the crowd had grown tired of watching the Christians suffer, the soldiers slaughtered all who remained alive, Perpetua among them. Just before they died, the martyrs embraced and gave each other the kiss of peace.

These deaths have inspired all the Christians of Carthage. The Lord himself could be seen in their love and sacrifice. Wherever martyrs are remembered, their names will be praised for the witness they gave to the Gospel!

THE POWER IN SEEDS

Tertullian, a Christian who witnessed Perpetua's death, said, "The blood of the martyrs is the seed of the Church." Describe how the deaths of Perpetua and her friends aided the growth of the Church.

CHRISTIAN WITNESSES

Eyewitness accounts can be very persuasive. After all, they're not based on hearsay or rumor. They're grounded in personal experience. During the first century A.D., many people became followers of Jesus because of the testimony given by people who had known Jesus in the flesh or had witnessed his appearances after his crucifixion. These disciples preached the Good News far and wide.

When the first witnesses to the Lord died, new people stepped forward to continue proclaiming the Good News. But the most powerful witnesses to Christ were those men and women who gave their lives to proclaim the Good News. People like Stephen, Bishop Ignatius of Antioch, and Perpetua followed Jesus while they lived, but in dying their witness became much more powerful. They were so committed to their faith in Jesus that they decided to die rather than to deny it.

Those who are willing to die for what they believe are known as martyrs. By their death, they give total witness to their faith in Jesus. People who see these deaths are moved often to conversion. As the stories of martyrs are retold, people are inspired by their example and choose to follow Christ.

The Church has painstakingly collected the stories of those who remained faithful. In their own words, the martyrs speak of their love for Christ.

> *Neither the pleasures of the world nor the kingdoms of this age will be of any use to me. It is better for me to die for Christ Jesus than to reign over the ends of the earth. I seek him who died for us; I desire him who rose for us. My birth is approaching.*
>
> SAINT IGNATIUS OF ANTIOCH

> *I bless you for having judged me worthy from this day and this hour to be counted among your martyrs.*
>
> SAINT POLYCARP

The Church honors people who die as martyrs by proclaiming them saints of God.

Mantegna, *Saint Sebastian.* 15th century.

Saint Sebastian, a third-century martyr, is the patron saint of soldiers.

Although very few Christians are called to die for the faith, every Christian is called to be active in the life of the Church and to be a witness to the Gospel. As people see how Christians live and act, faith in Jesus is communicated in word and deed. Whether you realize it or not, what you do and say influences what people think about Jesus.

Modern Witnesses

Christians continue to give their lives in martyrdom even today. They die because they preach the Gospel of Jesus, a message many people still do not want to hear. Although the people mentioned on these pages have not been officially declared saints by the Church, their witness continues to inspire people to follow Christ.

FRANZ JAGERSTATTER

Franz took off his uniform, handed it to the captain and said, "I cannot wear this sign of evil."

"If you do not fight for the fatherland you will be tried for treason and put to death," the captain responded.

"Then I will die," Franz responded.

Franz Jagerstatter was an Austrian farmer with a wife and three children. He was not a theologian and cared little for politics. But he loved the Lord greatly. When Franz heard the hatred preached by Hitler and the Nazi regime, he knew it was evil and refused to cooperate with it. He would not wear the German uniform and he would not fight in the war.

Tried and condemned to death for refusing to do his duty, Franz ignored all efforts to make him change his mind. "God will take care of my family," he wrote.

Franz Jagerstatter was beheaded on August 9, 1943, believing that his real duty was to follow the teachings of Jesus and proclaim his law of love. "For love will emerge victorious and will last for all eternity—and happy are they who live and die in God's love."

ITA FORD

The country of El Salvador was in turmoil. Death squads—military groups secretly backed by the government—were threatening to kill anyone who tried to improve the lives of the poor and oppressed Salvadoran people. The death squads were especially active against Christian missionaries who worked with the poor.

Sister Ita Ford refused to be frightened by the death squads. She was in El Salvador to proclaim the Good News of Jesus by her actions: she fed the hungry, healed the sick, clothed the naked, and educated the ignorant. On December 2, 1980, Sister Ita Ford and her companions—Sisters Dorothy Kazel, Maura Clarke, and lay mission worker Jean Donovan—were all murdered for preaching the Gospel.

In a letter to her niece written shortly before Sister Ita died, she described her own witness to the Gospel:

I hope you come to find that which gives life a deep meaning for you, something worth living for—maybe even worth dying for. Something that energizes you, enthuses you, keeps you moving ahead. I can't tell you what it might be.

For Sister Ita and her companions, that something worth dying for was their belief in Jesus.

JOACHIM RUHUNA

Hutu rebels murdered Archbishop Joachim Ruhuna of Burundi, a member of the Tutsi minority, on September 9, 1996. Also slain were a Burundian Missionaries of Charity sister and two lay catechists.

A car carrying the archbishop and the others was ambushed at Murongwe on the way to Gitega. The bishop's body was identified by a local deacon, although his body has not been recovered. Sources say that the bishop's body was taken away and mutilated by the rebels.

The archbishop had been booed recently during a speech when he begged both sides to stop the terrible bloodshed. "There are no names for this. I have seen it many times but I condemn violence on both sides," the bishop said. The bishop had received death threats because of his call for peace.

1. **What does it mean to be a martyr?**
2. **How does the example of martyrs help to spread the message of Jesus?**
3. **How can you be a living witness to the Gospel?**

You can tell the world about your love for Jesus by your words and actions. When you help friends solve a problem without violence, you are a witness to Jesus. When you convince a friend not to cheat or steal, you spread the Good News.

DO NOT BE AFRAID

In Matthew 5:3–12, Jesus taught how his followers should act. You can be a witness by living Christ's Beatitudes in your daily life. Read the following Beatitudes. For each, write one example showing how you can give witness to the love of Jesus. With a partner, dramatize one of your examples.

Blessed are the poor in spirit. _____

Blessed are you who mourn. _____

Blessed are the meek. _____

Blessed are you who hunger and thirst for righteousness.

_____

Blessed are the merciful. _____

Blessed are the clean of heart. _____

Blessed are the peacemakers. _____

Blessed are you who are persecuted in my name. _____

DAYS OF REMEMBRANCE

Martyrs are remembered on the day of their death—the day they were born into God's kingdom. On the feast day of a martyr, the priest wears red vestments, the color of blood—and the color of love. In your prayer, ask these martyrs to help you be a faithful witness to Jesus.

Saint Felicitas, Saint Stephen, Saint Ignatius, Saint Polycarp, Saint Justin, Saint Lawrence, Saint Cyprian, Saint Boniface, Saint Stanislaus, Saint Thomas Becket, Saint John Fisher, Saint Thomas More, Saint Paul Miki, Saint Isaac Jogues, Saint Jean de Brébeuf, Saint Peter Chanel, Saint Charles Lwanga, Saint Perpetua,

As you gave your martyrs the courage to suffer death for Christ, give us the courage to live in faithful witness to you.

You may not be aware of it, but your relationship with Jesus probably started in your own home. Who introduced you to Jesus? Take a moment to thank this person for being a witness of Jesus' love for you. Be sure to describe specific times and events and to tell what led you to see Jesus.

CATHOLICS BELIEVE

1. Disciples of Jesus are called to be faithful witnesses to the Gospel, in life and in death.
2. Martyrdom is the supreme witness given to the faith.
3. Christians follow Jesus by living the Beatitudes.

KNOW

1. What did Saint Ignatius of Antioch do to give witness to Jesus? _____

_____

2. What do you learn from the martyrdom of Saint Stephen? _____

_____

3. How did persecution help to spread the Good News? _____

_____

4. What are some ways that Christians can be witnesses to Jesus today? _____

_____

5. Why are Franz Jagerstatter, Sister Ita Ford, and Archbishop Joachim Ruhuna of Burundi considered modern-day martyrs? Explain how their deaths witnessed to Jesus. _____

_____

6. When do Catholics celebrate the feast of martyrs? Why do they celebrate on that date? _____

_____

SUNDAY MASS

After the Responsorial Psalm there is usually a reading from one of the New Testament letters (*epistles*). Many of these letters were written to encourage a persecuted Christian community to remain faithful to Jesus. Listen carefully this Sunday to this reading for such encouragement. Be prepared to report back to your class about what you learned.

PRINCE OF PEACE

CONTENT KEYS

1. **Jesus preached a message of peace and justice.**
2. **Jesus' followers work for justice.**
3. **Christians are called to be peacemakers.**

Love your enemies, and pray for those who persecute you.

MATTHEW 5:44

WHO IS MY NEIGHBOR?

A man fell victim to robbers as he went down from Jerusalem to Jericho. They stripped and beat him and went off, leaving him half-dead. A priest happened to be going down that road, but when he saw the man, he passed by on the opposite side. Likewise a Levite came to the place, and when he saw the man, he passed by on the opposite side. But a Samaritan traveler who came upon him was moved with compassion at the sight. He approached the victim, poured oil and wine over his wounds, and bandaged them. Then he lifted him up on his own animal, took him to an inn, and cared for him. The next day he took out two silver coins and gave them to the innkeeper with the instructions, "Take care of him. If you spend more than what I have given you, I shall repay you on my way back."

LUKE 10:29–36

Being a Neighbor

In your opinion, which of these three was a neighbor to the robber's victim? Explain your answer.

Good Neighbors

Jesus' message about loving one's neighbor has been heard and followed for the last two thousand years. Here are three stories about people who were each touched by Jesus' teaching and who tried to live it faithfully. These three people were born in different countries, lived in different times, and followed different religious traditions. What they have in common is the belief that in order for peace to enter the world, people had to be good neighbors.

LEO TOLSTOY

Count Leo Tolstoy came from a family of wealthy Russian landowners. Raised in the Russian Orthodox Church, Tolstoy was fascinated by Jesus' teaching. Tolstoy read the Gospel and saw a Jesus who liberated people from sin and freed them from fear, injustice, and oppression.

Tolstoy attempted to live Jesus' great commandment to love God and neighbor with passionate enthusiasm. Putting his beliefs into practice, Tolstoy worked to improve living and working conditions for the hundreds of workers on his family's land, who were treated little better than slaves.

Tolstoy believed wholeheartedly in Jesus' words, "Offer no resistance to evil. When someone strikes you on your right cheek, turn the other one to him as well" (*Matthew 5:39*). Tolstoy put this message into the many essays, short stories, and novels that he wrote later in his life. His message was simple: true happiness is found in taking the commands of Jesus seriously.

MOHANDAS K. GANDHI

Tolstoy's writings influenced many people. One of his books, *The Kingdom of God Is Within You,* changed the life of a young Indian lawyer, Mohandas K. Gandhi. Born into a wealthy Hindu family, Gandhi practiced law in South Africa. There, and later in his native India, Gandhi struggled to free people from unjust British colonial laws.

Gandhi had heard of Jesus from Christian missionaries, but it was the writings of Tolstoy that helped him understand Jesus' teachings on peace and justice.

Gandhi never became Christian, but Jesus' words inspired him to develop a system of nonviolent resistance to evil and injustice. By refusing to cooperate with oppressive governments, Gandhi's followers wore down the opposition. Gandhi led peaceful demonstrations, fasted, and prayed. The Indian people called him *Mahatma,* which means "Great Soul." His efforts led to independence for India—a revolution accomplished without violence.

A PRAYERFUL REVOLUTIONARY

Leo Tolstoy's writings about Jesus' message of peace also influenced Dorothy Day. Dorothy began her life as a rebel. As a young adult, she supported the socialist movement and rejected conventional values such as patriotism and marriage. But Dorothy did not find satisfaction in this way of life.

Dorothy began to search for meaning in her life. She found what she was looking for in the Gospel and the lives of the saints. In 1928, after the birth of her daughter Tamar, Dorothy was baptized a Catholic. A year later, when the Great Depression plunged millions of Americans into poverty and homelessness, Dorothy found her purpose in life.

With Peter Maurin, Dorothy began the Catholic Worker movement—a way of living the Gospel day-by-day. By sheltering and feeding people who were poor, finding them jobs, and offering them hope, Catholic Workers put Jesus' message to love your neighbor into immediate action.

Dorothy was a pacifist who believed that all war was wrong. She wrote letters and articles protesting the use of violence to resolve problems. She demonstrated publicly against American involvement in wars and against the development of nuclear weapons. At times, Dorothy was jailed for her beliefs. But she prayed, fasted, and remained faithful to the words of Jesus, who said this:

Love your enemies, and pray for those who persecute you, that you may be children of your heavenly father.

MATTHEW 5:44–45

1. **What inspired Leo Tolstoy, Mohandas Gandhi, and Dorothy Day to stand up against evil?**
2. **In what ways did each of these people show a love for their neighbor?**

A Message for Today

What would a good neighbor do in each of the following situations? Write your answers in the space provided.

1. Mrs. Santana is a poor widow with three very young children. She would like to attend an evening class to help her get a better job, but she can't afford to pay a babysitter. She's debating whether she should leave her children home alone or not take the class.

2. Mr. Franklin is nearly blind. He can no longer drive and the store is too far away for him to walk. He's wondering how he will be able to get food into the house.

3. Your parish is sponsoring three refugee families from Haiti. There are several twelve-year-old children in these families.

A Cry for Justice

Jesus was asked, "Which is the first of all of the commandments?" He answered,

> *The first is this: "Hear, O Israel! The Lord our God is Lord alone! You shall love the Lord your God with all your heart, with all your soul, with all your mind, and with all your strength." The second is this: "You shall love your neighbor as yourself." There is no other commandment greater than these.*
>
> Mark 12:28–31

Jesus was a student of the Scriptures. He knew the Jewish law. When asked to choose one law as the greatest, Jesus divided the law into two categories. One category was concerned with love for God, the other with love for one's neighbor.

Notice that Jesus does not offer a new teaching here. He doesn't have to. Jewish law is built around these two concepts. Jesus' message of love of neighbor was nothing new. It formed the cornerstone of Jewish belief. To love one's neighbor meant to treat each person with **justice.**

What Jesus added to the Jewish law is a broadening of who should be considered one's neighbor. It's easy to act kindly toward a brother, mother, or favorite aunt. You may even feel kinship with people who live in your town, state, or country. But what do you feel about people in your community who look, speak, and act differently from you? In Luke 10:29–36, Jesus says that you should treat everyone as your neighbor, not just those who look, act, or believe like you. That is, you should treat everyone with justice.

In John's Gospel, Jesus strengthened this teaching when he said to his disciples,

> *"I give you a new commandment: love one another. As I have loved you, so you also should love one another. This is how all will know that you are my disciples, if you have love for one another."*
>
> John 13:34–35

Jesus' meaning was clear. Those who would follow him were to love everybody and treat them with justice.

You can work for justice simply by treating others as you want to be treated. Show compassion towards everyone you meet, and treat people as children of God. By giving people the dignity and respect they deserve, you will help to ensure justice.

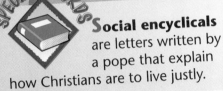

SPECIAL WORDS

Social encyclicals are letters written by a pope that explain how Christians are to live justly.

WORKING FOR PEACE

Jesus did not give his disciples a detailed list explaining what they should do to live justly. You are already familiar with the core of this teaching as expressed in Matthew 5:3–12 (the Beatitudes) and Matthew 25:31–45 (the Corporal Works of Mercy). Over the centuries, the Church has continued to offer guidance on how to act justly.

SOCIAL JUSTICE

In a speech to the United Nations, Pope Paul VI told the world's delegates, "If you want peace, work for justice." The word *justice* is often defined as "giving to someone what he or she is owed." But what does that mean? Can one person justly own all of the land in an area, while the people who work the land own nothing? Do you have a right to have more than enough food to eat, while someone is sitting at your backdoor dying of hunger? The Church would answer each of these questions "no!"

God's creation was meant for the benefit of all, not just for the benefit of a few. For this reason, everyone has the right to participate in the economic life of a community. One person's right to ownership is not greater than another's right to make a living. As Saint John Chrysostom wrote, "Not to enable the poor to share in our goods is to steal from them and deprive them of life. The goods we possess are not ours, but theirs."

Helping people to gain what is rightfully theirs is known as social justice. In the last one hundred years, various popes have written **social encyclicals** which explain in detail how Christians are to act justly today. Above all, Christians are called to do everything they can to help the poor and oppressed people of the world.

PEACEMAKING

Although not always seen in practice, Christianity is a religion of peace. Jesus' teaching was seen as a ban on all forms of violence: "Offer no resistance to one who is evil. When someone strikes you on your right cheek, turn the other one to him as well."

The Church's teaching on war was influenced by Saint Augustine's proposal of the just war theory. This theory said that Christians had the right and the obligation to defend the defenseless and fight evil. This theory still shapes Church teaching, although pacifism— refusing to use violence to resolve conflicts—is also part of the Church's long tradition.

1. **Why is justice an important part of peacemaking?**
2. **What is one way you can be a peacemaker today?**

PEACE ON EARTH

Henry Longfellow sat by his wounded son's bedside. Charles was wounded in the terrible Civil War, but now at last he was home.

As Charles slept, Henry went to his desk and picked up his pen. Sitting quietly, Longfellow heard church bells chiming through the cold December night. Christmas! He had completely forgotten. This was the birthday of the Prince of Peace, whose coming was proclaimed by an angelic song. "Glory to God in the highest and on earth peace to those on whom his favor rests" (*Luke 2:14*). Thoughtfully, Longfellow began to write:

> *I heard the bells on*
> *Christmas Day,*
> *Their old familiar*
> *carols play,*
> *And wild and sweet*
> *The words repeat*
> *Of peace on earth,*
> *good will to men.*

It was as though the message of the bells mocked Henry. Where was the peace in a world full of war? Where was the hope, with his wife dead and his son so ill? He put his bitterness on paper.

> *And in despair I bowed my head;*
> *"There is no peace on earth," I said,*
> *"For hate is strong*
> *And mocks the song*
> *Of peace on earth,*
> *good will to men!"*

MY BROTHER

Longfellow dropped his pen as he heard his son groan. As Henry drew near to the bed, Charles took his father's hand and held it tightly.

"You were right, Father," he gasped. "War is not about glory, but about blood and death. I saw the boy who shot me, at the moment my bullet hit him. He was a Southerner, but he could have been my brother! Can you forgive me?"

In answer, Henry held his son while they both wept. Outside, the church bells continued to ring, bringing the dawn of Christmas. In the morning light, Henry added a last verse to his poem, expressing his belief that peace was truly possible.

> *Then pealed the bells more loud and deep:*
> *"God is not dead, nor does he sleep!*
> *The wrong shall fail,*
> *The right prevail*
> *With peace on earth,*
> *good will to men!"*

Ode to Peace

Use this space to write a poem about being a peacemaker.

WORKING FOR JUSTICE

To be a peacemaker, you must work for justice. One way to do that is to identify the causes of problems and then think of practical steps to solve them. In the space provided, name three problems in your community, identify their causes, and think of a just solution for each.

Problem	Causes	Just Solution
1. _____ _____	1. _____ _____	1. _____ _____
2. _____ _____	2. _____ _____	2. _____ _____
3. _____ _____	3. _____ _____	3. _____ _____

INNER PEACE

Set aside five minutes each day this week to meditate quietly on what you can do to be a peacemaker. Use one of these brief prayers as a meditation starter.

Lord, make me an instrument of your peace.

PRAYER OF SAINT FRANCIS

Kindness and truth shall meet; justice and peace shall kiss.

PSALM 85:11

Let justice surge like water, and goodness like an unfailing stream.

AMOS 5:24

O Lord, make us children of quietness and heirs of peace.

SAINT CLEMENT

WITH YOUR FAMILY

You can work for peace in your own home by treating each person with dignity and respect. Don't call other people names or fight over minor matters. When you have a disagreement, find a way to resolve the issue without fighting.

CATHOLICS BELIEVE

1. Jesus taught his followers to treat people justly.
2. Jesus' followers work for justice by helping people participate in the social, economic, and political life of the community.
3. Christians work for peace by treating people with dignity and respect, solving conflict non-violently, and defending the rights of the defenseless.

KNOW

1. What did Jesus say about the importance of being a good neighbor?

   _____

2. How does being a good neighbor promote justice?_____

   _____

3. How was Count Leo Tolstoy influenced by Jesus' teaching of peace?

   _____

4. How were Dorothy Day and Mohandas Gandhi influenced by the writing of

   Count Leo Tolstoy? _____

5. What does it mean to be a peacemaker? _____

   _____

6. What is the purpose of social encyclicals? _____

   _____

SUNDAY MASS

Each Sunday at Mass, the Church prays for the needs of the community. Many parishes offer prayers for peace and justice at this time. Write your own prayers for peace and justice to be used during the Prayer of the Faithful. Pray for issues that concern you. During the sign of peace before communion, share Christ's peace with those around you by shaking hands or giving a hug.

20

THE SERVANT KING

The one who humbles himself will be exalted.

LUKE 14:11

CONTENT KEYS

1. Jesus called his followers to be generous.
2. Christians are to act with charity.
3. Generosity is shown by doing little things with love.

SERVANT OF THE SERVANTS

Cardinal Giovanni Battista Montini was no stranger to power. He had served as a Vatican diplomat for thirty years, meeting often with the most powerful people in the world. He knew the temptations of wealth and power. But he also knew the power of the Gospel.

When he was elected pope, Cardinal Montini—Pope Paul VI—thought often about the true meaning of wealth and power. The office of pope is one of the most powerful leadership positions in the world. One of the signs of the papal office had been a three-tiered golden crown covered with jewels. Up to the time of Pope Paul VI, this crown was placed upon the new pope's head as if he were a king. This crown symbolized the pope's authority as head of the Church, ruler of the Vatican state, and vicar of Christ. Pope Paul did not think this was the message he wanted to send to the people of the world.

Pope Paul VI realized that Jesus had spoken of a different type of power. Jesus had washed the disciple's feet and commanded them to be servants of others. If the pope was truly the *Servant of the Servants of God,* as the pope was traditionally called, then these symbols of worldly power would have to go.

Pope Paul VI gave the papal crown to charity so that it could be used to raise money for the poor. In its place, the pope wore the miter of a bishop. He seldom wore silk and velvet robes. He preferred a simple cassock—the traditional garment of a parish priest.

In 1965, Paul VI became the first pope to visit the United States. Speaking to the United Nations, the pope stood before the delegates as "a humble man, your brother," not as a worldly ruler or as a person of power. He said, "I long to serve you with humility and love."

SIGNS OF POWER

Pope Paul VI rejected the worldly signs of papal power to emphasize the signs of service. Draw a sign that shows the importance of service

WHAT KIND OF KING?

We had been out in the countryside with Jesus praying when he asked us the question. Of course, he was always asking us questions. It was part of how he taught. Sometimes he would joke with us, tease us about how slow we were to understand. But we could tell right away this question was serious.

"Who do the people say that I am?" he asked.

We scrambled for answers, remembering what we'd heard whispered in towns and villages.

"Some say you are John the Baptist, somehow back from the dead," we said, "or Elijah, come back to announce the kingdom, or some other prophet who has risen in our midst."

Jesus listened to all we said without making any move in response. After a few minutes of stony silence, Jesus looked at each of us and asked, "But who do *you* say that I am?"

Only Peter had the boldness to answer, "You are the Messiah of God."

TO RULE WITH HIM

We did believe that Jesus was the Messiah, but we scarcely had any idea of what that meant. I'm ashamed to say that right up to the end, we argued over foolish things, like what our rewards would be in his kingdom.

One very hot afternoon, when the stones in the road seemed sharper than usual, we began talking about what we would do once we gained power.

"When I'm governor of Galilee," I said grandly, "I'll pave all these roads with smooth stones. And I won't have to worry, because I'll be riding a horse!"

"You'll be lucky to be holding the governor's horses, Philip!" snorted Simon the Zealot. "Jesus will never choose you to rule with him."

"At least I speak Greek," I countered. "He'll need someone who can order the Gentiles around."

Simon spat in the dust. "Your Greek will do you no good when God casts all the Gentiles out of the kingdom!" he shouted. "Only faithful Jews like me will rule with the Messiah!"

Soon, we were all at it, each one claiming a higher office than the next. All, that is, but Jesus himself. He walked on ahead, not seeming to have heard anything we said. But when we reached the town, he asked, "What were you arguing about on the way?"

No one had the courage to answer.

FOLLOWING Jesus

Humble people recognize that they should give credit to God for all they accomplish. Jesus spoke often about the importance of being humble. Read *Luke 18:9–14* and act out or retell this story as it might happen today.

BE LAST TO BE FIRST

When we entered the house where we would be staying, a crowd had already gathered to hear Jesus speak. With all the commotion, none of us noticed a little child wedged into the corner, frightened by all these strangers.

Jesus went to her immediately. Gently, he took her into his arms. She was a tiny thing with big, solemn eyes.

Speaking to the crowd, but looking at us, Jesus said, "Whoever welcomes a little child like this one in my name, welcomes me. Whoever wishes to be first in the kingdom must be the last of all and the servant of all."

These shocking words really made me think. Jesus was comparing himself to a completely powerless person. He was explaining that his kingdom is not about commanding armies, or ordering people around, or having one's own way. He was saying that the greatest person in the kingdom is the one who is a servant to all.

I knew he was talking to us, but it took a long time before I understood what he meant. Not until after Jesus had given up his life did I see that the one who stands highest in God's kingdom is the one who is humble, the one who willingly sacrifices for the benefit of others.

Adapted from LUKE 9:46–48

MAKING CONNECTIONS

Read the following passages from Scripture: Matthew 5:41, Matthew 21:28–32, Luke 16:19–31, Luke 17:7–10, and Luke 18:18–30. Based upon what you have read, describe how a follower of Jesus can be a servant today.

Be Humble

Jesus spoke often on the need for his disciples to be humble. On numerous occasions he finished a parable with the phrase, "The first will be last and the last will be first."

After watching people choose their seats at a banquet, Jesus told them a fact of life: If you choose the place of honor, you will be embarrassed when you are asked to move to a less important spot. If you sit at the less important spot to begin with, you will be pleased when you are called to take a seat of honor. "For everyone who exalts himself will be humbled, but the one who humbles himself will be exalted" (*Luke 14:8–11*).

Not all of Jesus' lessons in humility were reserved to table etiquette. "Strive to enter through the narrow gate," Jesus said (*Luke 13:24*). By this, Jesus meant that claiming to be a Christian doesn't make you better than anyone else. Your words have to be backed up by your actions. As Saint Augustine later advised the Christians of North Africa, "Work as if all things depend on you. Pray as if all things depend on God." This is a sign of humility.

PEOPLE OF SERVICE

All Christians make a commitment to serve others in their baptismal covenant. For that reason, service is not an option. The question for a Christian is not "Should I serve others?" but "How should I serve others?"

There are millions of ways that you can serve others. No matter what life you choose or job you do, you can treat other people with honesty, dignity, and respect. You can choose a career in a caring profession where serving others is part of your daily work. What are some examples of professions that provide direct care for others?

You can serve others through marriage or the single life. Parents make sacrifices for their children regularly to provide them with food, shelter, and knowledge of a loving God. The couple serves each other as signs of Christ present in the world. Many people choose the single life to care for sick or elderly parents.

You can also serve others through the sacrament of Holy Orders or by choosing religious life. Bishops, priests, deacons, sisters, and brothers have dedicated themselves to lives of service for the Christian community. Through their personal sacrifice, people are cared for, children are taught, the sick are nursed to health, the poor are empowered, and the sacraments are celebrated.

A Personal Pledge

In the space provided, write a personal pledge to live up to your baptismal commitment of service to others.

THE LITTLE WAY

There was no doubt about it—Thérèse Martin was a pampered little girl. The youngest of five sisters in a loving French family, Thérèse was called "Baby" by her mother, "brat" by her nursemaid, and the "little queen" by her father. Though often ill, Thérèse had a very strong will. She would throw hour-long temper tantrums if she didn't get her way.

Thérèse's mother once attempted to joke her out of her high-and-mighty ways. "I'll give you a half-penny if you kiss the ground," her mother teased.

Three-year-old Thérèse thought a moment. A halfpenny would buy a great deal of candy, and the ground wasn't so far away. But then she shook her head firmly. "No, thank you, Mama. Queens do not kiss the ground."

I WANT IT ALL

There was another side to Thérèse, however—an unexpected side. She loved and imitated her older sisters, and even as a child she had a great love for Jesus. Thérèse always imagined Jesus as a child like herself. In the little queen's imaginary kingdom, Jesus was the king.

Thérèse also had a great love for life and joy in simple things. When her older sister Leonie offered Thérèse and another sister, Celine, their choice from a basket of old playthings, Celine chose a ball. Thérèse threw her arms around the whole basket. "I choose it all!" she declared.

Later, Thérèse would say that this choice set the pattern for her life. She chose to accept wholeheartedly everything God sent her way—both joys and sorrows.

DARK TIMES

When Thérèse was only four years old, her beloved Mama died. Suddenly, the playful, pampered child became timid and quiet. Her life became even more difficult when Thérèse's two oldest sisters, whom she looked on as other mamas, decided to become Carmelite nuns. The Carmelites are a cloistered order, who live lives of quiet, hidden prayer.

After recovering from a terrible mental and physical illness when she was a young teen, Thérèse decided that Jesus was calling her to become a Carmelite, too. At first, her family and the Carmelite superiors doubted her vocation. She was so young—only fourteen. And how could this pampered little child ever live a life of poverty, chastity, and obedience? Stubborn as ever, Thérèse set out to convince them all.

A SHORTCUT

Thérèse entered the Carmelite convent at the age of fifteen, after receiving the approval of the pope. Joining the Carmelites didn't change Thérèse, however. She still wanted things done her way.

Thérèse had difficulty adjusting to many of the convent routines. She found repetitive prayer boring and often fell asleep in the chapel. She had to remind herself over and over that she no longer owned anything. Even the pens and the ink she used to write in her spiritual journal belonged to the community. And she had a terrible time with charity, especially with imperfect people whose little failings most annoyed her. Gritting her teeth, Thérèse forced herself to show the greatest kindest to those who annoyed her the most.

Having read the lives of the saints, Thérèse wanted to follow their example. But how could she possibly do great deeds in the convent laundry room? For a person as stubborn as Thérèse, however, the little matter of living behind cloister walls could not stop her from achieving her goal.

Thérèse wrote in her journal, *"I decided to find a shortcut to heaven—like the elevators that rich people have in their houses. I will do every little thing as though it were a great deed. I will get to heaven by the little way."*

From being a pampered queen who expected everything to be done to please her, Thérèse dedicated her life to going out of her way to help others. She became like a little child, offering everything to Jesus as a child offers flowers to her mother.

Sister Thérèse of the Child Jesus died of tuberculosis at the age of twenty-four. Her spiritual journals, published after her death, are read around the world. Through her journals, Thérèse continues to inspire Christians to dedicate their whole lives, every little thing they do, to following Jesus.

1. **Why do you think humility was difficult for Thérèse?**
2. **Describe Saint Thérèse's "little way" to heaven.**
3. **What did Thérèse have in common with the little child that Jesus pointed out as an example of the "greatest in the kingdom"?**

My Little Way

You can follow the example of Saint Thérèse and show your love for Jesus simply by doing little things with great care. Make a list of five opportunities you have daily to show your love for others. Next to each item on your list, name one thing you can do to show your love for Jesus through this action.

Opportunities	My Response
1.	1.
2.	2.
3.	3.
4.	4.
5.	5.

HUMBLE SERVICE

In her "little way," Saint Thérèse taught that your attitude and action have to work together. It's not enough just to do things—you must also do them joyfully, seeing even the worst job as a chance to serve God. Look at the following words. Describe a situation where you have demonstrated your love for God in this way.

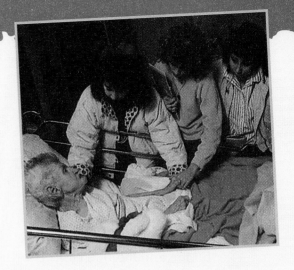

Humility _____

Respect _____

Generosity _____

Kindness _____

Sacrifice _____

Compassion _____

Concern for Others _____

GOOD AND FAITHFUL SERVANTS

We stand before you, Holy Spirit, conscious of our sinfulness, but aware that we gather in your name. Come to us, remain with us, and enliven our hearts. Give us light and strength to know your will, to make it our own, and to live it in our lives. Guide us by your wisdom, support us by your power, for you are God, sharing in the glory of the Father and the Son.

You desire justice for all: enable us to uphold the rights of others; do not allow us to be misled by ignorance or corrupted by fear or favor. As we gather in your name, may we temper justice with love, so that all our decisions may be pleasing to you, and earn the reward promised to good and faithful servants. Amen!

SAINT ISIDORE OF SEVILLE, SIXTH CENTURY

WITH YOUR FAMILY

Look for opportunities to do little acts of loving kindness for members of your family. Be especially kind to the one person with whom you have the most disagreements. Don't expect to be rewarded for anything you do. Let your acts of kindness be their own rewards.

▼REVIEW CHAPTER 20

CATHOLICS BELIEVE

1. Jesus told his followers to be servants to all.
2. Jesus told his followers to act with humility.
3. You can follow Jesus by doing little things with love and concern.

KNOW

Read the following quotations. For each, explain how you would apply the quotation to a specific situation.

QUOTATION	APPLICATION
"The first will be last and the last will be first." **Matthew 20:16**	
"For everyone who exalts himself will be humbled, but the one who humbles himself will be exalted." **Matthew 23:12**	
"Strive to enter through the narrow gate." **Matthew 7:13**	
"Work as if all things depend on you. Pray as if all things depend on God." **Saint Augustine**	
"I will do every little thing as though it were a great deed. I will get to heaven by the little way." **Saint Thérèse**	

SUNDAY MASS

At the conclusion of the Mass, the priest says, "Go in peace to love and serve the Lord." Think of one way that you can serve Jesus better during this coming week. In prayer, ask Jesus to help you to serve him better.

JESUS IS PRESENT

If you look closely, you can see Jesus present in the lives of the many people who follow him. Study each work of art and study its caption. Then under each photo, write a caption to explain how Jesus can be seen today in the work of his followers.

Roselli, *Sermon on the Mount.* 15th century.

Wherever Jesus went, crowds flocked to receive his healing touch. His compassion never failed.

In times of crisis, Jesus asked, "Where is your faith?" (Luke 8:22–25)

David, *The Marriage at Cana.* 15th century.

Jesus rejoiced in his Father's love.

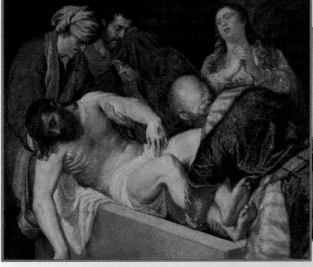

Titian, *Entombment of Christ.* 16th century.

Jesus goes before us in every human experience—even into death.

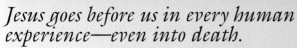

Where You See Jesus

Create a piece of art—a collage, mural, poster, or banner—
showing modern day examples of people following Jesus. Share
and explain your work.

LEARNING

1. Why do people pray before images?
Visual images help people express their devotion to Jesus and the saints and feel close to them.

2. How are Jesus' disciples called to live?
Disciples of Jesus are called to be faithful witnesses to the Gospel in life and in death.

3. What message did Jesus teach his disciples about justice?
Jesus taught his disciples that they should treat everyone as their neighbor, showing people the dignity and respect they deserve.

4. What did Jesus teach his disciples about serving others?
Jesus taught his disciples to be humble servants. Jesus taught this by washing the disciples feet and by telling them that the "first shall be last, the last shall be first."

LIVING

Choose one of the following projects to do on your own, with a partner, or as a class.

• Prepare and deliver a report on one of the following people: Saint John of Damascus, Dorothy Day, Pope Paul VI, Sister Ita Ford, Leo Tolstoy, or Saint Thérèse. Show how the person you chose is an icon of Jesus.

• Use any art form you like to create an image of Jesus. Let your image reflect what you believe and how you feel about Jesus.

• Plan or participate in an activity that fosters respect and problem-solving skills. Prepare a report about your experiences.

ASKING

1. When was the last time I served someone?
2. What can I do this week to witness my faith in Christ more fully?

PRAYING

All: In you, O Lord, we trust!

Group 1: Here is my servant whom I uphold, my chosen one with whom I am pleased, upon whom I have put my spirit.

Group 2: He shall bring forth justice of the nations, not crying out, not shouting, until he establishes justice on the earth.

All: In you, O Lord, we trust!

Group 3: Thus says the Lord, who gives breath to the earth's people, and spirit to those who walk the earth.

Group 4: I, the Lord, have called you for the victory of justice, I have grasped you by the hand!

All: In you, O Lord, we trust!

Group 5: I formed you, and set you as a covenant of the people, a light for the nation.

Group 6: To open the eyes of the blind, to bring out prisoners from confinement, and from the dungeons, those who dwell in darkess.

All: In you, O Lord, we trust!

Based on ISAIAH 42:1–7

Jesus, the Life

So faith, hope, love remain, these three; but the greatest of these is love.

1 CORINTHIANS 13:13

21

LOOKING TO THE FUTURE

Then I saw a new heaven and a new earth.

REVELATION 21:1

CONTENT KEYS

1. Only God knows what will happen in the future.
2. Jesus told his followers to be prepared at all times.
3. Christians look to the future in faith, hope, and love.

AT THE MOVIES

Many people enjoy scary movies. Among the most popular forms of the scary movie is the "Great Disaster." Some great danger—tornado, meteor, fire, disease, or alien invasion—threatens to destroy the whole earth. Look at the movie ad. Talk about your reaction to disaster movies.

COLOSSUS CINEMA
PRESENTS
AN EPIC MOTION PICTURE

Never before in the history of motion pictures has a spectacle of such dimensions been brought to the screen.

SEE   The earth ravaged by terrible earthquakes, tornadoes, and hurricanes.

SEE   Hideous monsters threaten the earth.
Only one man, a man on a mission, can defeat the forces of evil. If he fails, the earth is doomed!

YOUR TURN

Use this space to write or draw your vision of the future.

THE FUTURE IS NOW

Concerns about the future of the world are not new. People have always worried about what lies ahead for them and their children. Often their hopes and fears have been expressed through art and stories. They've searched for answers to their concerns in faith.

The poster on the previous page for the movie Final Judgment—inspired by the prophecy of the Book of Daniel, chapter 7—is an example of a faith response to concerns and fears about the future. The Book of Daniel, which is part of the Hebrew Scriptures, was written at least 2,100 years ago.

You would be mistaken, however, if you read the Book of Daniel looking for clues to when the world would end. Although the Book of Daniel seems to predict the end of the world, it is actually an example of **apocalypse.** The writer of the Book of Daniel was not interested in predicting the future. This unknown writer was offering confidence and hope to Jews who were being persecuted for their faith.

Apocalyptic writing is a kind of code. If you and your friends send coded messages, no one else will be able to understand you unless he or she knows the code you are using. That's what can make apocalyptic writing so interesting: you have to know the code in order to really understand it.

The Jewish readers of the Book of Daniel in 125 B.C.—about the time the book was actually written—knew the code, but their Greek oppressors did not. The Jews understood that the message was about the present, not the past or the future. Through Daniel's visions, they were reminded that God had promised to protect them. If they remained faithful, God would come to their rescue. The rabbis and scholars used this literary form to communicate God's message of trust and faithfulness to people in desperate need of encouragement.

THE CHRISTIAN APOCALYPSE

The Christian Scriptures contain one book of apocalyptic writing, the Book of Revelation. Revelation was written by a man called John of Patmos. Although John identified himself with the Apostle John, they were not the same person. The Book of Revelation was written around the end of the first century to the Christian churches who were suffering under Roman persecution. The complex images and symbolism used by John do not predict the end of the world nor do they have modern parallels. They are a code that communicates a message of hope to Christian readers, while keeping the message hidden from the Romans. Although the Book of Revelation, like the Book of Daniel, was written for people living in a particular time and place, John's lesson of the triumph of good over evil is a valuable message for people living in any age.

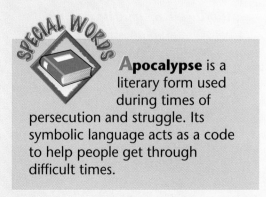

Apocalypse is a literary form used during times of persecution and struggle. Its symbolic language acts as a code to help people get through difficult times.

THE NEW JERUSALEM

The old man who called himself John was a prisoner on the rocky island of Patmos. Sentenced to exile and death in this abandoned place, he spent his days covering rolls of papyrus with spidery writing.

John's eyes were filled with visions. He saw battles raging in heaven between the forces of good and evil, with the stars and planets themselves joining in combat.

Then war broke out in heaven; Michael and his angels battled against the dragon. The dragon and its angels fought back, but they did not prevail.

REVELATION 12:7–8

The other prisoners thought of family and friends with longing or bitterness, but John's heart was with the Christians he had left behind, who were persecuted by the same Roman government that had condemned John to exile on Patmos. It was for them, his spiritual children, that John wrote, using splendid images to fire their hope and encourage their resistance to evil. He assured them that if they remained faithful to God, God would reward them.

I know your works, says the Lord. You have limited strength, and yet you have kept my word and have not denied my name. Because you have kept my message of endurance, I will keep you safe in the time of trial that is going to come to the whole world. I am coming quickly. Hold fast to what you have, so that no one may take your crown.

REVELATION 3:8,10–11

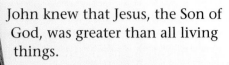

de Liebana, *Commentary on the Apocalypse.* 2nd century.

John knew that Jesus, the Son of God, was greater than all living things.

Do not be afraid. I am the first and the last, the One who lives. Once I was dead, but now I am alive forever and ever. I am the Alpha and the Omega, the first and the last, the beginning and the end.

REVELATION 1:17–18;22:13

While the other prisoners cursed their fate or wished they had never been born, John's heart was full of joy.

Then I saw a new heaven and a new earth. The former heaven and the former earth had passed away, and the sea was no more. I also saw the holy city, a new Jerusalem, coming down out of heaven from God. I heard a loud voice from the throne saying, "Behold, God will wipe every tear from their eyes, and there shall be no more death or mourning, wailing or pain, for the old order has passed away."

Adapted from REVELATION 21:1–4

God's Triumph

In the space, express your vision of God's triumph over evil. Use your faith and your imagination. Be as creative as you can.

WORDS OF WARNING

The followers of Jesus have a vision of the future that is not based on disaster movies. Their vision is based upon the life and teaching of Jesus. It is in Jesus that they trust.

Jesus' followers were very familiar with prophecies about the end of time, when God would judge the world. They asked Jesus, their teacher, for signs that the end was near. These teachings of Jesus are found in chapters 24 and 25 of the Gospel of Matthew. These passages teach three main ideas:

1. Only God knows the fate of the world.
2. You must be prepared at all times for God's coming.
3. You will be judged by how well you used your gifts and talents to serve others.

COMING IN GLORY

Christians believe that Jesus will return again in glory at the end of the world to judge the living and the dead. God's kingdom will not be fulfilled on earth until this final time. Until then, the Church and all of its members work to proclaim Jesus' message about the need for conversion, the forgiveness of sins, and the need to love God and neighbor unselfishly.

When Jesus returns in glory, he will reveal the good or evil in the heart of all people. Those who accepted God's grace and used it to follow Jesus in serving others will be welcomed into eternal life in heaven. Those who reject the salvation offered by Jesus will experience the punishment of eternal separation from God in hell.

Jesus referred to heaven as a wedding banquet, a mansion with many rooms, and paradise. He spoke of hell as a place where there will be much torment and fire. The greatest torment for people in hell is that they will be excluded for all times from God's love.

Those who die in God's grace and friendship are assured of eternal salvation. However, some people will not be ready to meet God immediately. They still need to be purified of their sins. The Church gives the name Purgatory to this final stage of purification. This is why Catholics pray for the dead, so that they might quickly enter the presence of God.

The early Christians expected Jesus to return again in their lifetime. Their prayer, *Maranatha* ("Come, Lord"), expresses this desire. (*Maranatha* is the last word in the Book of Revelation.) But as Jesus said, only the Father knows when the end will happen. So until that time, Christians watch, wait, and pray for the Lord's return.

1. **What do Catholics believe about the end of the world?**
2. **What do the words *heaven, hell,* and *purgatory* mean to you?**

KEYS TO CHRISTIAN LIFE

Jesus is the Alpha and the Omega—the first and last letters of the Greek alphabet—mentioned in the Revelation of John. Jesus is the beginning and end of all of life: the past, present, and future. All that was, is, and will be is in his hands.

Jesus knew that his message about the last days caused his disciples to worry about the future. At the Last Supper, Jesus spoke to their fears and told them not to worry. He would be with them always. He gave his friends—and, through them, the entire world—three keys for living as a Christian: faith, hope, and love.

Do not let your hearts be troubled. You have faith in God; have faith also in me. In my Father's house there are many dwelling places. I am going to prepare a place for you. I will come back again and take you to myself, so that where I am you also may be.

Adapted from JOHN 14:1–3

FAITH, HOPE, AND LOVE

Faith is the first key to the future. Through the eyes of faith, death—even death on a cross—is not the end. Faith looks at life as the road to the kingdom of God. When the time is right, Jesus will come back to bring you to that kingdom, the dwelling place he has prepared for you.

Jesus knew that even the strongest faith is tested and tempted, so he promised to send the Holy Spirit to comfort and lead his disciples. With this promise, Jesus gave his friends something else to look forward to: he gave them hope.

Amen, amen, I say to you, you will weep and mourn, while the world rejoices; you will grieve, but your grief becomes joy. When a woman is in labor, she is in anguish because her hour has arrived; but when she has given birth to a child, she no longer remembers the pain because of her joy that a child has been born into the world. So you are also now in anguish. But I will see you again, and your hearts will rejoice, and no one will take your joy away from you.

JOHN 16:20–22

Jesus reminded his friends that it is almost impossible to maintain faith and hope in the future all by oneself. Only by building strong ties of love and service to one another could the followers of Jesus face the trials that lay ahead.

If you love me, you will keep my commandments. If you love me, you will keep my word, and my Father will love you, and we will come to you and make our dwelling with you.

Catholics believe that God is in charge of life and will make all things new. They believe that they are working to build the kingdom of God. Make a commitment to try to give your best at everything you do. By dedicating your work to God, you are helping to build the kingdom.

Behold the hour is coming and has arrived when each of you will be scattered to your own home. But I am not alone, because the Father is with me. In the world you will have trouble, but take courage, I have conquered the world.

JOHN 14:15,23; 16:32–33

Love—the love of God, who is Father, Son, and Holy Spirit—is the final key to the future.

These three keys are known as the theological virtues. Through these gifts, poured into your heart by the Holy Spirit, you truly come to know God.

Jesus did not promise his followers that their way would be easy or that the future glory of God's kingdom would come without struggle. He suffered and died, showing that the way to resurrection was through suffering and death. He left behind the three keys of faith, hope, and love, so that all who followed him might succeed in their journey.

WORDS OF ENCOURAGEMENT

Design a poster that shows people acting with faith, hope, and love. Share your work with the class.

BEING PREPARED

Jesus told his followers to stay awake and watch carefully so that they might be prepared for his coming. In the chart below, list some choices or actions you face every day. For each, explain how the choice you make affects your future.

CHOICE OR ACTION	HOW IT AFFECTS MY FUTURE
You are offered drugs and alcohol.	
You are asked to visit the sick once a month.	
You are invited to join the parish youth group.	
You must choose between studying for an important test or watching TV.	
Your little sister needs someone to play with.	

THE LIFE OF THE WORLD TO COME

All: I will walk in the presence of the Lord in the land of the living.

Group 1: Gracious is the Lord and just; yes, our Lord is merciful. The Lord keeps the little ones; I was brought low, and he saved me. The Lord has freed my soul from death, my eyes from tears, my feet from stumbling. I shall walk before the Lord in the lands of the living.

All: I will walk in the presence of the Lord in the land of the living.

Group 2: How shall I make a return to the Lord for all the good God has done for me? The cup of salvation I will take up, and I will call upon the name of the Lord. Precious in the eyes of the Lord is the death of God's faithful ones.

All: I will walk in the presence of the Lord in the land of the living.

Based on PSALM 116

WITH YOUR FAMILY

Call a family meeting. At this meeting, discuss ways that your family can be prepared in case of emergencies: fire, earthquake, flood, and accidents. Write up your family plan and present it to the class.

▼REVIEW CHAPTER 21

CATHOLICS BELIEVE

1. Only God knows the fate of the world.
2. Jesus will come again to judge the living and the dead.
3. The theological virtues—faith, hope, and love—help Christians live for the present and the future.

KNOW

1. What is apocalyptic writing? What are two examples of this form of writing? _____

_____

2. Who is the author of the Book of Revelation? What is the message of this book? _____

3. What message did Jesus give his disciples about the end time?

_____

4. What will take place at the final judgment? _____

_____

5. What are the theological virtues? What is the purpose of these virtues? _____

SUNDAY MASS

The Sunday Mass brings together the past, present, and future. From the past it remembers Jesus' life, death, and resurrection. In the present, you join with the community of believers to celebrate God's love for you. The future is revealed in the glory that is Christ received in the Eucharist. During the Memorial Acclamation the Church acknowledges this mystery of faith when it prays, "Christ has died, Christ has risen, Christ will come again."

22

For we walk by faith, not by sight.

2 CORINTHIANS 5:7

HAVE FAITH

Peter was half asleep, thinking about Jesus. He and the other disciples were sailing across the Sea of Galilee. Jesus had promised to meet them on the other side. Peter didn't know how Jesus planned to get there or when he would arrive.

Very early in the morning, the winds grew strong. Peter's fishing boat began to toss violently about on the waves. Being experienced fishermen, Peter and the disciples jumped up and started to prepare the boat for the storm.

When the lookout called, everyone paid attention to where he pointed. How was it possible? Here was Jesus walking across the tossing water as if he were on flat ground! The disciples were frightened by what they saw. They must be seeing a ghost.

Sensing their fear, Jesus called to them, "Take courage, it is I. Do not be afraid."

Peter, still not quite sure, called "Lord, if it is you, command me to come to you on the water."

Jesus gave the order, "Come."

Peter was overcome with confidence. Putting aside all of his fears, Peter stepped bravely onto the water. One step. Two steps. Peter walked across the water focusing on nothing but Jesus. Amazed by what he was doing Peter thought, "I'm walking on water." That one little thought broke Peter's concentration. Now he felt the power of the wind and the strength of the waves. He became afraid and started to sink.

"Lord, save me," Peter cried.

Jesus reached out his hand and saved him, saying "Oh, you of little faith. Why did you doubt?"

Based on MATTHEW 14:22–33

von Kulmbach, *Saint Peter Walking on the Water.*

WALKING ON WATER

Describe a time when you accomplished something you never thought possible. What gave you the confidence you needed to succeed?

FAITHFUL PIERRE

With great ceremony, the bones of an African American man, a former slave, were removed from a grave in lower Manhattan and ceremoniously entombed in a crypt under the chapel altar of New York's Saint Patrick's Cathedral. The plaque on the new tomb reads simply, "Pierre Toussaint, Servant of God."

It was an ironic homecoming for the former slave who had once been turned away from a New York Catholic church—a church whose building fund he had directed—because of racial discrimination.

Pierre Toussaint was born into a life of slavery in 1766 on the island of Saint Dominique in what is now the country of Haiti. The slaveowners of Haiti were French Catholics, and Pierre was baptized as a child. (In English, his name would be "Peter All Saints.")

The Berard family, who owned Pierre, treated him fairly, as far as slaveholders went. He was allowed to be educated and joined the family for Mass in their chapel. He also traveled with the Berards to the United States to live in New York when rumors of a slave uprising threatened Haiti.

THE MAN WHO HELPED

In New York, young Pierre was apprenticed to a hairdresser. This was a time when wealthy women wore their hair in elaborate styles that sometimes took hours to prepare. Pierre soon became a popular stylist. Black and Catholic in a city that was prejudiced against both, Pierre was welcomed eagerly into the homes of the rich and powerful. Along with his combs and curling irons, Pierre brought faith. He shared his beliefs simply and eloquently and did much to overcome anti-Catholic sentiment among the people he met.

Pierre was faithful to people, too. When Mr. Berard died, and the family plantation in Haiti was destroyed by revolution, Pierre supported his owners with his earnings.

Pierre's charity extended to everyone he met—black or white, rich or poor—and many people he never met—orphans, French families impoverished by the revolution, a whole community of black Catholic sisters in Baltimore whose work he supported.

The rich women of New York trusted Pierre as a good listener and a man of common sense. He took their troubles as his own and did what he could to help them with their problems.

Meucci, Pierre Toussaint (detail). 19th century.

Pierre Toussaint was named Venerable *by Pope John Paul II in December 1996.*

As God Sends It

Pierre was a familiar figure on the streets of New York. He attended Mass each morning at Saint Peter's Church (from whose new building he would later be turned away) and then went about his work. When diseases like cholera spread through the tenements of New York, Pierre risked his own safety to help nurse the sick and bury the dead. His rooms in the attic of the Berard home became a center for all those in need of jobs, education, money, or shelter, no matter who they were.

Pierre was a man of great faith. He lived his life confident in the promises of Jesus. Because of his faith, Pierre brought the love of God to a life many people would find impossible.

Although he could have bought his freedom with the money he made, Pierre chose to care for his owner, Mrs. Berard, until her death. A free man at age 41, Pierre finally married. Unable to have children of their own, they adopted Pierre's niece, Euphemia, who they loved dearly. When she died of tuberculosis at a young age, Pierre and his wife were devastated. But instead of growing angry or bitter over the terrible things that happened to him, Pierre gained even more confidence in God.

Pierre Toussaint's life of faithful service and generosity would be remarkable in any age or place, but it was doubly amazing that he was able to accomplish what he did in the early years of the United States. In spite of slavery, prejudice, and disappointment, Pierre kept faith. More than that, he inspired faith in others.

1. **In what ways did Pierre Toussaint show his faith in God?**
2. **How can having confidence in God help you to live like Pierre Toussaint?**

Faithful People

Pierre shared his faith in God with others through his generosity and kindness. Describe a person in your life who helps your faith in God grow stronger.

THE MUSTARD SEED

Jesus had complete faith in God. Jesus' friends had seen this faith firsthand. They had watched Jesus heal and forgive people of their sins. They heard Jesus praise those who trusted in him. They had been at his side when he taught about the power of faith using parables and ordinary images.

Even after all they had seen and heard, the disciples still had trouble understanding just what Jesus meant by faith. Some even thought of faith as a substance that could be measured out or earned. "Lord," they said. "Increase our faith."

Jesus just looked at them and shook his head. Pinching his thumb and forefinger together, as if holding something very tiny, Jesus said to them,

If you had faith the size of a tiny mustard seed, you would say to this mulberry tree, "Be uprooted and planted in the sea," and it would obey you.

Based on LUKE 17:5–6

Jesus was telling his friends that it is not the size of a person's faith that matters, for faith cannot be measured. Rather, a person who has faith can accomplish much more than he or she ever could alone.

The word *faith* means to have trust, belief, or confidence in someone or something. It can also mean accepting a set of teachings as true. When Jesus spoke of faith, he meant having total trust in God.

Faith is a gift from God; it cannot be earned. Through faith, you are able to believe in and commit yourself to God. You can also grow stronger in faith through prayer, reading the Scriptures, and acting for the benefit of others.

Jesus did not provide a definition for the word *faith.* He used stories, parables, and comparisons to show what it means to have faith.

Having Ears to Hear

Jesus told stories to get his message across, and he would often end his stories with the words, "Whoever has ears ought to hear." These words suggested that there is a lesson here to be learned for those who are open to learning. What can you learn from the following stories about faith?

Everyone who listens to these words of mine and acts on them will be like a wise man who built his house on rock. The rain fell, the floods came, and the winds blew and buffeted the house. But it did not collapse; it had been set solidly on rock. And everyone who listens to these words of mine but does not act on them will be like a fool who built his house on sand. The rain fell, the floods came, and the winds blew and buffeted the house. And it collapsed and was completely ruined.

MATTHEW 7:24–27

ON GOOD GROUND

Jesus told a parable about a man sowing seed. Some of the seed fell on a path and birds ate it. Some of the seed fell on rocky ground. The seed sprouted quickly, but because the soil was not deep, the plants soon died in the heat. Some of the seed fell among thorns. The thorns choked it. But some of the seed fell on rich soil and produced great fruit.

Jesus explained this parable in this way:

The seed sown on the path is the one who hears the word of the kingdom without understanding it, and the evil one comes and steals away what was sown in his heart. The seed sown on rocky ground is the one who hears the word and receives it at once with joy. But he has no root and lasts only for a time. When some tribulation or persecution comes because of the word, he immediately falls away. The seed sown among thorns is the one who hears the word, but then worldly anxiety and the lure of riches choke the word and it bears no fruit. But the seed sown on rich soil is the one who hears the word and understands it, who indeed bears fruit.

MATTHEW 13:18–28

A MODERN PARABLE

With a partner, write a modern-day parable about the meaning of faith. Be prepared to share what you have written.

MARY'S FAITH

The Church honors Jesus' mother, Mary, as the model of faith. The Mother of God had moments of doubt and trouble, but she never lost her confidence in God. In Mary, the seed of faith fell on rich ground. She nurtured it and it bore great fruit.

Mary's total trust in God can be a model for you to imitate. Though the circumstances may be different, you can choose to say yes to God as Mary did.

- *When you make important choices.* Mary was asked to be the Mother of the Redeemer. She didn't hesitate to trust God with her whole future (*Luke 1:38*). How has faith helped you to make an important decision? _____

_____

- *When life doesn't go the way you planned.* After the panic of losing Jesus in Jerusalem and the joy of finding him again, Mary was confused by Jesus' words. Luke 2:51 says she "kept all these things in her heart." When have you been helped by your faith to demonstrate patience?

_____

_____

Just as physical exercise makes your muscles stronger, so spiritual exercise strengthens your faith. Choose one of these spiritual exercises to do each day for the next week: pray, read Scripture, read about a saint, or fast from treats in order to share your money with the poor.

- *When there doesn't seem to be a solution.* The host ran out of wine at the wedding party in Cana. Mary wanted to do something to ease the hosts' embarrassment. At first, Jesus refused her request to help. But Mary persisted, and Jesus worked his first public miracle (*John 2:1–11*). Tell of a time when your faith in God helped you persevere even when you had doubts. _____

_____

- *When everyone else gave up.* Mary, among a handful of others, stood at the foot of the cross as her son died in agony. She did not abandon him, and she welcomed his friends as her own children (*John 19:25–27*). Tell of a time when your faith helped you to accept God's will when it was different from what you wanted. _____

_____

Mantegna, *The Crucifixion*. 15th century.

1. What is the meaning of the word *faith*?
2. How did Jesus reveal his faith in God?
3. What does the Church mean when it calls Mary a model of faith?

KEEPING FAITH

Faith means believing in God, living as if tomorrow matters, and treating yourself, other people, and your world with love and respect. For each of the following questions, explain how you could put your faith into action.

1. A person you don't like very much gets a math problem wrong on the board.

2. You are asked to wash the dishes when you had planned to watch your favorite TV program.

3. You need ten more dollars to buy a video game. You know where your mother keeps her household money.

WITH YOUR FAMILY

Pierre Toussaint received his Catholic faith from slaveowners. Share Pierre Toussaint's story with your family. Ask an adult member of your family to tell you about a person they know who has demonstrated strong faith. Be prepared to share your findings with your classmates.

PSALMS OF FAITH

The psalms are songs of faith. These prayers, known and sung by Jesus and a part of the Church's liturgical heritage, celebrate the many moods of faith: questioning, joyful, shaken, repentant, thankful.

You can make the psalms your prayers of faith, too. Use a verse as a meditation-starter, or read the whole psalm.

When I lie down in sleep, I awake again, for the Lord sustains me.

Psalm 3:6

How long, O Lord, will you utterly forget me? How long will you hide your face from me?

Psalm 13:2

Even though I walk in the dark valley I fear no evil; for you are at my side.

Psalm 23:4

In you, O Lord, I take refuge. Into your hands I commend my spirit; You will redeem me, O Lord, O faithful God.

Psalm 31:2,5

A clean heart create in me, O God, and a steadfast spirit renew within me.

Psalm 51:12

▼ REVIEW CHAPTER 22 · · · · · · · · · · · · · · ·

CATHOLICS BELIEVE

1. Having faith means trusting in God.
2. Jesus used stories to teach about faith.
3. Mary is the model of faith.

KNOW

1. How was Peter's walking on the water an act of faith? What caused Peter to sink? _____

_____

2. How was faith a source of strength for Pierre Toussaint in difficult times? _____

_____

3. How did Jesus teach about faith? Use one example in your answer.

_____

_____

4. What does it mean to have faith? _____

_____

5. Explain why Mary is considered a model of faith. _____

_____

6. What are three ways in which you can show your faith in God?

_____

_____

SUNDAY MASS

At every Mass, Jesus' death and resurrection is remembered in the Eucharist. Each time that you receive the Eucharist, you express your own faith in God. Think about your commitment to God this Sunday. What can you do to strengthen this commitment?

GROWING IN HOPE

CONTENT KEYS

1. **Hope is a gift from God.**
2. **Jesus is the source of Christian hope.**
3. **Christians are called to share hope with others.**

Hold fast to the hope that lies before us.

HEBREWS 6:18

A SIGN OF HOPE

My family has been farming this same rich black Iowa soil for over one hundred years. My mother's great-grandparents Jan and Analise settled this land, breaking through the thick prairie grass sod with a plow pulled by two oxen. Newly immigrated from Holland, they came to America to fulfill a dream. They wanted a bright future for their children. They knew that life would be difficult as they made a new home, but they believed that, with God's blessing, they would succeed.

Farming is never easy. All spring you plow and till the fields until the weather is right for planting. All summer long you weed, cultivate, and irrigate the fields, praying each night for rain, but not too much rain. When the weather is right, the crop is bountiful and the harvests are joyful celebrations. When the weather fails, so do the crops. Those harvests are sad times, as farmers wonder if they can hang on for one more year.

Although I'm only thirteen, I know that I will be a farmer like my parents before me. I will plant the seed and tend it. I will celebrate in joy when the first green stalks push out of the ground. And I will give thanks to God, because for another year, God's promise is fulfilled. I am a farmer. I am a person of hope.

ANOTHER SEASON'S PROMISE

CONSIDER YOUR OWN LIFE. WHERE DO YOU SEE SIGNS OF HOPE?

HOPE IN JESUS

Six months after Jesus' crucifixion, people all over Judea were still stunned by what had happened. Many people were disappointed. They had hoped that Jesus was the Messiah who would overthrow Roman rule. Their hopes had been crushed by the cruelty of Roman justice. Jesus' death meant that they had been deceived once more.

Not everyone had lost hope at Jesus' death because not everyone had expected an earthly kingdom. As news of Jesus' resurrection spread among his disciples, their hope grew and flourished. They began to share their hope in the resurrection with their friends. Not everyone was open to this message. Although they had been friends for a long time, Zachary was having trouble convincing Joshua to believe in the resurrection.

HOPE IN DEATH?

"Hope?" Joshua asked Zachary. "How can you talk about hope? Give up. He's dead. That's it. Forget him and get on with your life."

Zachary shook his head. "We've been friends for a long time, Joshua. You've given me good advice in the past. But you're wrong about this. You're talking about something you don't understand."

"Don't tell me that, Zach. I know all about Jesus. I saw him, remember? I heard him preach. I witnessed his healings. He was a great man. But he was crucified. You saw it. He's dead. It's over."

Zachary stopped walking and laid a hand on his friend's shoulder. He spoke softly, but his voice was firm. "I don't expect you to understand, Joshua. At least, not yet. But I tell you this—and I'll tell you again and again until the day I die: Jesus lives. He is the Messiah. God's reign is now."

Joshua snorted. "You're spending too much time with those disciples of his. Their craziness is rubbing off on you!"

Zachary took a deep breath. "If they're crazy, Joshua, it's a craziness the world needs. Jesus' followers are filled with joy. And hope—yes, Joshua, hope. And love. They take care of one another. No one among them goes hungry. No one suffers without being comforted. They pray and break bread together. These are good people, Joshua, the best."

"They may be good people, but they're not reasonable. Already they're in trouble with the authorities. To continue associating with them is to put yourself and your family in danger. And for what?"

"For truth, Joshua."

"Truth?"

"Jesus promised new life through baptism. I was baptized and now I have new life. Jesus promised his Spirit. I have that, too. His Spirit is within me. Jesus promised God's love and forgiveness and I feel loved and forgiven. Come with me, Joshua. Meet the people who knew him. Hear what they have to say."

A NEW LIFE

Joshua hesitated at Zachary's argument. What was it that made Zachary so willing to believe in a man who had died? How could he be so hopeful in a situation that offered so little possibility? "I don't understand, Zach," Joshua said at last.

Zachary responded, "If you knew what I have, Joshua, you'd want it, too. Jesus offered us a new life in God. Because of that new life, I don't worry any more about the Romans. Someday their rule will be over. They'll be gone. They will not be able to defeat God's promise. Think of those who are ill or crippled. I believe that they'll be whole one day. Because of Jesus, I have hope that those who sorrow will one day laugh and those who die will live again."

Joshua stood speechless in the road, silenced by his friend's passion. Zachary waited patiently for him to speak. "It's a beautiful vision, Zach," Joshua said at last.

Zach answered, "I can't make you believe it, but if you can open your heart—even a crack—to the Spirit of Christ, you will believe. Come with me, Joshua. Meet Jesus' disciples. Talk to them. Pray with us."

Joshua hesitated. Again, Zachary allowed his friend time to think.

"All right," Joshua said after a pause. "I'll do it for you. For our friendship." Zachary smiled. "Do it for hope," he said.

WHY FOLLOW JESUS?

Zachary's hope in the promises of Jesus led Joshua to faith. In this space, offer two reasons for having hope in Jesus.

THERE'S HOPE

The ancient Greeks, who believed in many gods, had a myth about the origin of hope. The first human being created by the gods was a woman named Pandora, whose name means "all gifts." The gods gave Pandora all of the wonderful things of the Earth, but they locked all evil things away in a box and warned Pandora not to open it.

If someone gave you a present and told you not to open it, would you be able to overcome the temptation? Pandora couldn't. Out of the opened box flew a black cloud of evil—war and sickness, poverty, hatred, and death. But the gods had not left Pandora—or humanity—defenseless against evil. At the bottom of the box Pandora found the gift of hope.

This myth is a poetic way of saying that no matter how bad things are, the gift of hope will help humanity overcome their problems. Christians also believe in the importance of hope, but they know that the source of this great gift is the One God and Father of Jesus Christ.

Like a stubborn plant that grows up through a snowbank or a cracked cement sidewalk, hope is almost unstoppable. As the proverb says, "Where there's life, there's hope."

Christian hope is rooted in faith in God, the reason for hope. Hope provides you a stable tether when you are buffeted by waves of fear and despair. That's why an anchor is the traditional sign of hope. Just as an anchor keeps a ship from drifting away at sea, Christian hope holds you fast to Christ.

Christian hope helps you overcome discouragement and persevere in difficult times. Because of hope, you can be generous with your time and treasure. Hope is expressed and nourished in prayer, especially in the Lord's Prayer, which expresses the goal of all hope.

A theological virtue, Christian hope looks beyond this world to the world of eternity with God, who is both the source and the fulfillment of hope.

For in hope we were saved. Now hope that sees for itself is not hope. For who hopes for what one sees? But if we hope for what we do not see, we wait with patient endurance.

ROMANS 8:24–25

1. **What is the importance of hope?**
2. **What is the source of hope for Christians?**

A FIRM ANCHOR

In the space provided, create your own sign of hope.

PEOPLE OF HOPE

Christians are living signs of hope. No matter how bad a situation may seem, they see that God's love is always there for them. Because of their belief in Jesus and their confidence in his promises, they can be generous with their time and treasure to help people in need. Look at some of the ways that Christians bring Christ's hope to others.

Generosity is a virtue that flows from hope. There are many ways that you can be generous. Offer your time to tutor another student or participate in a hunger walk. Offer your talents to lift others' spirits with art, comedy, or music. Offer your treasure by sharing your wealth with people in need.

At Chicago's Bonaventure House, the residents are accustomed to being thought of as "hopeless cases." They're poor. They were homeless. Many of them had been drug addicts or prostitutes. And now they are all living with AIDS. But at Bonaventure House, the Alexian Brothers, Franciscans, and other volunteers who live with and care for the residents see them as children of God. That's how God sees them, too.

With their lives ahead of them, children should be living signs of hope. They offer the full possibility of God's promise. Yet in cities and towns all over the world, children suffer from disease, poverty, homelessness, crime, violence, and sexual abuse. Salesian priests, religious and lay volunteers—dedicated like their founder, Saint John Bosco—work to welcome these children into loving homes.

HOPE BREEDS HOPE

In all of these situations, and thousands of others like them, people of hope are at work. But it's not only the priests and lay volunteers, or the nurses and counselors who share the gift of hope. Those they serve are people of hope, too.

- A man dying of AIDS gives his last few dollars to a volunteer to buy flowers for the funeral of a woman too new to the residence to have made any friends.
- A ten-year-old Colombian street child, whose own mother had sold her as a prostitute, carefully sews a bright new quilt for an abandoned toddler.
- A seventeen-year-old girl gives a childless couple the baby they long for.
- An aging cancer patient, his face lined with pain, always has a new joke to share with his nurses. Hope gives birth to hope.

1. **What are two of the biggest problems in your community? What could people of hope do to help resolve these problems?**
2. **What are three examples of people of hope at work in your parish or neighborhood?**
3. **How can you be a person of hope?**

At shelters like Saint Anne's home in Los Angeles, pregnant unwed teens are treated with love and respect. They receive the care they need to deliver healthy babies. They're encouraged to talk things through with family members. They're helped to consider the best options for themselves and their children, such as adoption. The people who work at Saint Anne's help young women choose hope—for themselves and their babies.

DID YOU KNOW?

Father James Keller, a Maryknoll priest and founder of the Christophers, was inspired by the Chinese proverb, "It is better to light one candle than to curse the darkness." Today the Christophers (whose name means "Christ-bearers") continue to light the candle of hope by witnessing to the Good News in their everyday activities.

Imagine that you are in prison, locked behind bars for more than a year. How do you feel? Thousands of young teenagers experience this feeling of fear and abandonment every day. Detention ministers volunteer to visit children in jails and juvenile halls. They listen to these young people, pray with them, and work with them to build a future and to break the hopeless cycle of imprisonment.

Words of Hope

When people are feeling down, sometimes all they need to feel better are words of hope. What words of hope would you offer in the following situations?

1. Your friend is feeling depressed about grades. Her mom and dad are upset about her poor performance. She has confided in you that she may run away from home rather than show her parents her latest report card.

   _____

2. Joey has a problem. The class bully is looking to beat him up. He seems to be very upset.

   _____

3. Fran's mom died last year of cancer. She was the one Fran always talked to when she felt bad. Now she feels all alone. Her dad's so busy, he doesn't have time to talk to her.

   _____

   _____

With Hope

Lord, help me to be a doer, not a talker.
Help me to say, "It can de done," not "It can't be done."
Help me to improve, not merely disapprove.
Help me to get into the thick of things, not just sit on the sidelines.
Help me to point out what's right with the world, not always what's wrong.
Help me to light candles, not blow them out.
Lord, fill my heart with hope that looks for good in people, with hope that discovers what can be done, with hope that pushes ahead, with hope that opens doors, with hope that carries on.
Amen!

Father James Keller, THE CHRISTOPHERS

WITH YOUR FAMILY

Pray the Christopher's prayer with members of your family. Discuss with your family things that you can do to be signs of hope for people in need.

▼ REVIEW CHAPTER 23 ....

CATHOLICS BELIEVE

1. Hope is a gift of God.
2. Christian hope is founded on the promises of Jesus.
3. Christians are called to be signs of hope to the whole world.

KNOW

Write two sentences explaining how each of the following is a sign of hope.

1. A farmer planting a field. _____

   _____

2. An anchor. _____

   _____

3. A sick, old man sharing money with a newborn baby. _____

   _____

4. The Resurrection. _____

   _____

5. Helping homeless people find a place to live. _____

   _____

6. Being a disciple. _____

   _____

SUNDAY MASS

In each of the Eucharistic prayers, the Church, as a sign of hope, prays that God will remember all of those who have died in Christ's peace. This Sunday, join your prayer with the Church for everyone in your family who has died. In your prayer, be sure to mention people by name.

CELEBRATING LOVE

CONTENT KEYS

1. Jesus described heaven as a banquet of love.
2. To prepare for the heavenly banquet, you must love others.
3. Love reaches its fullness in heaven.

God is love, and whoever remains in love, remains in God and God in them.

Based on 1 JOHN 4:16

SPEAKING OF LOVE

Paul knew that the Corinthians were an unruly bunch, but he loved them nonetheless. They took to Christianity with a passion not found in many other places Paul had been. But because of their passion, the Corinthians tended to do things to an extreme. Paul had heard from a friend that the Corinthian church was in danger of self-destructing, and so he wrote them about the meaning of love.

If I speak in human and angelic tongues, but do not have love, I am a resounding gong or a clashing cymbal. And if I have the gift of prophecy, and comprehend all mysteries and all knowledge; if I have all faith so as to move mountains, but do not have love, I am nothing. If I give away everything I own, and if I hand my body over so that I may boast, but do not have love, I gain nothing.

Love is patient, love is kind. It is not jealous, it is not pompous, it is not inflated, it is not rude, it does not seek its own interests, it is not quick-tempered, it does not brood over injury, it does not rejoice over wrongdoing but rejoices with the truth. It bears all things, believes all things, hopes all things, endures all things. Love never fails.

1 CORINTHIANS 13:1–8

THE BOOK OF LOVE

Using Saint Paul's description of the meaning of love, offer three examples that show what love is.

1.

2.

3.

I Am the Resurrection

"**I**t's time," Father Matt nodded. Joe took his mother's arm and went to stand with the rest of the family behind Grandpa's coffin.

At the doorway to the church, Father Matt sprinkled Grandpa's coffin with holy water as a sign of his Baptism. The white pall over the coffin was another baptismal sign, Joe knew—a reminder of the white garment Grandpa had worn when he was baptized as a baby.

Walking down the aisle behind the coffin, with his cousin Ted leading the way and carrying the cross, Joe nearly grinned at the thought of Grandpa as a baby. That strong, gruff man had never been little or helpless. But then a wave of sadness swept over Joe. Grandpa was gone!

EVEN IF HE DIES

Joe's mother held his hand tightly all through the first two Scripture readings. Joe tried to concentrate on the words, but all he could hear was his own voice on that last afternoon.

Grandpa and Joe had been in the front of the store, restocking shelves. Joe was a little bored and anxious to find out how the football game on TV was going. He missed much of what Grandpa had said.

"So there'll be some good years left in this business when you take it over," he heard Grandpa say.

"No way," Joe shouted louder than he meant to. "I'm going to college and getting a real job."

They went on working together. Grandpa didn't say anything, and Joe was too embarrassed to apologize. The next day, Grandpa died from a heart attack while working at the store. Now all Joe could remember was the look of hurt he had caused on his Grandpa's face by his remarks.

LOVE GOES ON

Father Matt got up to read the Gospel. It was about how Jesus had raised Lazarus, the brother of Martha and Mary, from the dead.

> *Jesus told Martha, "I am the resurrection and the life; whoever believes in me, even if he dies, will live, and everyone who lives and believes in me will never die. Do you believe this?"*
>
> JOHN 11:25–26

Joe listened to this reading very closely. "If only Jesus would bring Grandpa back for just one minute, so I could tell him I'm sorry!" Joe thought.

Through the rest of the funeral Mass, Joe prayed that God would welcome Grandpa into heaven. He prayed that his mother would have the strength to keep on going in her grief. And he prayed for Grandpa's forgiveness.

Friends and family gathered back at the house after the burial at the cemetery. Joe thought it was kind of neat that people needed to share food and be together in sad times as well as in happy ones.

Almost everyone had gone when Mr. Brannock, who owned the bookstore next door to Grandpa's store, took Joe aside and handed him a package. Joe didn't know what was going on. He looked at Mr. Brannock in surprise.

"Your Grandfather bought you this book on the morning before he died," Mr. Brannock said. "He wanted me to send it to you, but when I heard what happened, I held it aside to bring it to you myself."

Joe opened the brown paper package. Inside was a big world atlas. Page after page was filled with colorful maps and pictures of faraway places. On the first page was a note in Grandpa's careful printing.

"Joe," he had written, "I understand. Go where you need to go. I'll always love you. Grandpa."

Joe cried a little when he read the note. His mother cried a lot when he showed her the book and explained the note. She looked at the picture of Joe's dad, who died in the Marines. "Jesus was right," she said. "Love goes on." And then both cried some more.

1. **How did Joe hurt his grandfather? How did Joe experience forgiveness?**
2. **Why do you think people gather after a funeral to share a meal and tell stories?**
3. **What does Jesus' promise of eternal life mean to you?**

THE FEAST OF LOVE

When Jesus was asked to describe the kingdom of God—the goal and reward of all believers—he returned again and again to the image of the heavenly banquet.

It was a natural choice. After all, the kingdom of God is, at heart, pure and perfect happiness. And human beings, who are not yet pure and perfect, get their best glimpse of that happiness when they gather to celebrate with food, drink, and music.

God's People had always seen banquets as a foretaste of eternal happiness. Psalm 23 envisions the joy of being forever in God's presence:

You have spread the table before me in the sight of my foes. You anoint my head with oil; my cup overflows.

PSALM 23:5

The prophet Isaiah, speaking to a people made poor by exile, described the reward of faithfulness in terms of God's nourishing love:

All you who are thirsty, come to the water! You who have no money, come, receive grain and eat. Come, without paying and without cost, drink wine and milk!

ISAIAH 55:1

The riches of the heavenly banquet were always tied to loving faithfulness to God's covenant. Israel's land of covenant, the Promised Land itself, was described as "a good and spacious land, a land flowing with milk and honey" (*Exodus 3:8*).

THE BANQUET OF LOVE

One day, when Jesus was sharing a meal with some of his followers, someone called out, "Blessed is the one who will dine in the kingdom of God!" Jesus responded with a parable.

A man gave a great dinner to which he invited many. When the time for the dinner came, he dispatched his servant to say to those invited, "Come, everything is now ready." But one by one, they all began to excuse themselves.

Then the master of the house commanded his servants, "Go out quickly into the streets and alleys of the town and bring in here the poor and the crippled, the blind and the lame." Learning that there was still more room, the master commanded, "Go out to the highways and hedgerows and make people come in that my home may be filled."

LUKE 14:15–23

Another time, Jesus compared the heavenly kingdom to a wedding feast, for which it was important to be dressed in one's finest and prepared to celebrate (*Matthew 22:1–10*). And he praised those who, like wise wedding attendants, kept themselves awake and ready to celebrate even when it seemed the bridegroom—the Messiah himself—was delayed in arriving (*Matthew 25:1–13*).

In every word and action, Jesus taught his followers how to prepare themselves for the heavenly banquet. The proper wedding garment, the brightly lit lamp, the "yes" to God's invitation show the same unselfish love—the love that feeds the hungry, shelters the homeless, forgives the sinner, and lays down its life for others.

The best expression of the banquet of love is the Eucharist. At the Table of the Lord, God's eternal love nourishes and saves. In the Eucharist, Jesus, the Lord of love, is present in the celebrating community.

That is why the early Christians called the Eucharist the *agape* meal, the feast of love. The Greek word *agape*, which means "unselfish love," is often translated into English by the word *charity*. It is this love that Saint Paul described to the Corinthians. It is this love that allows you to put into practice the teachings of Jesus.

1. **What does the image of the banquet tell you about the kingdom of God?**
2. **Why is the Eucharist a "feast of love"?**

A Vision of Love

The love that Saint Paul wrote about in his letter to the Corinthians is not the romantic love mentioned in songs or the feelings of affection you might have for a favorite pet. Saint Paul was talking about the love that leads all people to God. It is the unconditional love of neighbor that Jesus announced as the New Commandment.

Saint Paul wrote that no one will know the fullness of love until the experience of God in heaven. He wrote,

At present we see indistinctly, as in a mirror, but then (in heaven) we will see face to face. At present I know partially; then I shall know fully as I am known. So faith, hope, and love remain, these three; but the greatest of these is love.

1 Corinthians 13:12–13

A HEAVENLY VIEW

The fourteenth-century Italian poet Dante Alighieri wrote an epic story—The Divine Comedy—about his journey through hell and purgatory on his way to heaven. Dante's guide through hell and purgatory was the great Roman poet Virgil. For Dante, the pagan Virgil stands for the voice of reason. But Virgil (reason) is not able to guide Dante to heaven. A new guide is needed for that.

The great love of Dante's life, Beatrice, died when she was only twenty-four. Dante mourned her loss. It is Beatrice—her name means "blessed happiness"—who becomes Dante's guide into heaven.

Beatrice tells Dante that it is because of his spiritual love for her that he is allowed to glimpse heaven. She explains that all human loves have the possibility of leading one either to heaven or hell. If people say "yes" to real love, they are drawn up to God like a turning wheel moved by a gear. Heaven itself is a state of perfect love, and God is "the Love that moves the Sun and other stars." God is the source and summit of all love.

SHARING LOVE

Who guides or inspires you to turn to God in love? Describe your inspiration.

FOLLOWING Jesus

Love is the greatest virtue. All other virtues flow from it. Love is seen in your kindness and generosity towards others. Organize a fund-raising effort for your parish food bank. Give generously of your own time, talent, and treasure to help those in need of your love.

GLIMPSES OF HEAVEN

Dante was granted a vision of heaven because of his love for Beatrice. Anyone can glimpse heaven when he or she experiences real love, for heaven is love. Look at the following pictures. Briefly describe how love is shown in each.

_____

_____

_____

_____

_____

_____

_____

_____

A PILGRIM IN THIS WORLD

Like Dante in his vision, you are a traveler trying to find your way to God. This prayer for pilgrims is attributed to Pope Clement XI.

Lord, I believe in you: increase my faith. I trust in you: strengthen my trust. I love you: let me love you more and more. I am sorry for my sins: deepen my sorrow.

I want to do what you ask of me: in the way that you ask, for as long as you ask, because you ask it.

Let me love you, my Lord and my God, and see myself as I really am: a pilgrim in this world, a Christian called to respect and love all those whose lives I touch.

Amen!

SHOW LOVE!

Draw a picture of yourself showing love for others.

WITH YOUR FAMILY

Find an appropriate way to show unselfish love to every member of your family. Offer to do the dishes when it is not your turn. Teach a younger brother or sister how to play one of your games. Give your parents big hugs and tell them thanks for all they do for you.

▼REVIEW CHAPTER 24········

CATHOLICS BELIEVE

1. Jesus frequently used the image of a loving feast to describe the kingdom of heaven.
2. To prepare to enter the kingdom, Christians must follow the new commandment of loving their neighbors.
3. Heaven is absolute happiness: it is a communion of life and love with God.

KNOW

Using Paul's teaching about love from 1 Corinthians 13, provide examples showing how a Christian should show love.

Love is patient.

Love is kind.

Love is not jealous.

Love is not pompous, inflated, or rude.

Love does not seek its own interest.

Love rejoices in the truth.

SUNDAY MASS

Receiving the Eucharist is a taste of the heavenly banquet. Look for all of the images of love you see in the Mass. What message of love do you hear during the Liturgy of the Word? In what ways is Jesus' love for you shown in the Liturgy of the Eucharist? How are you called to share your love with God and your neighbor?

KNOWING JESUS

But put on the Lord Jesus Christ.

ROMANS 13:14

The Mind of Christ

According to Saint Paul, Christians should "have the mind of Christ" (*1 Corinthians 2:16*). This oneness with the Lord takes some effort. It requires continual attention to the presence of Jesus within you. You can meet Jesus in many ways. Some of them are described here.

You can learn the mind of Christ from studying the Scriptures. During the week, read the next week's Gospel and think about what it means. On Sunday, listen to the Gospel reading at Mass. Pray about what you have studied and heard. You can grow close to Jesus through prayer. Pray the Lord's Prayer often. As Saint Teresa of Avila wrote,

The Master is never so far away that disciples need to raise their voices in order to be heard: he is always right at your side. I want you to understand that, if you are to recite the Lord's Prayer well, one thing is needful: you must not leave the side of the Master who has taught it to you.

You can grow closer to Jesus by celebrating the sacraments frequently. Attend Mass each Sunday and receive the Eucharist whenever possible. Examine your conscience daily. Ask God for forgiveness for what you have done wrong and for what you have failed to do. Celebrate the sacrament of Reconciliation regularly.

As a baptized follower of Jesus, you are a living member of the Communion of Saints. You can learn a lot about Jesus from studying the lives and writings of the saints.

Saint Teresa of Avila

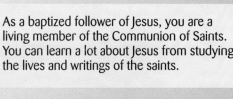

Jesus said that anything you do for those who are suffering, you do for him. You will meet Jesus in each kind deed you do for others that you undertake in the Name and Spirit of Christ.

Jesus identified with those who were persecuted. It takes courage to stand up for what is right. When you work for peace and justice you are living as Jesus called you to live.

A Friendship Plan

Make a plan for growing in knowledge and love of Jesus during your school break. In the space provided, express your plan in words or with a drawing.

UNIT  6 REVIEW ....

LEARNING

1. **What three keys did Jesus leave his followers to prepare them for the future?**
   Jesus left his followers the theological virtues of faith, hope, and love.
2. **What is the virtue of faith?**
   Faith is a gift from God that allows a person to have confidence in Jesus and all he taught.
3. **What is the virtue of Hope?**
   Hope is the gift from God that helps a person stay focused on the promises of Jesus even during difficult times.
4. **How is the virtue of love expressed?**
   As lived by Jesus and explained by Saint Paul in his letter to the Corinthians, love is expressed in unselfish actions done generously for one's neighbor.

LIVING

Think of a real problem in your family, school, or community. Write a short story or skit about young people dealing with the problem using the theological virtues of faith, hope, and love.

ASKING

1. How do I show faith, hope, and love in the way I treat other people?
2. How do my actions as a Christian make a difference in the world around me?

PRAYING

All: Bless the Lord, O my soul, and all my being, bless God's holy name.

Group 1: The Lord redeems our lives from destruction, crowns us with kindness and compassion, and fills our lifetime with good: our youth is renewed like the eagle's.

All: Bless the Lord, O my soul, and all my being, bless his holy name.

Group 2: As a father has compassion for his children, so the Lord has compassion for us. For the Lord knows how we are formed; God remembers that we are dust, and can be swept away with the wind.

All: Bless the Lord, O my soul, and all my being, bless his holy name.

Group 3: But the kindness of the Lord is from all eternity, and God's justice belongs to our children's children. God is the Lord of heaven, and rules over all the world.

All: Bless the Lord, O my soul, and all my being, bless his holy name.

Based on PSALM 103

I Am a Catholic

CONTENTS

THE MASS

The first Christian communities followed Jesus' command to remember him; they kept their Jewish tradition of reading the Scriptures, singing the psalms, and praying. They added the reading of the letters from missionaries like Paul and, later, the reading of the Gospels. They took strength from their celebration of the Lord's Supper. In all these things, Jesus was present. Jesus is also present today during the Eucharist.

- In the Liturgy of the Word, it is Jesus who speaks in the Scriptures, the Word of God.
- Jesus is present in the priest who presides at the Eucharist.
- Jesus is present in Holy Communion. You are united with Jesus and with others into the one Body of Christ, the Church.
- Jesus is present in the gathered community.

Every Mass follows the same pattern:

- *Introductory Rites:* Entrance Procession, Greeting, Penitential Rite, Glory to God, Opening Prayer
- *The Liturgy of the Word:* First Reading (Old Testament), Responsorial Psalm, Second Reading (New Testament), Gospel Acclamation, Gospel, Homily, Profession of Faith, Prayer of the Faithful
- *The Liturgy of the Eucharist:* Preparation of the Gifts, Offering of Gifts, Preface, Eucharistic Prayer, Memorial Acclamation, Great Amen, The Lord's Prayer, Greeting of Peace, Breaking of the Bread, Communion, Prayer after Communion
- *Concluding Rites:* Closing Prayer, Blessing, Dismissal

THE SACRAMENTS

Sacraments are signs of God's love and sources of God's grace. More than just symbols that stand for a greater reality, the sacraments actually bring about what they symbolize.

- *Sacraments of Initiation:* Baptism, Confirmation, Eucharist

- *Sacraments of Healing:* Reconciliation, The Anointing of the Sick
- *Sacraments of Service:* Marriage, Holy Orders

FEASTS OF JESUS

In a way, every day of the Church Year is a feast of Jesus. The Church recalls and celebrates his saving love at every Mass. In addition to the major liturgical seasons and feasts, the Church celebrates certain days as commemorations of Jesus' power and presence. Here are some of these feasts of the Lord.

- *The Presentation of the Lord.* This feast recalls Joseph and Mary's journey to Jerusalem to offer Jesus to God in the Temple, fulfilling Jewish law. It is celebrated on February 2.
- *The Feast of the Body and Blood of Christ.* This feast was added to the calendar during the Middle Ages, when Lenten fasting made it inappropriate to truly celebrate the gift of the Holy Eucharist on Holy Thursday. It is also known as the Feast of Corpus Christi and is celebrated on the Thursday after Trinity Sunday.
- *The Feast of the Sacred Heart of Jesus.* Devotion to the Sacred Heart of Jesus, the sign of his great love, was promoted by Saint Margaret Mary Alacoque. This feast is celebrated on the Friday following the Second Sunday after Pentecost.
- *The Feast of Christ the King.* On this final Sunday of the Church Year, you look forward to the second coming of Christ, who will establish forever the kingdom of God. It is celebrated on the Last Sunday of Ordinary Time.

MARY'S DAYS

Mary, the Mother of Jesus, has many feast days during the Church Year.

- *Feast of the Nativity of Mary.* No one knows when Mary was born. But from very early times, Christians have celebrated September 8 as her birthday. In many parts of the world, this day is also celebrated as a harvest festival. The finest grapes and wheat are presented before Mary's statue and then shared with the poor.
- *Feast of the Immaculate Conception.* On December 8, the Church celebrates that Mary was fully part of God's kingdom from the very first moment of her life. Under this title, Mary is the patroness of the United States.
- *Feast of Our Lady of Guadalupe.* Mary is celebrated as patroness of all the Americas on December 12.
- *Feast of the Annunciation.* March 25 celebrates when Mary received the Good News that she was to be the Mother of the Savior. For many centuries, this feast was celebrated as New Year's Day in Europe.
- *Feast of the Assumption.* At the end of Mary's life, she was taken, body and soul, into heaven. Christians celebrate this event on August 15. In many parts of the world, the flowers, fruit, and medicinal herbs grown in summer are blessed on this day.

CELEBRATE

ADVENT

- Advent is the liturgical season made up of the four weeks before Christmas. It is a time of prayer and preparation for the great Feast of the Nativity of Jesus Christ. The word *advent* means "coming."

- Christians are people who live in three dimensions: past, present, and future. During Advent, Christians identify with God's People in the past, who lived with the tension of waiting for the promised Messiah.

- Christians live in the present of Advent as they prepare, now, today, to celebrate the birth of Christ. The best way to do that is to live as though God is with you always. Instead of being preoccupied with what you might get at Christmas, think about what you can give. Instead of getting caught up in the hustle and bustle of pre-Christmas preparations, take some time for quiet prayer and reflection.

- Past and present are not enough for the followers of Jesus. Christians are called to live as future people, too, showing by their actions a glimpse of the kingdom of God that is yet to come in its fullness. You prepare the way for the Lord when you live every day as though this world, this life, is not the end. You prepare the way for the Lord when you make this world and this life better for all God's People, in hope of the kingdom to come.

CHRISTMAS

- Christmas, the Feast of the Nativity of the Lord, celebrates the mystery of the Incarnation—God's own Son born in our human flesh.

- We celebrate the birthdays of many famous men and women, but the celebration of Jesus' birth is quite different. Even though Jesus is probably the most famous person in the history of the world, we don't know the day of his birth. No records exist to tell us the precise day and hour when Mary gave birth to her Child.

- Very early in the Church's history, the commemoration of Jesus' birth became associated with the pagan Roman feast of Saturnalia, held in midwinter to celebrate the "birthday of the sun"—the point at which winter's dark days begin to grow longer as the earth turns toward spring.

- Of course, Christians have always been curious about the details of Jesus' birth. The Gospels of Matthew and Luke contain infancy narratives—stories of the events surrounding the birth of Jesus, seen through the eyes of faith.

LENT

- Before he began his public ministry, Jesus spent time alone in the desert wilderness. For forty days, the Gospels tell us, Jesus fasted, prayed, and faced temptation.

- Each year, in Lent, Christians spend forty days in prayer, self-discipline, and doing works of justice, preparing for the joy of Easter. This Lenten retreat is also the final preparation for the candidates who will receive the sacraments of initiation at the Easter Vigil.

EASTER

- Easter, the Feast of the Resurrection, is the central feast of the Christian year. This feast celebrates Jesus' conquest of sin and death, and the Christian hope of eternal life with God.

- Easter is all about *belief*. You can't see eternal life. You can only touch the risen Jesus with the eyes and hands of faith. For this reason, you can consider Saint Thomas the Apostle the patron saint of Easter.

- Christians pray and practice self-discipline during Lent for the same reason that Jesus prayed and fasted in the wilderness: to strengthen themselves against temptation.

- Prayer focuses your mind and heart on God. It helps you listen to God's will for you. Silent prayer, meditation, and reflection all open you up to God's presence.

- Fasting—limiting the amount of food you eat—and abstinence—going without something—are ways to develop self-discipline. Self-discipline keeps you from becoming spiritually lazy and helps you identify with those who do not have enough to eat.

227

WHAT IS PRAYER?

Prayer is what happens when people are struck by and respond to the wonder of God's presence, a presence recognized in simple ways:

- in deeds of kindness
- in the enjoyment of others
- in longing, frustration, joy, and pain

WHEN IS THE TIME FOR PRAYER?

Followers of Jesus are people of prayer.

You are heirs to a rhythm of prayer that is formed by the lives of people who are special to you, and that is as ordinary as the pages of the calendar and the hours on the clock.

1. You can pray seasonally. Each of the seasons of the Church Year has its special flavor and feel.
2. You can pray to remember and celebrate others. Your life has been touched by the lives and example of others—heroes and heroines, family members, and saints.
3. You can pray weekly. The rhythm of the week, especially that established by Sunday, surrounds your life.
4. You can pray at life's special moments. This means that the rhythm of life also summons your prayer: birth, caring, nourishing, gathering, departing, hurting, healing, and dying all mark important points in your life.
5. You can pray daily. Think of a normal day: You awake, wash, eat, play, share, rest, sleep. God's people recognize God's presence in this daily rhythm and respond with prayer.

PERSONAL PRAYER

Your relationship with God will grow as you develop the habit of holding private conversations with him. Here are some suggestions to help you with your conversation.

- Quiet down and listen for God. God is already closer to you than your own heartbeat.
- Get comfortable and take several deep breaths.
- Feel God's loving presence flowing through your body.
- Say something to invite God into your thoughts and feelings.
- Tell God about what's on your mind.
- Listen for God's word in your heart.
- Take your time. Be patient. Wait for God.
- Thank God for your time together.
- Write about your prayer experience in your personal journal.

CATHOLICS PRAY TO THE BLESSED TRINITY

SIGN OF THE CROSS

In the name of the Father, and of the Son, and of the Holy Spirit. Amen.

GLORY TO THE FATHER

Glory to the Father, and to the Son, and to the Holy Spirit, as it was in the beginning, is now, and will be forever. Amen.

CATHOLICS PRAY TO GOD THE FATHER

THE LORD'S PRAYER

Our Father, who are in heaven, hallowed be your name. Your kingdom come; your will be done on earth as it is in heaven. Give us this day our daily bread, and forgive us our trespasses as we forgive those who trespass against us. And lead us not into temptation, but deliver us from evil. Amen.

CATHOLICS HONOR MARY

HAIL MARY

Hail Mary, full of grace, the Lord is with you. Blessed are you among women, and blessed is the fruit of your womb, Jesus. Holy Mary, Mother of God, pray for us sinners, now, and at the hour of our death. Amen.

ROSARY TIMES

- *Joyful Mysteries:* (1) The Annunciation, (2) The Visitation, (3) The Nativity, (4) The Presentation of Jesus in the Temple, (5) The Finding of Jesus in the Temple.
- *Sorrowful Mysteries:* (1) The Agony in the Garden, (2) The Scourging of Jesus, (3) The Crowning with Thorns, (4) The Way of the Cross, (5) The Crucifixion.
- *Glorious Mysteries:* (1) The Resurrection, (2) The Ascension, (3) Pentecost, (4) The Assumption of Mary into Heaven, (5) Mary Is Crowned Queen of Heaven and Earth.

CATHOLICS PRAY FOR VIRTUE

ACT OF FAITH

O my God, I believe that you are one God in three Divine Persons: Father, Son, and Holy Spirit. I believe that your Divine Son became man and died for our sins, and that he will come again to judge the living and the dead.

I believe these and all the truths that the Catholic Church teaches, because you have revealed them, who can neither deceive nor be deceived. Amen.

ACT OF HOPE

O my God, relying on your almighty power and infinite mercy and promises, I hope to obtain pardon of my sins, the help of your grace, and life everlasting through the merits of Jesus Christ, my Lord and Redeemer. Amen.

ACT OF LOVE

O my God, I love you above all things with my whole heart and soul, because you are all-good and worthy of all my love. I love my neighbor as myself for the love of you. I forgive all who have injured me and ask pardon of all whom I have injured. Amen.

CATHOLICS ASK FOR FORGIVENESS

ACTS OF CONTRITION

My God, I am sorry for my sins with all my heart. In choosing to do wrong and failing to do good, I have sinned against you whom I should love above all things. I firmly intend, with your help, to do penance, to sin no more, and to avoid whatever leads me to sin. Jesus Christ suffered and died for us. In his name, dear God, forgive me. Amen.

O my God, I am heartily sorry for having offended you. And I detest all my sins because of your just punishments, but most of all because they offend you, my God, who are all good and deserving of all my love. I firmly resolve, with the help of your grace, to sin no more and to avoid the near occasion of sin. Amen.

Lord Jesus Christ, Son of God, have mercy on me, a sinner.

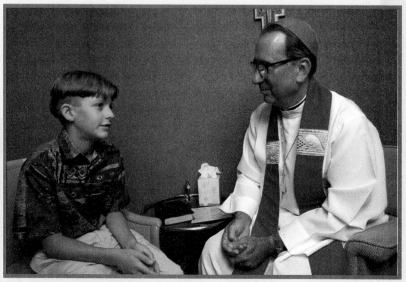

Catholics Pray Always

Morning Prayer

Almighty God, You have given us this day; strengthen us with your power and keep us from falling into sin, so that whatever we say or think or do may be in your service, and for the sake of your kingdom. Amen.

Evening Prayer

Lord, watch over us this night. By your strength, may we rise at daybreak to rejoice in the resurrection of Christ, your Son, who lives and reigns forever and ever. Amen.

Blessing before Meals

Bless us, O Lord, and these, your gifts, which we are about to receive from your bounty, through Christ our Lord. Amen.

Grace after Meals

We give you thanks for these and all your gifts, almighty God. You live and rule forever. Amen.

Family Prayer

Heavenly Father, you have given us a beautiful example in the Holy Family of Jesus, Mary, and Joseph. Give us openness to your Spirit, so that we may follow through in the practice of family virtues. Strengthen our bonds of love. Grant us the courage to reach out to others and to do your will. Amen.

SAINTS AND STORIES

Do you realize that each and every person is called to be a saint? When you were baptized you joined the Communion of Saints. Men and women who are called "saints" are people who dedicated their lives to proclaiming the Good News of Jesus in word and deed.

SAINT FRANCIS OF ASSISI

Francis Bernadone was born to a wealthy Italian family. While a sick and imprisoned young soldier, Francis decided to change his life. He gave away everything, including the clothes he wore. As a poor man, he found true riches. With God's love, Francis learned to love the earth, its people, and even its animals. Francis influenced other people to follow him and live as he did. These people are now called Franciscans. Francis was declared a saint shortly after his death. His feast day is October 4.

SAINT ELIZABETH ANN SETON

Elizabeth Ann Bayley Seton was the mother of five. Widowed at the age of 29, she worked hard to support her children. Tragically, two daughters died in childhood. She became a Catholic in 1805. She started the first Catholic grade school in the United States, and founded the American branch of the Daughters of Charity. Elizabeth became the first American-born female saint in 1975. Her feast day is January 4.

SAINT TERESA OF AVILA

Teresa of Avila lived in Spain. She was a woman of action and of prayer. She reformed the Carmelite order of nuns and wrote great books on mystical prayer. Teresa was a very good friend of God. She talked to God directly and told God exactly what she thought and felt. In 1967, Teresa was proclaimed a Doctor of the Church. This means that her writings and holiness have helped many people learn about God. Her feast day is October 15.

SAINT JOHN BOSCO

John Bosco was born to a poor family near Turin, Italy. Often, the Boscos went to village fairs, where young John studied the jugglers and acrobats. With practice, John became an expert juggler. Later in life, Father Bosco used his entertaining skills to draw people to God. In Turin, he cared for poor, homeless boys nobody wanted. He founded the Salesian Order to continue his work. He died in 1888. His feast day is January 31.

SAINT BENEDICT

Benedict was born into a noble Roman family in the last days of the Roman Empire. Benedict soon chose a life of seclusion and poverty. He lived alone so that he would have more time for prayer. Benedict wrote *The Rule of Saint Benedict* to guide how religious men and women live. Benedictines still follow the Rule. He was proclaimed the patron saint of Europe in 1964. His feast is July 11.

SAINT CATHERINE OF SIENA

Catherine Benincasa always seemed older than her years. At six, she had a vision of Jesus. As sixteen, she became a lay member of the Dominican Order. Unable to join the convent, she lived convent life at home. She served the poor and sick during the plague. She couldn't write, but others recorded her conversations with Christ in *The Dialogues.* She became a trusted advisor for the pope. She is a Doctor of the Church. Her feast is April 29.

233

THE TEN COMMANDMENTS

1. I am the Lord, your God. You shall have no other gods besides me.
2. You shall not take the name of the Lord, your God, in vain.
3. Remember to keep holy the Sabbath day.
4. Honor your father and your mother.
5. You shall not kill.
6. You shall not commit adultery.
7. You shall not steal.
8. You shall not bear false witness against your neighbor.
9. You shall not covet your neighbor's wife.
10. You shall not covet anything that belongs to your neighbor.

Based on EXODUS 20:2–17

THE BEATITUDES

Blessed are the poor in spirit, for theirs is the kingdom of heaven.
Blessed are they who mourn, for they will be comforted.
Blessed are the meek, for they will inherit the land.
Blessed are they who hunger and thirst for righteousness, for they will be satisfied.
Blessed are the merciful, for they will be shown mercy.
Blessed are the clean of heart, for they will see God.
Blessed are the peacemakers, for they will be called children of God.
Blessed are they who are persecuted for the sake of righteousness, for theirs is the kingdom of heaven.

Based on MATTHEW 5:3–10

THE PRECEPTS OF THE CHURCH

1. Take part in the Eucharist every Sunday and holy day. Do no unnecessary work on Sunday.
2. Celebrate the sacraments frequently.
3. Study the Good News of Jesus Christ.
4. Follow the marriage laws of the Church.
5. Support the People of God.
6. Do penance.
7. Support the missionary efforts of the Church.

THE CORPORAL WORKS OF MERCY

Feed the hungry.
Give drink to the thirsty.
Clothe the naked.
Shelter the homeless.
Visit the sick.
Visit the imprisoned.
Bury the dead.

THE SPIRITUAL WORKS OF MERCY

Help the sinner.
Teach the ignorant.
Counsel the doubtful.
Comfort the sorrowful.
Bear wrongs patiently.
Forgive injuries.
Pray for the living and the dead.

EXAMINATION OF CONSCIENCE

Use these questions to help you think about your choices
and prepare for the sacrament of Reconciliation.

1. How do I show love for God?
   Do I put God first in my life?
   Do I avoid relying on superstition or magic?
2. How do I respect God's name?
   When I make promises, do I take them seriously?
   Is my language respectful?
3. How do I participate at Mass?
   Am I a part of my parish family?
   Do I take time for prayer and spiritual growth?
4. What contribution do I make in my family?
   Am I obedient to my parents and others in authority?
   Do I show love for my brothers and sisters?
5. How do I respect God's gift of life?
   Do I take care of my health and the well-being of others?
   Do I avoid violence and fighting?
6. How do I show respect for the human body and for God's
   gift of sexuality?
   Do I avoid situations, entertainments, and conversations
   that make fun of God's gift of sexuality?
   Am I modest and chaste in my thoughts, my words, and
   my actions?
7. How am I honest?
   Do I take care of my possessions and respect the
   belongings of others?
   Am I careful to make sure that others get their
   fair share?
8. How do I show gratitude?
   Do I run others down out of envy?
   Do I let material possessions control my life?

WHAT CATHOLICS BELIEVE

Use these statements to review what you know about Jesus and the Church.

1. Jesus is the Son of God, both fully human and fully divine, who came to announce God's reign of love.
2. Jesus died to save all people from sin and death.
3. Jesus rose from the dead and returned to his Father.
4. Jesus is present in the world today.
5. Jesus received support for his divine mission from Mary, his mother, and Joseph, his foster father.
6. Jesus' life in Nazareth provides examples of how a person should live.
7. Jesus' public life began with his baptism by John in the Jordan River.
8. The Church is apostolic; it is based on the tradition of the Apostles.
9. Jesus invites everyone to participate in the kingdom of God.
10. Jesus Christ is the full revelation of the Father.
11. Easter is the most important Christian feast.
12. Jesus' divine glory was revealed at the Transfiguration.
13. God becoming human is the mystery of the Incarnation.
14. Mary is truly the Mother of God.
15. Jesus promised to send the Holy Spirit, the Advocate, to his disciples.
16. There is one God revealed as the Blessed Trinity: Father, Son, and Holy Spirit.
17. Jesus is present in the Scriptures, in the Eucharist, in the Church, and in the sacraments.
18. The Church is the Body of Christ.
19. Christians are called to care for all people as their brothers and sisters.
20. Jesus taught his followers to serve others.

NICENE CREED

We believe in one God, the Father, the Almighty, maker of heaven and earth, of all that is seen and unseen.

We believe in one Lord, Jesus Christ, the only Son of God, eternally begotten of the Father. God from God, Light from Light, true God from true God, begotten, not made, one in Being with the Father. Through him all things were made.

For us and for our salvation he came down from heaven: by the power of the Holy Spirit he was born of the Virgin Mary, and became man.

For our sake he was crucified under Pontius Pilate; he suffered, died, and was buried. On the third day he rose again in fulfillment of the Scriptures; he ascended into heaven and is seated at the right hand of the Father. He will come again to judge the living and the dead, and his kingdom will have no end.

We believe in the Holy Spirit, the Lord, the giver of life, who proceeds from the Father and the Son. With the Father and the Son he is worshiped and glorified. He has spoken through the Prophets.

We believe in one, holy, catholic, and apostolic Church. We acknowledge one baptism for the forgiveness of sins. We look for the resurrection of the dead, and the life of the world to come.
Amen

G L O S S A R Y

Abba An Aramaic term of endearment that means "papa" or "daddy;" the title by which Jesus addressed his Father, God.

Abortion The grave sin of purposely causing the death of an unborn child.

Absolution The forgiveness of sin offered in the sacrament of Reconciliation.

Alleluia A Hebrew exclamation that means "Praise the Lord!"; the song of Easter.

Alpha and Omega A title for Jesus, the beginning and end of all things (from the first and last letters of the Greek alphabet).

Amen In Hebrew and Aramaic, a word that means, "May it be so!"; the traditional end to our prayers.

Anointing of the Sick The sacrament in which the Church continues the healing ministry of Jesus.

Apocalypse A literary form used during times of persecution and struggle.

Apostle A special friend and follower of Jesus; one who is sent.

Aramaic The everyday language spoken by Jesus.

Ark of the Covenant The container for the tablets of the Law.

Baptism The sacrament of initiation that gives new life, frees you from sin, and makes you a member of the Church.

Beatific vision The experience of being in the presence of God; the complete and perfect happiness of heaven.

Beatitudes Short sayings of Jesus, found in Matthew's Gospel, that sum up the values of God's kingdom.

Bible The book of God's Word, the Scriptures. The Bible is made up of many books whose writers were inspired by God.

Bishop The leader and shepherd of a diocese. The fullness of Holy Orders.

Blessed Sacrament Another name for the real presence of Jesus in the Eucharist.

Blessed Trinity The name for the mystery of the one God who is Father, Son, and Holy Spirit.

Body of Christ The Church, the living presence of Jesus in the world; the unity of all Christians; the Eucharist.

Catechumen A person preparing to receive the sacraments of initiation.

Catholic A word that means "universal, open to all;" a baptized Christian who acknowledges the authority of the pope and the bishops.

Celibate A person who chooses not to marry for the sake of the kingdom.

Charity Unselfish Christian love; *agape*.

Christ A Greek title for Jesus that means "Messiah, the Anointed One."

Christian A follower of Jesus.

Church The community of believers; the building in which the community gathers for worship.

Communion Another name for the Eucharist.

Communion of Saints The unity of all baptized followers of Jesus, living and dead.

Community Literally means "those who live within the same walls."

Confession Telling one's sins to the priest; one step in the sacrament of Reconciliation.

Confirmation The sacrament of initiation that seals and completes Baptism by strengthening us in the Holy Spirit.

Conscience The gift of God that helps you tell right from wrong.

Contrition True sorrow for sin and the willingness to do better; showing contrition is a step in the sacrament of Reconciliation.

Conversion Changing one's life for the better; turning away from sin.

Council A gathering of bishops to clarify Church teaching and Catholic practice.

Covenant A binding agreement; the relationship between God and the Jewish people through Abraham, Moses, and David; God's relationship with all humanity through Jesus.

Deacon An ordained minister who helps the priest and bishop serve the Christian community; the first level of Holy Orders.

Diocese A portion of the universal Church made up of a number of parishes in a given area, led by a bishop.

Discernment The skill of evaluating choices.

Disciple A follower of Jesus; one who learns.

Eucharist The Mass; the sacrament of Jesus' real presence; Holy Communion; a sacrament of initiation. The word *eucharist* means "thanksgiving."

Evangelist A title for the Gospel authors, from the Greek for "bringer of Good News."

Exodus The journey of God's People out of slavery in Egypt; the biblical book that tells of the journey.

Faith The gift of believing and trusting in God through the Church.

Free will The gift of God that allows human beings to choose freely whether to accept or reject God's love.

Fruit of the Spirit The effects of the Holy Spirit's presence, seen in the lives of Christians (*Galatians 5:22–23*).

Gentiles Non-Jews, people outside the covenant.

Gospel A New Testament account of the life and teachings of Jesus; another name for Jesus' message. There are four accounts of the Gospel: Matthew, Mark, Luke, and John. The word *gospel* means "good news."

Grace A share of God's own life and love within us. *Sanctifying grace* is the new life you receive in the sacraments; *actual grace* gives you the strength to live as a follower of Jesus.

Heaven The state of eternal happiness after death; being in the presence of God forever.

Hebrew The language Jesus used for prayer; the formal religious language of the Jews; the language of the Old Testament.

Hell The state of eternal separation from God after death; the punishment of those who choose evil.

Holy Family Jesus, his Mother, Mary, and his fosterfather, Saint Joseph.

Holy Land The part of the Middle East, centered around Jerusalem, where the events of the Bible took place.

Holy Orders The sacrament of service that celebrates the call to serve God's People through the ordained ministry of deacon, priest, or bishop.

Holy Spirit The Advocate or Helper promised by Jesus.

Humility The virtue of self-honesty and the avoidance of false pride; from a word meaning "bound to the earth."

Idolatry The worship of false gods; the sin of allowing created things to come before their Creator in our hearts.

Ikon Greek for "image;" a picture or image of Jesus, Mary, the saints, or angels used as the focus of prayer and devotion.

Incarnation The name for the belief that Jesus Christ, the Son of God, became man and was born of the Virgin Mary.

Israel The collective name for the Jews, the People of God, from a name given by God to their biblical ancestor, Jacob; the Old Testament kingdom of the Jews. The modern nation of Israel carries the name of this biblical kingdom.

Jerusalem The holy city, sacred to Jews, Muslims, and Christians.

Jews The name by which God's People were known at the time of Jesus, from Judah, one of Jacob's sons; members of the Jewish faith today.

Judgment When Jesus comes again to bring the kingdom of God, he will judge all people, living and dead, on how well they have followed the Law of Love. This is called the *Last Judgment*. At the time of death, each person also faces a *personal judgment*.

Justice The virtue of treating all people, especially those most in need, with fairness, respect, and mercy.

Kingdom of God A name for God's power and love working in the world.

Lectionary The book of Scripture readings used at Mass, arranged according to the liturgical cycle.

Litany A form of prayer in which short petitions are interspersed with a repeated response.

Liturgy The Church's public worship of God, including the Mass and the sacraments; Greek for "the work of the people."

Lord A biblical title for God or for Jesus Christ that acknowledges God's greatness and power.

Magisterium Latin for "teaching body;" the Church's authority, given by Jesus Christ and sustained by the Holy Spirit, to teach what is true.

Marks of the Church Signs of the Holy Spirit's abiding presence in the Church; the Church is "one, holy, catholic, and apostolic."

Marriage The sacrament of service that celebrates the covenant between a man and a woman to be faithful for life, to welcome children, and to serve the Christian community.

Martyr A person who dies for his or her faith; Greek for "witness."

Messiah The Hebrew word that means "Anointed One;" the Savior promised by God. Jesus is the Messiah.

Ministry Loving service to others. In Baptism, every Christian is called to the ministry of service.

Miracle A dramatic sign of God's power and love at work in the world.

Mission The work each person is sent by God to do.

Missionary Someone sent to share the Good News of Jesus.

Morality The teaching that guides the choices we make. Christian morality, built on the Beatitudes and the Ten Commandments.

Mystagogia The period of time in which newly-baptized Christians come to understand the Church and their role in it; Greek for "teaching of the mysteries."

New Testament The part of the Christian Bible that contains the Gospels, the Acts of the Apostles, the Letters (or *Epistles*), and the Book of Revelation.

Old Testament The part of the Christian Bible that contains the Hebrew Scriptures and other sacred writings from before the time of Jesus.

Oral tradition Describes how history is passed on accurately by the careful retelling of events.

Ordination Reception of the sacrament of Holy Orders.

Original sin Separation from God that has been part of the human condition since people first chose to turn away from God's love.

Parable A special kind of teaching story, common among Jewish rabbis and preachers, used by Jesus to announce the kingdom.

Parish A local community of Catholics who gather to celebrate Mass and the sacraments, to share the faith through religious education, and to serve one another's needs.

Paschal Mystery The saving death and resurrection of Jesus; the mystery of our faith; from the word *Passover*, Jesus is the ultimate Passover Lamb.

Passion The agony, arrest, trial, suffering, and death of Jesus, commemorated in Holy Week.

Passover The Jewish feast of the Unleavened Bread that commemorates the Israelite's passage from slavery to freedom; celebrated with a special meal called the *seder*.

Pastoral letters Letters written by a bishop or group of bishops to advise Catholics (and sometimes society in general) about matters of Church teaching, practice, and social justice.

Penance Active undertaking to make up for sin.

Pentecost The feast that commemorates the sending of the Holy Spirit, celebrated fifty days after Easter.

Pope The bishop of Rome and the successor of Saint Peter; the head of the universal Church on earth.

Prayer Communication with God in any way. The five purposes of prayer are adoration, blessing thanksgiving, petition, and contrition.

Priest An ordained minister who assists the bishop and serves the Christian community by sharing the Word and celebrating the sacraments; the second level of Holy Orders.

Prophet One who calls others to follow God's Word and to live in justice.

Psalm A sacred song used in worship; a sung prayer. The Book of Psalms in the Bible contains 150 of these songs.

Rabbi The Hebrew word for "teacher;" the title by which Jesus' disciples addressed him; the spiritual or educational leader of a Jewish congregation.

Reconciliation The sacrament of healing that celebrates God's loving forgiveness of sin, restores sanctifying grace, and reunites us with God and with the community.

Repent To turn away from sin, to show contrition.

Resurrection The mystery of Jesus' rising from death to new life, commemorated on Easter and at every Sunday Mass; the belief that all faithful followers of Jesus will share in new life, body, and soul, when the kingdom comes.

Revelation The showing forth of God's power and love in Jesus Christ, in the Scriptures, and in God's People. Divine revelation and sacred tradition are the sources of the Church's teachings.

Sabbath The Lord's Day, set aside for worship and rest. Sunday, the day of the Lord's resurrection, is the Christian Sabbath.

Sacrament Signs of God's love and sources of God's grace, given by Jesus to his Church. The Church celebrates seven sacraments: Baptism, Confirmation, Eucharist, Reconciliation, the Anointing of the Sick, Marriage, and Holy Orders.

Sacrifice Something precious offered to God out of love and worship or in sorrow for sin; something difficult given to or done for another's good; Jesus' saving action on the cross, commemorated in the sacrifice of the Mass.

Saint A title meaning "one who is holy." All Christians are called to holiness by Baptism. The Church honors specific saints who have been *canonized,* formally recognized as model followers of Jesus.

Salvation God's great act of love and mercy, sending Jesus to save human beings from sin and death. Salvation is a gift; you have the freedom to accept or reject it.

Satan A name that means "the Adversary, the one who opposes;" the biblical name for the devil, the personification of evil.

Scripture A word that means "writings;" sacred Scripture is "holy writing"—the Bible, the Word of God.

Second Coming The return of Jesus Christ in glory at the end of the world to judge all people and bring the fullness of God's kingdom.

Sin The deliberate choice to do wrong; the condition of separating oneself from God and the community (from a Hebrew word that means "missing the mark"). Sin can be personal or social in its effects. *Mortal sin*, or grave wrong, is serious sin chosen freely and with full knowledge of its seriousness; mortal sin robs the soul of the life of grace. *Venial sin* is less serious wrongdoing.

Social encyclicals Letters written by a pope that explain how Christians are to live justly.

Son of God The title given to Jesus by his followers.

Son of Man A biblical title for the Messiah, used by Jesus to refer to himself.

Soul The immortal or eternal part of your being, God's own life in you.

Synagogue A Jewish neighborhood house of worship and religious study.

Tabernacle The container for the Blessed Sacrament in a Catholic church.

Temple The central place of worship for the Jews, located in Jerusalem. The last Temple was destroyed by the Romans in A.D. 70; some modern Jewish congregations refer to their houses of worship as "temples."

Ten Commandments The laws of the Sinai covenant, given by God to Moses. Followers of Jesus honor the Ten Commandments, which Jesus summed up in the Great Commandment (*Luke 10: 25–28*).

Torah The first five books of Hebrew Scripture: Genesis, Exodus, Leviticus, Numbers, and Deuteronomy.

Tradition From the Latin word for "handing on," knowledge and customs passed from one generation to the next; sacred tradition is the collected teaching and practice of the church.

Vice A sinful habit or practice. The seven vices or *deadly sins* are traditionally listed as pride, greed, lust, anger, gluttony, envy, and sloth.

Virtue A practice that leads to goodness and holiness. The three *theological virtues* are faith, hope, and love. Prudence, justice, temperance, and fortitude are the *cardinal* or *moral virtues.*

Vocation A call from God to serve others in God's name. Marriage, committed single life, priesthood, and religious life are all Christian vocations.

Vow A sacred promise or pledge made to another person or to God, often with the community as witness, such as the vows of Marriage.

Wisdom A gift of the Spirit.

Witness To express one's beliefs in words and in action; to testify.

Word of God A title for Jesus Christ; a name for the Scriptures.

Works of Mercy Practices that help bring about God's kingdom by serving others. Works of Mercy can be *Corporal* ("for the body") or *Spiritual* ("for the soul").

Worship Praise and honor given to God alone.

INDEX

240